PRAISE FOR

VENUS ENVY

"Fascinating . . . inside scoops. . . . Plenty of off-the-court gossip."
—*San Francisco Chronicle*

"Explosive. . . . Jon Wertheim has done the game a good service."
—*Tennis Week*

"Wertheim['s] . . . book has the fly-on-the-wall perspective that you'd expect from a veteran tour observer. He depicts the pro tennis circuit in all its theater-of-the-absurd glory [and] backs up these guilty pleasures with solid reporting."

—*Washington Post*

Sports Illustrated

About the Author

L. JON WERTHEIM is a senior writer for *Sports Illustrated* and tennis columnist for CNN/SI.com. He lives in Manhattan with his wife.

VENUS ENVY

POWER GAMES, TEENAGE VIXENS, AND MILLION-DOLLAR EGOS ON THE WOMEN'S TENNIS TOUR

L. JON WERTHEIM

Perennial

An Imprint of HarperCollins*Publishers*

For Ellie

First Perennial edition published 2002.

Designed by Jackie McKee

The Library of Congress has catalogued the hardcover edition as follows:

Wertheim, L. Jon.
    Venus envy : a sensational season inside the women's tennis tour / by
L. Jon Wertheim.—1st ed.
        p. cm.
    ISBN 0-06-019774-9
    1. Women tennis players—Biography. I. Title.

GV994.A1 W45 2001
796.342'082'0922—dc21
    [B]   2001024314

ISBN 0-06-095749-2 (pbk.)

02   03   04   05   06   WB/RRD   10   9   8   7   6   5   4   3   2   1

CONTENTS

VENUS ENVY

VOLLEY OF THE DOLLS

AN HOUR AFTER HER EXHILARATING VIC-
tory in the finals of the 2000 U.S. Open, Venus Williams was being led
through the bowels of the National Tennis Center and into a CBS television booth to take a phone call. "President Clinton wants to congrat-
ulate you," an excited production assistant told her. Venus wasn't too
impressed. She entered the soundproof room, plopped into a swivel
chair, clipped a microphone to her yellow tennis dress, and awaited her
gentleman caller.

The President, who had been in the stands earlier that day, phoned
in a few moments later from his Westchester home, assuming no
doubt that he would pass along some pro forma praise and then get
back to dinner with the First Lady. Suddenly he was being grilled as if
he were facing the White House press corps. Showing no signs of letting up, Venus made Clinton adjust to her rules, her tempo—just as
she had done with Lindsay Davenport earlier in the evening. All the
while she wore a broad, faintly sadistic smile.

First, she chided the President for not being at her match. "So what
happened? Where'd you go?" she said. She then tweaked the President and other members of the Millennium Summit for the traffic
gridlock between Manhattan and Queens. "You know, we suffered

through traffic, while you guys shot straight through. That's okay, though. You got special privileges." While Clinton hemmed and then hawed, Venus moved to her next topic: fiscal policy.

"Do you think you could lower my taxes? Mr. President, did you see me today? I was working hard."

"Uh," Clinton responded uneasily. "What state do you pay in?"

"I'm in Florida, so I pay a high property tax."

"Yeah, down there . . ." Clinton stammered.

Venus cut him off. "So what can you do about it?"

"Not much right now. There may be something coming out soon. Um, we're working on it. I think there ought to be special rules for athletes."

"Oh," Venus said, laughing. "Can I read your lips?"

After grilling Clinton for a few more minutes, Venus was ready to get off the telephone. She wished good luck to the President's wife in her upcoming New York senate election. "Tell her, 'all the way,' you know."

"Yep, you take care," Clinton mumbled.

"Thank you," said Venus, as she clicked off.

The line went dead, and as Venus removed her earpiece and microphone she saw that the CBS crew in the booth were staring at her, astonished. Had she really just jousted with the President of the United States? Venus looked around the room and shrugged. "What?" she said. "I'm not really intimidated by anyone. Why should I be?"

Venus Williams's bravado that day was a stark contrast to her mood at the same site a year earlier. After the 1999 U.S. Open final, Venus was shrouded in a black hooded sweatshirt, her hands holding up her chin, as she looked on lugubriously, barely able to bring herself to clap as her younger sister, Serena, held the U.S. Open trophy aloft. Serena had beaten Martina Hingis, the player who had dramatically taken out Venus the day before. That loss to Hingis would lodge in Venus' consciousness and spawn nightmares for the next nine months. Venus was genuinely happy for her sister, but she still couldn't help but think that fate had played a cruel joke at her expense. "It wasn't supposed to be like that, the younger sister winning a Grand Slam first," said the girls' mother, Oracene Williams, who likened Venus' defeat to a death in the family. "I won't lie: it shook her up."

That loss to Hingis would eat at Venus for a long, long time. It may also have been the best thing that ever happened to her.

In the year 2000, Venus wouldn't just surpass her little sister; she would establish herself as the dominant player in women's tennis. In addition to claiming the U.S. Open and Wimbledon titles, she would run off a thirty-five-match winning streak and win gold medals in both singles and doubles at the 2000 Summer Olympics. To top off what had already been a pretty good year, she signed a $40 million endorsement deal with Reebok that made her the richest female athlete in history.

A few years ago, the Women's Tennis Association was an oatmeal-bland collective of moonballing baseliners struggling for fans and respect. No less than Martina Navratilova derided the circuit in 1995 as "Steffi and the Seven Dwarfs." Pat Cash, the former men's Wimbledon champ, said that comparing women's tennis to men's tennis was like comparing manure to harness racing. "Lazy, fat pigs" is how another past Wimbledon champion, Richard Krajicek, assessed the field.

Then they came—a Generation Next, equal parts attitude and pulchritude, raised in an era of heroine chic, in which Buff is Beautiful, and trash talking is just keeping things real. Mixing tennis with fashion, sex appeal, the Internet, and the kind of postfeminist swagger that enables a player to talk smack to the President of the United States, the WTA Tour has been transformed into the sport of queens—with a few divas thrown in for spice. "These aren't just good tennis players," says Arnon Milchan, the Hollywood mogul who, fittingly, produced the movie *Pretty Woman* and bought the worldwide television rights to the women's tour. "They are performers giving us a dramatic show."

At a time when reality-based entertainment is the rage, the Tour's

" 'tude brood" has made women's tennis the ultimate cinema verité sport, equal parts March Madness and *Survivor*. As in an eleven-month soap opera, tensions mount from week to week, loyalties shift, families splinter and come together, feuds escalate, characters fade in and out, fortunes fluctuate, careers are made and broken. It's prime-time fare— except that on the WTA Tour, the episodes are more outrageous and the plotlines more surreal.

Like any successful serial, women's tennis has a delectably rich cast of characters: Two proud and athletic sisters, weaned on the game in an L.A. ghetto, battle skepticism, scorn, and racism as they try to fulfill the pronouncements of their bombastic Svengali—who may or may not be insane; the crafty, undersized, former Eastern European, who clings desperately to her top ranking as she slays opponents with her guile—and her sharp tongue; the luminous Russian Bond girl, who hauls in a small country's GNP in endorsements but has yet to win a tournament; an affable but tough-talking California girl who just wants to be a jock in a culture that demands sex appeal; there's the req- uisite tragic heroine, a former top player who was stabbed by a deranged fan, lost her father to cancer, and labors like Sisyphus to regain her touch; and there's the psychologically fragile French/ Canadian/American trying to become known for something other than her abusive, manipulative father. The end result is a constellation of stars that most other sports would kill for.

In the year 2000, the WTA Tour set records for attendance and prize money and regularly drew television viewership that eclipsed men's tennis and compared favorably to MLS soccer and NHL hockey. A *USA Today* poll determined that 75 percent of tennis fans prefer the women's game to the men's; and even the Tour's most strin- gent critics are starting to see the light, or at least lighten up. John McEnroe, who's been mocking women's tennis as long as he's been throwing tantrums, has encouraged the male players to allow the women equal prize money ... while the offer is still available. "You can't deny it," he says. "Right now the women have the better product."

The quality of tennis has something to do with this belle epoque. Moonballs and interminable, topspin-heavy baseline rallies have become as anachronistic to the women's game as pleated skirts, cable sweaters, and, for that matter, modesty. But there's something else going on. Never before have players been so athletic, so powerful, so balletic, so muscular, so ambitious. So unabashedly sexy.

This popularity explosion parallels the surge in women's sports everywhere: nearly 100,000 fans cram into the Rose Bowl to watch a women's soccer match, and a women's basketball league that plays in the middle of summer can draw 20,000 fans for a game. And it doesn't hurt that men's tennis could use some Viagra, as its two most marketable players, Pete Sampras and Andre Agassi, are in their autumn years, and the rest of the field has all the personality of a TV test pattern.

Women's tennis—for now, anyway—is also free of the blemishes that mar most big-time sports. No carpetbagging franchises strong-arming towns for better stadium leases. No penurious owners putting profits ahead of performance. No players reneging on contracts, no lockouts, no holdouts, and precious few dropouts. Nobody's choked a coach, recorded a rap album full of misogynistic and homophobic bile, or had their lover gunned down in a drive-by shooting so they could avoid paying child support. And no paternity suits.

It's hard, however, to exaggerate the force of personality. The repertory troupe is an engaging mix of characters that cuts the kind of impossibly wide swath one normally sees on Benetton ad campaigns and college admissions brochures. They're black and white. They're young and old. They're straight and gay. They're battle-tested veterans reluctant to go quietly into that good night and they're impetuous arrivistes who share the dotcom culture's disdain for the establishment. And, like most contemporary heroines—Cher, Madonna, Hillary— the luminaries of women's tennis are surnameless. Mention Venus, Serena, Martina, Anna, Lindsay, Monica, and Mary on virtually any street corner in the world and most people know you are talking tennis.

Which is understandable, because these racketeers are everywhere, endorsing everything from dotcoms to sports bras to fruit juice. Their faces grace not only the covers of *Sports Illustrated* but also magazines like *GQ, Forbes,* and *Elle*. Their likenesses are re-created at Madame Tussaud's. They spawn computer viruses. They're asked to present Grammy Awards, they have roles in Jim Carrey movies, and they sit on the couches of Jay, Dave, Regis, Conan, and Rosie. They got milk. "It's this simple," explains Serena Williams, among the many players who drips with self-confidence. "Women's tennis is where it's at."

The players know it and flaunt it. On a cold November morning, a reporter boarded an elevator at the U.N. Plaza Hotel in Manhattan. It was the week of the Chase Championships, the year-end tournament for women's tennis. Before the doors shut, Anna Kournikova jumped on wearing a black leather jacket and navy sweatpants. The reporter asked when she would be playing her first match. "Tuesday," she said, her gaze locked on the illuminated numbers overhead. After an awkward pause, the reporter suggested that the reservoirs of dead time must be the worst part of being a pro tennis player. "Please," Kournikova said, tossing her long blond tresses as the elevator stopped at her floor and the doors opened. "We are not tennis players. We are stars."

THE LAND OF OZ

ACROSS BETWEEN A GREEN ROOM AND REC room, the players' lounge is the equivalent of backstage in tennis. With no home clubhouse or permanent locker room, it is here that the nomads on the WTA Tour while away downtime at tournaments and minimize their social displacement between matches. They shoot pool, gab on their cell phones, surf the Net, play Ping-Pong, nap on comically overstuffed couches, and nibble snacks as they await their next court call.

The 2000 Australian Open is the first major event on the calendar, and the indoor/outdoor, two-tiered lounge in the catacombs of Rod Laver Stadium percolates with activity, adrenaline, and anticipation. As though it were the first day back at school after a long summer hiatus, the players arrive on the Melbourne campus happy to see their pals—exchanging hugs, showing off their new outfits, hairstyles, and tans, and telling tales of newly minted romances. Just as in a high school cafeteria, there's an "in table" in the lounge where players like Lindsay Davenport, Lisa Raymond, Mary Joe Fernandez, and Corina Morariu catch up. Mingling around them are both Tour veterans with the confident, forceful personalities of seniors and Tour rookies with the endearingly awestruck look of freshmen. Everyone discusses who's wearing what labels, who's eating what, who's sleeping with whom, who's dissing whom. Gossip and rumors bounce around the room at warp speed: *Did you hear Arantxa is getting married in July? I heard Steffi was going to be here with Andre. Julie will probably quit after this year, you know. Nathalie is supposed to be writing some kind of tennis book. Joe is coaching Alexandra but Samantha is driving him absolutely nuts. Is it true Mary fired Michael and needs a new coach?*

The lounge, which features a melange of tongues and a medley of nationalities, is as close as tennis gets to a nerve center. Genial and modest Lindsay Davenport is getting the third degree from her friends about her fledgling relationship with Baltimore Ravens tight end Ryan Collins. Pressed for details by Mary Joe Fernandez and Pam Shriver, Davenport blushes and gets up from the table. "Don't bring it up again," she pleads. Suddenly there's a hush worthy of an E. F. Hutton ad. Trailed by an entourage of her mother, Alla, her coach, Eric Van Harpen, and two representatives from an endorsement company, Anna Kournikova sweeps in. All eyes fix on her, mostly to see which male player is by her side. A few days ago, she was seen locking lips with Australian Mark Philippoussis in the tennis center's courtesy car area, but other players spotted her earlier in the week with Ecuadorian Nicolas Lapentti.

Across the room, Martina Hingis sits quietly with her mother, Melanie Molitor, and Molitor's companion, Mario Widmer. Like Nick Carraway eyeing the lights of East Egg, Hingis stares longingly at Davenport holding court at the popular table. Before anyone can meet her gaze, Hingis turns back to her pasta lunch. Off to the side, removed from the other clusters, Serena Williams and her mother, Oracene, laugh uproariously at some private joke. Serena's older sister Venus, the other half of the small but self-sustaining Williams clique, is conspicuous in her absence. There are already rumors about why Venus isn't playing at the Australian. It has been four months since Venus watched sullenly as her little sister won the 1999 U.S. Open, the first Grand Slam title for the House of Williams. The following day, Venus and Serena won the doubles title but the older sister was still glum. Asked whether the doubles trophy was any consolation for her loss in singles, Venus shook her head. "It doesn't help at all," she said bitterly. "It never helps. I'll never forget."

Venus insists that there is no sibling jealousy in her heart, but it had to sting when she double-faulted during the doubles final and a fan yelled, "Let Serena serve!" A few weeks after the U.S. Open, at the Grand Slam Cup in Munich, Serena beat Venus for the first time in four meetings. Now, Venus' official explanation for missing the Australian Open is tendinitis in her wrists; but it is no secret that the psychic wounds she suffered at the U.S. Open haven't fully healed. "Maybe she's lost interest in tennis," suggested Davenport. "Right now, no one really knows."

Scheduled in December at the end of a grueling season, the Australian Open used to be played on the sloping grass courts of Kooyong, a tony, private suburban Melbourne club that, not unlike Forest Hills in Queens, was ill-suited to host a big-time event. Many players balked at making the trek to Australia at the end of a wearying year. Chris Evert, for instance, made only six appearances in Melbourne in her nineteen-year career. (Though she did reach the finals every time there.) That Barbara Jordan and Chris O'Neil—who?—are former Australian Open champions says plenty about the diluted fields. In 1988, the tournament turned things around. It moved to a state-of-the-art, downtown facility, the National Tennis Center at Flinders Park, and changed from grass to the more democratic rubberized surface Rebound Ace. The center court has a retractable roof, obviating rain delays and, at times, protecting players from a merciless sun that can push on-court temperatures to over 110 degrees. Organizers also rescheduled the tournament to the *beginning* of the year. Within a decade of that move, the Australian Open became the country's most popular annual sporting event.

And now, the players like it too—once they get over the biorhythm-bending, twentysomething-hour flights from the United States and Europe, and recover from the inevitable jet lag. Although they are tethered to their rankings from the previous fifty-two weeks' worth of results, a cumulative GPA as it were, the prevailing sentiment in Melbourne is that everyone is starting the year anew. Promise and possibility linger in the air. Marginal players fantasize that this will be their breakthrough year. The top players, who endlessly grumble that tennis's off-season is too short, arrive fresh and full of optimism, ready to rumble.

Nicknamed "Oz," Australia is a faraway fantasy land to most of the players, where, as Davenport puts it, "everything's easy and the people couldn't be any nicer." The two main player hotels, the Hyatt and the Crown Casino, are both within minutes of the courts. The city is inexpensive, clean, and quiet. The usual swarm of gadflies—the media, the agents, the representatives from racket and shoe companies, assorted hangers-on—are largely absent, unwilling to make the long and expensive trip from the U.S. or Europe. Like some cosmic Coriolis force, everything in Australia (not just the bathwater in the drain) seems to swirl in a different direction. "It's all just so manageable," says Lisa Raymond. "You come down here and wonder 'Why can't all of our tournaments be like this?' " The Australian Open has the prestige and ranking points of a Grand Slam, with the relaxed pace and negligible chaos of a mixed doubles scramble at a suburban racket club.

The one knock that the women have against the Australian Open was that, even in the year 2000, it still awarded them less prize money than the men. The disparity was slight, just 6 percent, roughly $3.4 million for the blokes and $3.2 million for the Sheilas. The $200,000 difference is less than what a top player can make for a weekend exhibition. And the Australian Open purse was closer to equity than the French Open and Wimbledon, which paid women, respectively, only 86 and 80 percent of the men's wages in 2000. But the disparity in Melbourne was particularly galling for the female players because after years of fighting, the women had been bestowed equal prize money there in the early nineties, only to have it taken away in 1995, when the women's game was about as riveting as the Weather Channel. Tennis Australia told the WTA Tour that there would be purse parity again when women's tennis became more competitive and television ratings were comparable to the men's. By 2000, television ratings were often *higher* for women's matches; and on the whole, female players were more marketable. Even in Australia, which claimed three of the top twenty men and no women in the top forty, there was as much buzz for Serena, Anna, Martina, and Lindsay as there was for Andre Agassi, Pete Sampras, Pat Rafter, and Gustavo Kuerten. Still, the tournament had given no indication that parity would be restored.

The day before first round matches began, Paul McNamee, a former Wimbledon doubles champ and the tournament director of the Australian Open since 1995, stopped by the WTA Tour players' meeting in the Hyatt's second-floor ballroom. He had just come from the men's meeting, where he had slapped a few backs, made a fill-in-the-blanks welcoming speech, and then left. When he entered the women's meeting, he was surprised to see more than seventy players lying in wait and ready to pounce on him. After some cursory introductory remarks he opened the floor to questions and was peppered with complaints about prize money. His first line of defense—"I catch hell from my wife about that issue all the time"—didn't play too well, as the masses leveled him with hostile stares.

He then offered the tired response that men play best-of-five set matches while women only play best-of-three. Rennae Stubbs and Kim Po were among the chorus who countered that entertainment, not quantity, is what matters most. Nicole Pratt, the Che Guevara of the Tour, a feisty, articulate Australian veteran who has an informed opinion on virtually every issue affecting women's tennis, stood up and said that if duration were all that mattered, marathon runners would earn more than sprinters. Other players added that fans aren't exactly clamoring for five-set matches. Besides, American Debbie Graham added, "that doesn't explain the disparity in doubles, where both men and women play best-of-three sets until the finals, but the men earn more money throughout."

McNamee played nervously with his hands and became increasingly defensive. It wasn't his decision, he asserted; a change in prize money distribution would ultimately lie with a twelve-member board. Pam Shriver, a former player still deeply involved with Tour issues, suggested that the WTA Tour contact the makers of Equal, the artificial sweetener, to subsidize the difference. Finally McNamee raised his hand in surrender, smiled, and said: "I guess I just don't understand you because I'm a man and you're women." This almost got him killed. Like a comedian deaf to the boos, he slipped out of the room, stopping only to say, "Thanks for inviting me, girls," as seventy players gnashed their teeth in unison. But it turned out their protests were heard: by the end of the year, Tennis Australia would announce that the men's and women's purses would be equal at the 2001 Australian Open.

In 1999, when Lindsay Anne Davenport arrived at the Australian Open, she flew to Melbourne from Sydney, where she had just beaten Martina Hingis, the world's No. 1 ranked player, in the finals of a hard-court tune-up. Davenport tried to board the plane carrying her overstuffed Wilson racket bag, but a Quantas agent stopped her at the gate. "You'll have to check your rackets," the attendant said. "They're too big to take on board." Davenport calmly pointed out that only moments earlier Martina Hingis, who was also on the flight, had carried *her* rackets on board, no questions asked. "Well, *that* was Martina Hingis," the attendant whispered reverentially. "She needs them for her matches."

So it goes for one of the best players in women's tennis. Davenport stands nearly six three, as tall as any female player in history; she has won more Grand Slams than any other player over the past three years and she is the best American woman since Chris Evert. But so long as she shares the stage with the sassy, brassy divas who are drawn to the spotlight as if it were a divining rod, she'll always be overlooked. Who, after all, wants to read about a 24-going-on-34-year-old who would rather play with her infant niece than attend a red-carpet movie premiere? Who wants to photograph a player who takes to putting on makeup the way cats take to baths, who's most comfortable in wet hair, sandals, and a T-shirt? What kind of buzz can a player generate whose gaudiest piece of jewelry is a copper bracelet designed to alleviate wrist pain?

The one adjective invariably used to describe Davenport is "sweet."

Davenport is many things—down-to-earth, funny, polished, intelligent, unfailingly honest. She remembers the names of the security guards at her Laguna Beach community and always says hi. She writes thank-you notes to tournament directors, is punctual, proofreads her e-mail for spelling errors, and hates riding in limos. At tournaments, she'd rather find a local greasy spoon like the Villanova Diner in suburban Philadelphia than go out to the trendy, see-and-be-scene restaurants. But sweet? No.

Sweet wouldn't compartmentalize pressure and coolly serve out Grand Slam titles with the world watching. She wouldn't call Kournikova, the hottest commodity in tennis, "a total circus act." She wouldn't toss off enough creative variations of the word "fuck" to make a longshoreman blush. Nor would she sport a tattoo of the Olympic rings on her, um, lower back.

Sweet? Davenport didn't even give her father, Wink, a *chance* to become one of those domineering tennis dads. As a kid, she cringed when she watched her father get worked up at one of Lindsay's sisters' volleyball games. A week later, at one of Lindsay's junior matches in Southern California, Wink groaned aloud and shook his head when his daughter, then ten or eleven, made a sloppy error. Lindsay stopped her match, calmly walked to the fence, and summoned her father. When he leaned in, she said, "Dad, if you do that one more time, you'll never get to come watch me again."

"People who think I'm nice would be surprised to know what goes through my head on the court," she says, laughing. "I'm a total bitch out there. I get so pissed. Even when I'm playing a friend and she hits a winner, I'm like, 'Who the hell do think you are?' That's how I think, I can't help it. If you look at my face, I look like the meanest girl out there."

And it's not just tennis. She admits that she had to stop playing board games with friends long ago because she became insanely competitive. She and her coach rarely play points in practice because they invariably end in a dispute. To cut Davenport off in traffic is to put your life at risk. While some were shocked at the story that sweet Lindsay once kicked Alexandra Stevenson's bag across the locker room, Davenport's friends nod knowingly. "That totally sounds like Lindsay," says Rennae Stubbs. "She's great but she doesn't stand for any shit."

Davenport also practices the kind of plain speaking that would make Harry Truman proud. In Australia, she said of the Williams sisters: "Who knows what's going on with that family. Serena's more friendly. At least she can bring herself to say hi. Venus can't—or won't—even speak. Venus likes to give the impression that she's so great, that she's 'Da Bomb,' or whatever. She can say it all she wants but that just means she doesn't have it. She gets psyched out in big matches. She's not happy with her sister winning and the pressure is really falling on her."

And don't even get Davenport started on the politics of the WTA Tour. Coated in Teflon, Davenport is willing to say in public what other players only think. "Women's tennis is so hot right now. We sell out all the time, we're on television more than ever, tournaments are dying to have us, and the Tour doesn't help the players. Why doesn't prize money go up?" (It increased less than five percent between 1999 and 2000.) "They say tournaments aren't making money. Bullshit, they're not." What can be done to fortify the Tour? "It would help to have a CEO who played hardball and worked more with the players. [Bart McGuire] won't even walk up to us at sponsor parties. The Tour asks us to do a lot and we'd be so much more receptive if we felt they were really on our side."

Davenport is just as tough and edgy as her more glamorous contemporaries, but that doesn't mean she wants to change her public persona, however misguided it may be. She has carved a niche with Madison Avenue as tennis's counterprogramming to the "Spice Girls." Davenport may not be ideal for endorsing a risqué sports bra or selling lip gloss, but she is well suited for Rolex, American Express, and Nike, companies that pay her in excess of $4 million a year combined. She also figures that the dearth of hype allows her more time to play tennis. "I'm glad we have girls like Martina and Anna who like [the glamour component] because it means I don't have to do it," she says. "If not posing for calendars and not getting makeovers means that I don't get as much attention, well, I'm fine with who I am."

Watching Davenport in Melbourne—confident, opinionated, always surrounded by friends—it's hard to believe it was once very different. Davenport's ad for American Express say she's been "Standing Tall Since 1997." It refers, of course, to the duration of her status as a card member, but it could just as easily be taken literally. When Davenport was growing up in Southern California, she was so embarrassed about her height that her parents would constantly prod her in the back, a reminder to stand up straight. At sixteen, she was nearly a foot taller than most of the girls in her high school class. She still has vivid memories of traveling to tournaments with her birth certificate in hand, knowing that some rival's parent would demand proof that Davenport belonged in her age group. "I was like a lot of teenage girls," she says. "I didn't have a lot of confidence and you can't fake it."

That she weighed more than two hundred pounds when she turned pro and heard other players call her "Dump Truck" behind her back didn't help her self-image. Nor did the extramarital affair she claims her father had at the beginning of her career, which ended her parents' marriage after nearly thirty years and threw Lindsay into a tailspin. "It was just a horrible time," she says. "I'm one of those people who doesn't play well when things off the court are bad." Her nadir came at the year-end Chase Championships in 1995 when she lost an ugly match to Gabriela Sabatini. She felt bad about her tennis, her body, her career. Something had to change. She stayed up all night, agitated, and took the first flight home from New York in the morning. A few days later, she hired Robert Van't Hof, a former pro and NCAA champion, who had just finished a tour of duty with Todd Martin, as her coach.

Van't Hof sized Davenport up immediately: her strokes were immaculate, her technique flawless, her hands deceptively quick. But her footwork and fitness were a disaster. Not only was Davenport glacially slow on the court but she hated exercising. Van't Hof set about making training tolerable, if not outright enjoyable, by varying the drills and doing them with Davenport. One day they'd throw a football and run fly patterns on the beach, the next day they'd climb stairs, the next they'd play basketball. "If someone tells me to go to the gym, I'm like, 'yeah, whatever,' and I'll drive home," says Davenport. "But when you have a coach work out with you, it's energizing."

Four years later, Davenport had shed more than thirty pounds and had vastly improved her conditioning. Her self-confidence grew in proportion. When she won the 1998 U.S. Open, her big breakthrough, it was poetic justice that she chased down a drop shot on match point. She came to Australia in 2000 in perhaps the best shape of her life, not only reaching balls that didn't even merit a glance a few years ago, but arriving with sufficient time to unspool a wicked riposte. "I think what speaks highest of Lindsay is that she hasn't let up since she became No. 1 in 1998," says Van't Hof. "She's taken the comments about her physique and used them as fuel."

Still, manifestations of her once poor self-image endure. Davenport despises being photographed or filmed. She panics when she sees TV cameras. She hates reading about herself to the point that if a story contains too many words about her, she'll ask Van't Hof to peruse it and wait until he tells her it's fit for her consumption. "It's tough to read bad things no matter how confident you are," she says. "I'm still sensitive." Several years ago when Davenport was still an also-ran, *Inside Tennis,* a magazine distributed almost exclusively in California, noted that Lindsay had purchased lottery tickets for a charity. A throwaway line at the end of the article said sarcastically: "What a shock, Davenport didn't win the big prize." Davenport cried when she read that item and hasn't given the magazine an interview since. She's inherently leery of crowds. Celebratory dinners, player parties, and even big weddings make her wince. "When I get married," she says, "it's going to be twenty people on a beach in flip-flops."

So too is she mercilessly hard on herself. Davenport may curse an opponent under her breath, but she directs plenty of venom at herself as well. In her second round match in Australia against the young American Marissa Irvin, Davenport played listless tennis. As the camera panned to her, it took something less than a lip-reading expert to discern Davenport mouthing, "This is so fucking bad" and then "Fuck me!" Her attitude and body language were so defeatist—head down, shoulders slouched, eyes rolling like dice—it looked as though she had just lost her favorite pet. Van't Hof was so disgusted that he left Davenport's box and exited the arena mid-match. "If she loses, fine," he said. "But I have a hard time when she competes like that." After Davenport won, 6–4, 7–5, the mellow-to-the-core Van't Hof told her it was the worst match he had seen her play in two years. Though it was nearly ten at night, they went to the practice court for a hitting session.

It's easy to dismiss Davenport's self-flagellation as lingering insecurity—which to some extent, it probably is. But it is also a manifestation of the supreme confidence she now has in her tennis ability. When she's at her best, she feels no player should be able to stay with her. Her epiphany came at Wimbledon in 1999 when she won her semifinal match and then eagerly looked forward to playing Steffi Graf in the final, instead of the much lower-ranked Mirjana Lucic. "I thought I was going to win and I wanted to beat the best player," says Davenport. "Earlier I would have been praying for the easier [opponent]." She ended up blitzing Graf, a seven-time champion, in straight sets. In Australia, the prospect of losing never entered her thoughts. "I expect tough matches, but I expect to beat everybody and I know I can win any tournament. It didn't always used to be this way, but now my attitude is: I deserve to be where I am."

In mid-January, with buckets of money and ranking points on the table, the prevailing wisdom is that players should be close to top form. Yet at the Australian Open, both members of tennis's famed sister act were still deep in hibernation. Venus Williams had pulled out of Australia because of persistent tendinitis in her wrists. Serena had decided to make the trip at the last minute, but she might as well have stayed in Florida. Having won the previous Grand Slam—the 1999 U.S. Open—Serena would have been a fair bet to win the title in Australia, particularly on a surface that was playing uncommonly fast, infusing her ballistic strokes with even more pop. But her game was coated in rust. She hadn't played a tournament since October, and she skipped a tune-up event in favor of taking fashion courses at the Art Institute of Fort Lauderdale with Venus. She didn't even arrive in Melbourne until three days before her opening match.

Her first opponent, Australian Amanda Grahame, didn't figure to keep her on the court for long. An unknown twenty-year-old from Canberra, Grahame was ranked 275th in the world. Before the match, Serena said of her opponent: "I wouldn't have been able to recognize her even if she was standing in front of me."

If Serena wasn't ready to impress anybody with her ground strokes, at least she was ready for the catwalk. Serena took the court in an airtight red and black Puma one-piece with a "Geronimo!" neckline and red leather tennis boots, eliciting gasps from the crowd and even a double take from the chair umpire. Once Williams and Grahame got on the court, there was little indication that 272 ranking slots separated the two players. A swashbuckling lefty bolstered by the enthusiasm of a partisan crowd, Grahame confused Williams with her serve and unleashed some nifty winners from the baseline. Williams took the first set 6–4, but Grahame capitalized on a break point to level the match at a set apiece. Staving off a monstrous upset, Williams shook off her torpor and closed out the match, 6–4, 4–6, 6–4 but she was appropriately disgusted with her play.

Serena acquitted herself only slightly better in her next match against Nicole Pratt, another Australian. After falling behind 1–3 in the first set, committing a bevy of sloppy errors from the baseline, Williams steadied herself and methodically banged out a 7–5, 6–1 win. She was still off in her following match against Sabine Appelmans, racking up wholesale errors, but she escaped 6–2, 7–6.

It wasn't lost on the rest of the field that Serena had labored to beat three pedestrian opponents ranked outside the top fifty. When a top player struggles on the court, a palpable schadenfreude bubbles among other players. With the morbid curiosity of rubberneckers gawking at a bloody wreck on the interstate, they crowd around the televisions in the locker room and even inconspicuously take an empty seat in the stands to witness the carnage firsthand. In Australia, one group of players clustered to watch excitedly on the monitor in the locker room as Serena flailed about. Another gathered around an overhead television in the players' lounge to watch.

It's a rite of passage in women's tennis that a top young player is ostracized by the rest of the field. Steffi Graf was persona non grata when she broke onto the circuit. Even Monica Seles, now universally loved, was teased and ignored by older players like Martina Navratilova when she was a teenager. But antipathy for the Williams sisters runs deeper than any hazing ritual—one player reported that as Serena stumbled through the early rounds, "girls who had barely met before were giving each other high fives."

Everyone had a diagnosis for Serena's woes. One player suggested that she was struggling because her older sister wasn't by her side. Another noticed a loss of the muscle mass that had made her so indomitable at the U.S. Open. "It's obvious they need an experienced coach," added another. In the press room, the most popular explanation was that Serena was suffering from hubris that enabled her to believe she could still win after four months of inactivity and such scant preparation.

In fact, what was really "ailing" both Serena and Venus was the multiplicity of their outside interests and something less than a wholehearted commitment to tennis. It ought to be considered wonderfully refreshing that in the months following her U.S. Open title Serena went to school—even if it was a fashion school—instead of wallowing in the endorsement dollars from Madison Avenue. (Serena is majoring in evening wear, Venus is concentrating in ready-to-wear garments.) Or that Venus will skip practice if she has too much homework. When it suits them, the tennis poo-bahs collectively salute these kinds of priorities and outside interests. But when the Williamses' extra-tennis pursuits threaten a promoter's ability to sell tickets and sponsorships, the knives come out. Suddenly, the sisters are betraying the sport. "I wish they'd put down their sewing needles or whatever the fuck they're doing, and play more events," says one tournament director. Clearly, had Serena not taken a full course load in the fall, she would have been in better form in Melbourne. On the other hand, as she pointed out, had she skipped school, "I would never have learned a thousand things I'll need to know when tennis is over."

Serena's lack of preparation caught up with her in her fourth round match with Elena Likhovtseva. A tall, lithe Russian, Likhovtseva is a free spirit who, after playing Fed Cup in California in the fall of '99, made an impetuous detour to Las Vegas. There, she and her boyfriend, Misha, an affable, chain-smoking, former University of Moscow food technology student, got married at Caesars Palace. Among the better athletes on the Tour, Likhovtseva hardly had to summon her gifts against Serena. After trailing 3–1, Likhovtseva rattled off eight straight games and watched with delight as Williams drove shot after unimaginative shot past the court's outside lines. Williams's thirty-second unforced error ended her miserable day at the office, 6–3, 6–3.

Serena is usually charming, quick and engaging. But after a loss, she snarls at the media. With a cap pulled down low, she gave distracted, monosyllabic answers during the postmortem. One intrepid writer asked her to assess her coaching situation. "I don't understand," Serena responded acidly. "My mother is here, she's my coach, and she's been there throughout my entire career. What part of that is such a big problem for everybody to understand?" Moments later, Serena stormed out of the room. She was on a flight back to Florida by the next morning. After all, she had thirty-eight fashion drawings due in two days and wanted to miss as little class time as possible.

Insiders knows that at the Grand Slams, the women's draw doesn't really start until the second week. Unlike the men's brackets, which are riddled with upsets, the women's side invariably follows form through the first week. For all the talk of improved depth in women's tennis, there's still a vast chasm separating the top half dozen players from the rest of the field. Ultimately, it benefits the game because it increases the visibility of the top players; fans of Lindsay Davenport, for instance, know that she'll be around for six or seven rounds. Also, the imbalance of talent on the women's tour heats up the rivalries among the top players, who clash more frequently in the high-stakes matches. The drawback is that it can be a snooze watching the top seeds prance through forty-five-minute creampuff matches in the early rounds. And so, without fail, the first-week media coverage of Slams is dominated by the off-court intrigues that make women's tennis at once so alluring and repulsive. It is the storm before the Week Two calm. At the Australian Open—as well as at Wimbledon and the U.S. Open—the major first-week story was Damir Dokic, the most recent example of tennis's large legion of deplorable dads.

There's very little sociological data on tennis fathers, the hard-driving, overbearing creeps who plague the women's game. Some say the first one was John Roosevelt, an uncle of FDR. The proud father of Grace and Ellen Roosevelt, two top Americans players in the late nineteenth century, John trained his daughters on the family court. The sisters were national doubles champions in 1900; Ellen was also the U.S. singles titleholder that year. According to a contemporary, John "coached and treated them like show ponies, closely monitoring their diet and sleep while the rest of the girls giggled and had a good time." Others claim that the avatar was Suzanne Lenglen's father. A century ago, "Papa" Lenglen, a former professional bicycle racer, placed handkerchiefs in various corners of the court and ordered his prodigy to hit hundreds of balls at them. Known as much for her rebellious dress and propensity to swig cognac at changeovers as for her dozens of titles, Suzanne Lenglen died in 1938 at age thirty-nine. Since then, the species of domineering tennis fathers has grown in proportion to the sport's prize money and international platform.

In the past two decades, prominent ill-behaved fathers have included Roland Jaeger, Peter Graf, Marinko Lucic, and Jim Pierce. To paraphrase Tolstoy, each churlish tennis father is different in his own way. Some, like Pierce, abused their daughters physically and berated them in public. Others, like Graf, isolated their daughters from the rest of the Tour and embarrassed them with their conduct. Still others, like Stefano Capriati, ran their daughters into the ground—but not before making millions.

The dysfunctional tennis father has some striking characteristics. He has often quit his full-time job—the telltale sign of trouble—to manage his daughter's career. He dresses like a player, clad in a silky sweat suit or in shorts, socks, and white shoes, all invariably provided gratis from the daughter's sponsor. He usually shoves his wife deep into the background. In many cases, he was an athlete of modest distinction who never quite fulfilled his promise. "A lot of the problem is that these guys are living vicariously through their daughters," says Michael DeJongh, a coach on the Women's Tour who's worked with Mary Pierce. "When their daughters fail, it's like they're losing to a girl."

Damir Dokic, a bearded, burly former boxer and truck driver, relocated his family from Croatia to Serbia and then to Australia in the early nineties. Until friends provided tables and chairs, the Dokic family lived in a small, unfurnished apartment in a working-class Sydney neighborhood. Around the time it became clear his daughter, Jelena, was a gifted player, it also became obvious that Damir was trouble. During Jelena's junior career, he received three warnings from the New South Wales Tennis Association for disruptive behavior that included berating officials. There were also suspicions that Damir physically abused Jelena. In January 1998, during the Australian ITF Junior Hardcourt Championships in Melbourne, local police received a complaint alleging that Damir had assaulted Jelena. Police investigated and reported bruises on Jelena, but she and her father both denied the assault. The bruises, she suggested to investigators, were the result of intense training. After a court hearing, in which Damir promised that he would not physically abuse his daughter, no formal charges were filed.

Clearly intoxicated at a 1999 Wimbledon tune-up event in Birmingham, Damir was evicted from the stadium for excessive cheering. He then lay down in traffic outside the stadium, ranted about NATO's presence in the Balkans, and was finally detained by police. When asked about Damir's outburst, Jelena maintained that the police had overreacted. "I definitely think the English are a bit fussy," she said. Yet Damir didn't seem to impair Jelena's play—two weeks later, she upset Martina Hingis in the first round of Wimbledon.

At the 2000 Australian Open, the Dokic family was back in the news. As her country's lone female ranked in the top fifty, Jelena was expected to do well in Melbourne. But in her first round match against qualifier Rita Kuti Kis of Hungary, Dokic played listless tennis and lost in three sets. Instead of attending a mandatory press conference, she left the grounds with her father, later claiming she had gone to church to pray for better results. When she returned to the stadium five hours later, she read a prepared statement that described Kuti Kis as someone who has "never been a player and I guess probably never will be." She added: "If anyone saw my practices, there's probably not more than three or four players at the moment that could beat me." Outside the interview room, Jim Fuhse, the WTA Tour's director of player promotions, shook his head. Fuhse had strongly suggested that Jelena begin by apologizing for her tardiness. "Instead she reads that statement," Fuhse said, throwing up his hands. "We try to look out for the players, but they seem to say whatever they want." The Tour fined Dokic $2,500 for ducking the post-match press conference. That should have been the end of the incident.

Instead, apparently at her father's urging, Jelena told the *Melbourne Sun-Herald* that WTA Tour administrators were rigging draws against her because they hated Damir. It was a patently ludicrous charge, made all the more absurd given that she had just dismissed her previous opponent as a nobody. Jelena later claimed she had been misquoted by the newspaper and blamed her management firm, Octagon, as well as the WTA, for failing to come to her defense. The behavior only provoked the Australian media. When an Australian television crew filmed Damir outside the Hyatt where the family was staying, he grabbed a camera and tried to eject the tape as he walked away. When the crewman demanded his camera back, Dokic stripped off its microphone. Suddenly realizing that he was being filmed, Dokic offered to pay the cameraman five hundred dollars for the tape. He refused and Damir's bizarre outburst became a lead story on the national news. More episodes were to follow.

Tennis is a hothouse for pushy parents and dysfunctional father-child relationships in a way that other sports aren't. Money is one of the reasons—the financial risks and rewards are far greater than in most other exploits. It can cost upward of $50,000 a year to send a talented child to a junior academy and pay for training and international travel for tournaments. A family can easily go into hock to support a precocious ball-striker. On the other hand, a player that breaks into the top ten is set for life. Stefano Capriati, who famously bragged about making his daughter do sit-ups in her crib, was once asked why he was pushing Jennifer onto the pro tour at the age of thirteen. With eerie prescience, he said: "Where I come from the saying is: 'If the apple is ripe you eat it.' So Jennifer may burn out—God only knows—but then she'll have more money than I could have given her." The proliferation of big money also makes it easier for parents to accompany their children on Tour and stay more visible. "The 'Daddy Factor' always existed," says Dr. Julie Anthony, a pro in the 1970s who is now a psychologist in Aspen. "The difference is that now you can afford to bring your dysfunctional father to every tournament."

The development timeline for a tennis player also encourages close parental supervision. There's no such thing as a teenager picking up a racket for the first time and going on to win Wimbledon. Most of the top players hit hundreds of balls every day before they were tall enough to see over the net. The parents made the choice for them—and invariably made wholesale sacrifices for their kids' junior careers—and thus feel inextricably tied to their results. And their winnings.

What's more, tennis is an easy sport to grasp. Unlike gymnastics or even golf, which involve a variety of technical skills, tennis consists of just a half dozen basic strokes. Overbearing fathers who have no formal training in the game—and usually look as though they couldn't run from one baseline to the other without having a lung collapse—nonetheless feel qualified to coach their offspring. Were Jelena Dokic a standout pianist, a chemistry whiz, or even a gifted golfer, Damir would undoubtedly have no delusions of being qualified to coach her. Tennis is different.

The thornier question is what makes female tennis players more susceptible to tyrannical fathers than their male counterparts? Sonya Jeyaseelan, the highest-ranked Canadian player, observes: "You can look at a men's draw and find maybe three players who have had a [dysfunctional] relationship with their father. With the girls you might find three who *don't*." When Jeyaseelan showed signs of talent at age six, her father, Reggie, quit his job in Vancouver and moved with her to a Florida tennis academy. Her mother stayed in Canada, earning the family's only income. In Florida, Reggie cooked Sonya's meals, washed her clothes, and looked on as she hit thousands of tennis balls each day. Sonya says her father would do "controlling, manipulative things" such as hide her dolls to keep her focus on tennis. She alleges that physical abuse followed. "He would tell the media I'd win Wimbledon at age eighteen; I didn't have friends because of him," says Sonya. "He wanted it more than I did."

Jeyaseelan thinks gender roles are to blame for the proliferation of overbearing fathers on the women's tour and their relative absence on the men's tour. "Women have been brought up to please men," she says. "You don't push a son too much because he is going to be the Man of the House someday, and he'll have to make decisions, so we let boys grow up on their own. With the woman, if she pleases the man, the man will take care of her."

Another explanation is that women reach their competitive peak in tennis earlier than men. Whereas four of the top ten WTA Tour players in 1999 were eighteen and under, the average age among the top ten men was over twenty-five. A teenager embarking on a pro career at age sixteen invariably requires parental supervision. Others claim that physical considerations play a significant role in tennis fathers dominating daughters and not sons. A USTA coach tells the story of a promising American junior boy with "a total fucking nightmare" for a father. By age sixteen, the kid was over six feet tall. One day, his five-nine dad was looking up at him while unleashing a tirade. The son looked down and laughed. "I don't deny that bonds between a parent and child are thick," says the USTA coach. "But it's a lot harder to manipulate and intimidate someone when they can kick your ass."

The WTA Tour does what it can to combat the blight of ill-behaved fathers, an ongoing public relations battle. In 1994, the Tour established the Age Eligibility Rules. An unqualified success, the rules restrict the number of events players under eighteen may enter, allowing them to mature away from the high-intensity lighting of the professional game. Under a mentoring program, teenage players are paired with former pros, who, unlike father-coaches, know the rigors of the circuit firsthand. All WTA Tour coaches—parents included—are subject to the Coaches Code of Ethics, which has the authority to ban aides de camp who compromise "the psychological, physical or emotional well-being of any player."

Not every bad father leads to a sad story. At age eighteen, Jeyaseelan mustered the courage to break from her overbearing father. "I had to tell him, 'You're losing a daughter, not just a tennis player,'" she says, choking up. "I told him, 'I don't want to have success and make millions under these unhealthy conditions.' It took me ten years to realize that, and even then I doubted myself."

At first she moved in with friends and struggled with the change, but eventually, she found her way. She got her own apartment in downtown Toronto, made friends on Tour, and away from the parental pressure her game flourished. She was outside the top two hundred when they split; within a year she was in the top hundred. That, she says, wasn't a coincidence. She finished 2000 ranked in the top fifty for the first time in her career, beating players such as Conchita Martinez and Nathalie Tauziat at Grand Slams. Five years after cutting the cord, she and her father have reconciled. "It's never going to be perfect," she says of their relationship. "He still wants to be a part of my career so badly. But he understands that he can't just hold on to me forever. We're still working on things, but it's so much healthier now than it was."

A unique feature of women's tennis in this soap opera age is how tournaments often become as famous for their controversies and contretemps as for their tennis. In 1999, Martina Hingis won her third straight Australian Open and reclaimed the top ranking from Lindsay Davenport, but the tournament will be best remembered for the headlines Hingis generated when she called her opponent in the final,

Amelie Mauresmo, a muscular and broad-shouldered out-of-the-closet lesbian, "half a man." Likewise, the 1999 French Open may be as remembered for Hingis's epic meltdown in the final as it will for Steffi Graf's emotional victory. In that match, Hingis was booed mercilessly when she took a prolonged mid-match bathroom break, emerged with a new hairstyle, trespassed to Graf's side of the net to argue a call, and served underhanded. Having been three points from victory, Hingis lost in dramatic and melodramatic fashion, then left the court in tears and slapped a WTA Tour representative who had summoned her back on the court for the trophy ceremony.

Hingis returned from the outskirts of Burnoutville to finish 1999 with the top ranking; but she arrived in Australia desperately seeking a fresh start. Her image had taken a pummeling in the previous year. She is a player who doesn't embarrass easily, but even she knows that she looked like a jerk. "Let's not even go there. I was all messed up," she said, pursing her lips. "If I never have another year like that, I'd be happy."

If ever a top athlete needed an image consultant, it was Hingis. Yes, she has her moments. But contrary to popular belief, she can be rather charming. She is also bright and has a good sense of humor. So why was it that the *New York Observer* once asked, "Has there ever been a less endearing champion than Hingis?" Why is she portrayed as "one of the most conceited people on earth" (as one British paper wrote during the Australian Open)? The answer: because she draws no distinction between what she thinks and what she says. In a sport in which players usually serve up a bottomless buffet of second-rate clichés—"I take it one match at a time," "I'm not looking ahead past the next round," "I need to stay aggressive"—Hingis is an Uzi of candor. At her best, she is a throwback to a time when public figures could actually speak their minds. At her worst, she spends hours with one of her Adidas shoes in her mouth, a small mouth that curves on the corners, as if to say, "I know something you don't." Ask Hingis about another player and she's likely to paint an unsparing portrait of a talentless pretender. Once asked to assess her rivals, she said that her lead in ranking points was so sizable that she had none.

The American pro Justin Gimelstob, who had a brief romance with Hingis, was astounded by her bluntness. "She would just trash another player in an interview—she would say something like, 'I beat her every time and her serve is really weak, so I'm not worried at all'—and I'd shake my head. I'd say to her, 'How could you have said that?' She'd look at me funny and go, 'How could I have said *what*?' I'm not sure she's all that cocky. I think she just doesn't get it."

Those around her often bristle when she speaks out. "I tried to convince her to be more prudent," Mario Widmer, Molitor's omnipresent companion, and Martina's de facto stepfather, said with a sigh in Australia. "I've told her for years not to be so cocky." But, so far, she's still queen of the diss. In the wake of her summer of 1999 meltdown, Hingis went to a media relations workshop at the behest of the WTA Tour and Octagon, her management firm. A reporter saw Hingis a few days later and asked whether it had been worthwhile. "No," she said without hesitating. "They didn't tell me anything I didn't already know." The one highlight for her was a video on athletes' bad habits featuring Baltimore Orioles outfielder Brady Anderson. Why was it funny? Hingis looked around the room to make sure there were no eavesdroppers and then said furtively: "He's Amanda's boyfriend, you know," referring to Amanda Coetzer.

The Tour's media relations personnel often give Hingis talking points—"don't forget to mention the crowd and praise your opponent"—before press conferences, and they also instruct her to curtail her monologues. On the other hand, Bart McGuire, the Tour's CEO, acknowledges, "We don't want our players to be bland, and I don't think there's any risk of that with Martina."

At the Australian Open, Hingis claimed that she had done some soul-searching during the off-season and was going to watch her mouth. No sooner had she arrived in Melbourne, however, than the international press corps (for whom Hingis is a godsend) tried to goad her into trashing her rival, Serena Williams. Nothing doing. Surely Hingis would have something to say about the latest outburst of Damir Dokic. No comment. Did Martina at least have some advice for poor Jelena? "I've made so many mistakes in saying things," Hingis responded. "I shouldn't say."

At six-one, Pam Shriver was hard to miss striding across the grounds of Melbourne Park. She had made the trip to Australia for a number of reasons. The former Tour veteran had been hired to provide television commentary for the matches, she had a few corporate speaking engagements, and, as a United States Tennis Association board member, she also had business concerns. But above all, she was desperate to get back to the familiar world of tennis and the Tour, a refuge after a nightmarish fall.

A lanky serve-and-volleyer with an unruly head of curly hair, Shriver burst on the tennis scene in 1978 when, at sixteen, she reached the finals of the U.S. Open. "It was a big thrill," she recalls, "and then I went back to high school the next Monday." A notch less talented than contemporaries Chris Evert and Martina Navratilova, she would never reach another Grand Slam singles final, but she retired in 1997 as one of the most accomplished doubles players in women's history. Something else set her apart: Shriver had a brain capable of thinking thoughts other than tennis. Driven, bright, and socially polished, she had been the player the Tour summoned whenever it needed a spokeswoman; she served on countless committees; as her career wound down, she bought a minority ownership interest in her hometown baseball team, the Baltimore Orioles. These days, defiantly youthful in her late thirties, she moves easily among tennis's various factions, young and hip enough to befriend the players but sufficiently removed to be a credible commentator and critic.

In 1996, Shriver had been girding for retirement when she was invited to have dinner in San Diego with former pro Liz Smylie and her husband, Peter. The Smylies had also invited their friend, Joe Shapiro, a retired corporate lawyer. Joe was fifteen years older than Pam, he was Jewish (she's Episcopalian), and he was almost a half foot smaller. He was an ambitious Harvard Law School graduate who had scaled the corporate ladder at Disney. As the company's general counsel, he was in

charge of negotiating Disneyland Paris and liked to boast that he had
flown from L.A. to Europe fifty times in an eighteen-month period. "I
was like 'Wow, what a great guy,' " Shriver recalls thinking. "I thought
to myself, now tell me: when am I ever going to see him?"

After dinner, Shapiro drove Shriver back to the La Costa Spa and
Resort. Lingering outside her room, Joe broke the ice when he looked
up at Shriver and said: "Would you mind standing downhill?" Early
into their courtship, he warned Pam that there was a serious drawback
to starting a relationship with him. Two years prior he had been diagnosed with non-Hodgkins' lymphoma, a type of cancer affecting the
immune system. It was in remission, but Shriver's stomach dropped.
She was already all too fluent in cancer-speak. Her older sister, Marion, had been battling cervical cancer since 1991. (She passed away in
1997.) Was she prepared for what might follow? "In every relationship, you come to a point where you can just say, 'Uh, look, it's been
fun, but I'm outta here,' " Shriver says. "In this case, I got to that point
and I said to myself, 'Pam, you're falling for a guy with a complicated
medical history.' Well, I decided not to take the easy way out, and it
was the best decision I ever made."

Joe and Pam married on December 5, 1998, in an intimate ceremony at the La Quinta resort in the California desert. What she calls
"six blissful months" followed. Then, in July of 1999, Pam traveled to
Massachusetts for a USTA board meeting. When she called Joe that
night, he sounded enervated. She had a bad feeling. A few days later, a
biopsy showed that his cancer had returned full force. Shriver spent
the next two months scrambling from one oncology unit to the next.
As Joe's cancer spread, an array of treatments, including heavy doses of
a powerful biotherapy drug, ravaged his organs. On September 23,
1999, Joe died at age fifty-two with Shriver next to him, holding his
hand. "Not too many women I know envision themselves as a widow
at thirty-seven," says Shriver. "Well, there I was."

She gradually started piecing her life back together. She did some
television work and held her annual charity exhibition in Baltimore in
November. She also started seeing a therapist. On her one-year marriage anniversary she and five friends chartered a sailboat off Marina

Del Ray and scattered Joe's ashes in the Pacific. On New Year's Eve, she went to the Brentwood Country Club, where Joe had been a long-time member, and poured white wine into the cup on the eighth green, the last hole of golf Joe ever played. "Happy New Year, honey," she whispered.

At the 2000 Australian Open, she had already been a widow for four months. Her moods sometimes changed from minute to minute. On the flight over, she was daydreaming when a Backstreet Boys song came on the headphones. It triggered a poignant memory and a torrent of tears.

As she stared at a bowl of cereal on the top floor of the Grand Hyatt one morning during the second week of the tournament, she reflected on the previous few months. "You know what's really helped me deal with this? Tennis," she said. "You obviously can't compare losing a tough three-set match to losing a spouse, but the lessons stick. You learn to recover from loss and you learn how to be resilient. I had losses on the court that were so devastating I'd go back to my room and sob inconsolably. When you're a teenager, you cry; when you're twenty-five you break a racket; and when you're thirty you pour yourself a drink and say 'what the hell.' But you learn to cope and you come back strong."

Her therapy has helped her to make some sense of the tragedy. For better or worse, her perspective on life has forever changed. So in Melbourne, when Shriver heard that Alexandra Stevenson wasn't speaking to her because, as Stevenson had been complaining to other players, "Pam trashed my game on television," Shriver could only shrug. At one point, it might have bothered her. Now, it was laughable. "Life's way too short to stress over little things like that," she said, gazing out the window at a panoramic view of Melbourne shrouded in gray clouds. "I've vowed to stay strong, get back into a ritual, and keep going. And I will. I will. But I sure have had enough sadness for a while."

For Jennifer Capriati, the Australian Open offered yet another chance to get back her former glory. After countless failed comebacks, she finished 1999 ranked in the top twenty for the first time since 1994. At age twenty-three, she was hopeful that she could finally put her check-ered past behind her and return to the top. When she arrived in Mel-bourne, she was radiating confidence. Under the direction of her coach, Harold Solomon, she was playing perhaps the best tennis of her career, pounding the ball as usual, but doing so with purpose for the first time. She had also been working out during the winter with Karen Burnett, her personal trainer at the Saddlebrook resort outside Tampa, and was fitter than she'd ever been. Jennifer's mother, Denise, often caught her daughter admiring her new ripples and bulges in the mirror. "You could just tell how good she was feeling about herself and her body," says Denise. "She felt like she worked hard, she was in shape, and she deserved to win her matches."

At the same time, it was clear that she was starting to think and act like a grown-up. During a leisurely breakfast at the Crown Casino Hotel, Jennifer and Denise were poring over a Melbourne newspaper trying to find a publicity photo taken for the Australian Open that fea-tured Jennifer posed in front of a fountain. Thumbing through the paper, Jennifer fought back tears when she read an article about a local player who felt her back stiffen on the court one day—what she had assumed was a strained muscle turned out to be inoperable bone cancer.

The story consumed Jennifer's thoughts during her first round win over Barbara Schwartz. By the end of the day, Jennifer and Denise had called CanTeen, an adolescent cancer support group in Melbourne, and invited a group of teenage patients to be their guests for a day at the matches. The next day, Denise picked them up in a courtesy car. The kids were given choice seats at Rod Laver Arena and were allowed into the locker rooms. They ate lunch in the players' lounge, sat in on Serena Williams's press conference, and finished the day watching their hostess and her partner, Jelena Dokic, defeat Els Callens and Dominique Van Roost in doubles. "I was just so moved by the story, I wanted to help, especially since they were so into tennis," said Capriati, who was still fir-ing off e-mail to the kids a year later. But there was another reason she was deeply affected. A year earlier, doctors had found a tumor in the groin area of her younger brother, Steven. It was successfully removed and he went back to school at the University of Florida, but the experience had been frightening. "It's so easy to get wrapped up in the tennis and forget what a great life you have," said Denise. "I think Jennifer realizes that any moment your life can change."

Not that she has to read a newspaper to know that. Virtually overnight, Capriati went from being tennis's Next Big Thing to being its poster child for burnout. Despite reaching the semifinals of Grand Slams and winning an Olympic gold medal, she's far better known for her mug shot, a raccoon-eyed, addled teenager, arrested for possession of marijuana in a fleabag south Florida hotel. In truth, her "path of quiet rebellion," as she euphemistically calls it, hardly entailed earth-shattering depravity. She was a rebellious teenager saddled with pressure including the breakup of her parents' marriage, who got caught shoplifting a cheap ring from a department store, experimented with recreational drugs—which may or may not have included crack and heroin—and did multiple stints in rehab. It's nothing we'd want for our own kids, but a poll of a freshman dorm at Harvard or Yale would certainly unearth transgressions and excesses just as worrisome.

In fits and starts, Capriati tried to extricate herself; but her efforts were halfhearted. In the spring of 1999, Capriati's father, Stefano, had called up Harold Solomon, perhaps the most highly regarded coach in the game, and begged him to work with his daughter. Solomon had tried to whip Capriati into shape several years earlier, but his style had been too intense for a player whose confidence had been so severely buffeted. "I told him 'no way' unless I heard from Jennifer herself," says Solomon. Capriati invited him to her house and the two spoke for hours. She pledged to work harder this time. Two months later, she won a French Open tune-up event in Strasbourg. It was her first tournament victory in six years.

In Australia, Capriati had never appeared more relaxed or comfortable with herself. While she usually endured press conferences the same way kids endure eating vegetables—speaking, um, like, a strain of Valley Girl-ese, ya know—she was also downright engaging. And playing her best tennis since the early nineties, she reeled off five wins in Melbourne and reached her first Grand Slam semifinal since 1991.

After Capriati savaged Ai Sugiyama to reach the semis, one reporter mischievously asked, "If anybody had told you a year ago that you would win a Grand Slam quarterfinal 6–0, 6–2, would you have asked what they were smoking?" Capriati grinned and fiddled with her diamond bracelet. "No comment." When the laughs subsided, she answered, "A year ago, maybe not. But a couple years ago, yeah." Why did she seem so much happier with herself than she had in the past? "I don't know." Capriati sighed. "I guess I've stopped thinking what the world thinks of me." In the corridor outside the locker room, Denise Capriati was ecstatic. "She's becoming a woman." Denise smiled. "I knew this day would come, it's just hard to believe she had to go through so much to get here."

Capriati's inspired run ended with her semifinal match against Davenport, who had caught fire. Davenport hadn't come close to dropping a set since her desultory second round effort against Marissa Irvin. Capriati and Davenport were born just months apart but they couldn't have taken two more divergent career paths. "When I was thirteen, Jennifer was a hero to me," Davenport says. "Obviously, things changed." Conversely, Capriati scarcely remembers Davenport from junior tennis, but acknowledges the irony that Davenport attended her senior prom and graduated from high school in the spring of 1994, the same time that she entered drug rehab. And here they both were, a match away from a Grand Slam final. During ninety minutes of high-quality, hard-hitting tennis, they traded fusillades. In the end, Davenport's superior consistency and big-match experience carried the day, 6–2, 7–6. Still, it was a huge confidence boost for Capriati, who, a year later, would come back to Melbourne and complete her transmogrification from cautionary tale to fairy tale by winning her first Grand Slam.

When Davenport walked into the locker room after the match, the first person to greet her was Martina Hingis, who had been watching on television. "You look tired, Leen-see," Hingis said with a shy smile. Like a grade school girl admiring her high school idol, Hingis is oddly reverential toward Davenport, the player who poses the most consistent threat to her dominance. Perhaps it's because Hingis feels a kinship with Davenport in their alignment against the Williams sisters. Perhaps it's because Davenport is one of the most popular players in the locker room, a modern-day Chris Evert who can tell dirty jokes to her friends and then charm the adults outside. Perhaps it's because Hingis envies Davenport's well-adjusted life, the healthy detachment she has from her parents, that her existence is devoid of drama and soap opera histrionics.

"I *am* tired," Davenport said, smiling.

"Let me get you some water," Hingis said eagerly.

With that, the world's top-ranked player bounded out of her chair and fetched the world's second-ranked player a small bottle of Evian.

A short time later, Hingis took the court against her semifinal opponent, Conchita Martinez. The match looked nothing like the slugfest between Davenport and Capriati. Power was supplanted by guile; resounding strokes gave way to delicate slices; drop shots and angles replaced unremitting depth. Raw power threatens Hingis's hegemony, but she is impregnable against a mere retriever like Martinez. Hingis covers the court well and she can execute every shot in the book. In the quarterfinals, Hingis had needed barely forty minutes to handle Arantxa Sanchez Vicario for the thirteenth straight time. "Easy day at the office," she said afterward with a devilish wink.

Her 6–3, 6–2 destruction of Martinez wasn't as close as the score indicated either. Hingis, it seemed, would indulge Martinez in a baseline rally for a while and then, suddenly tiring of the adagio tempo, flick a winner up the line or throw in a cold-blooded drop shot. Like most of Martinez's matches, though, this one seemed to last an eternity. Part of that is because her service toss scarcely rises above her head; thus she generates little power and wins few easy points on her serve. But her matches also drag on because of her maddening idiosyncrasies. In addition to never stepping on the lines, she insists on serving every point with the same ball. Time and again she would walk to the baseline to serve and signal the ballboys to retrieve the ball from the other end of the court.

Hingis was gleeful after the match. She was in the finals, two sets away from winning her fourth straight Australian Open singles title. Her confidence was peaking along with her tennis. Was she surprised that her match against Martinez had gone so smoothly? "It shows how well I played overall this tournament and, you know, it's not a surprise anymore," she said. "I beat all the players." So there.

During the late seventies and early eighties, it was said that the world's best doubles team was "John McEnroe and anyone." On the WTA Tour, the same could now be said for Hingis. Heading into the 2000 season, Hingis had won as many career doubles titles—twenty-six—as she had playing solo. Since turning pro, she has also blithely taken on and discarded partners the way most people change long distance carriers. As Hingis herself joked to a reporter, "It's like how Anna treats her men." Davenport, who played with Hingis only once, says, "Martina takes on a doubles player for a year, figures them out, and then moves on."

Hingis arrived in Melbourne with an eighteen-match Australian Open winning streak in doubles that included three titles, each with a different partner: Natasha Zvereva, Mirjana Lucic, and Anna Kournikova. For the better part of 1998, Hingis had a wonderful run with Jana Novotna, but they parted company. Hingis announced publicly that Novotna, at the doddering age of thirty, was "too old and slow." (Novotna responded by calling Hingis "stupid.") Hingis played well with Kournikova for most of 1999, but unceremoniously dumped her after the two won the year-end Chase Championships. Kournikova's controversial coach, Eric Van Harpen, believed that he was the cause of the breakup, alleging that Hingis's mother, Melanie Molitor, wanted her daughter to have nothing to do with him. "He's right," says Hingis. "He's a pain in the butt."

Regardless of how shabbily Hingis treats her partners, there will always be a queue of suitors because, simply put, she is a doubles savant. She has adequate power, an unparalleled grasp of tactics, and can win her partner a lot of money. Playing mostly alongside Hingis,

Kournikova won $325,205 in doubles in 1999, nearly as much as she won playing singles. Hingis's most recent fling was with Mary Pierce, who although never mistaken for a standout volleyer or strategist, slugs the ball with blistering pace. More important, Pierce hit it off with Hingis socially, giggling with her during changeovers, solicitously putting her arm around her, and hanging out with her in the players' lounge. In Australia, the two cruised to the finals, where they met Lisa Raymond and Rennae Stubbs.

The match was a classic encounter between two great individual players and one great team. Raymond and Stubbs have been partners since 1995 and won more than a dozen titles. Best friends off the court, each shares an almost telepathic sense of what the other is doing and where she is going. Their strategy before the match was simple—hit every ball to Pierce—but they departed from the template when Hingis unaccountably proved to be the weaker partner that day. Hingis's serve was flat and Raymond and Stubbs were able to pick off her returns with savvy poaching. In the third set, Hingis chucked her racket after missing a floater. As the crowd whistled disapprovingly, a disgusted Molitor exited her front row perch and left Rod Laver Arena.

While Raymond is a talented top thirty singles player who would reach the Wimbledon quarterfinals later in the year, Stubbs, twentynine, was in the biggest match of her life. A native of Sydney, nearing the end of an unremarkable, injury-plagued singles career, Stubbs was playing her equivalent of a Wimbledon singles final. Her father, a milk vendor, had driven eleven hours through the night to be on hand, as had a half dozen other family members. On her second match point in the third set, she dove headlong for a volley she had no realistic chance of reaching. When she and Raymond converted their next match point moments later, Stubbs shrieked with joy and fell to the ground.

The crowd responded with a raucous standing ovation. In part this was because Stubbs is a died-in-the-wool Aussie. But the fans also appreciated how much the moment meant to the underdogs. Had Hingis won, she would have pocketed the $120,000 in prize money— what she makes for one exhibition—and immediately turned her attention to the singles final. For Stubbs, it was the match of her career.

Mark Woodforde, a fellow Aussie and longtime friend, ducked out of the players' lounge and rushed onto the court to give her a hug. Put in the unfamiliar position of giving a victory speech, she could barely get the words out. "Relax, Rennae," a teary-eyed Pam Shriver bellowed from courtside. "Take your time."

As Hingis walked off the court and headed toward the locker room, Molitor was waiting for her. In front of several other players, Molitor dressed down her daughter for her sloppy play and carefree attitude. Molitor told Hingis that if she were going to play like she didn't care, she shouldn't bother to go on the court. As Hingis approached Stubbs after the match, she was wearing her usual wry smile. "Can you believe how bad I played?" she said. "Have you ever seen me when I've returned so badly?" Stubbs is usually as volatile as a live hand grenade and so intense that she has been known to bark profanities at Raymond mid-match. But now she was too dumbfounded to react. She simply stared at Hingis and then responded drolly: "Well, Martina, now you know how us mortals feel."

Hingis had committed yet another breach of etiquette. Here it was, Stubbs's shining moment, a Grand Slam title that ended 6–4 in the third set, and Hingis, in so many words, had told her she had gotten lucky. When Davenport heard about Hingis's remarks, she shook her head. "This was the biggest win of Rennae's career. You just can't say stuff like that." Hingis, for her part, couldn't believe that another player could derive so much giddy pleasure from winning a Grand Slam doubles trophy. She, after all, had already won seven and she was still a teenager.

Aware of the criticism, Hingis later consulted Pierce, wondering whether she had committed a faux pas. When Pierce explained that even if you feel you've played poorly, it's polite to credit your opponents, Hingis nodded. Another lesson learned the hard way. Asked at the Amelia Island tournament ten weeks later if Hingis had ever apologized for being such an ungracious loser, Stubbs laughed. "Please tell me you're kidding."

A few hours after the doubles final, Lindsay Davenport laughed out loud. Reclining in her hotel suite at the Crown Casino, she was icing the sore left thigh that had forced her to withdraw from the doubles draw. She was only half-watching an REM-inducing men's semifinal match between Magnus Norman and Yevgeny Kafelnikov, when the cameras cut away to show Martina Hingis, her face etched in grim concentration, practicing on a back court with her mother. It's rare for a player to put in more than an hour of cursory hitting the day before a final. Yet here was Hingis, less than twenty-four hours away from defending her Melbourne title, whacking balls after having played three sets of doubles. "I was like, 'you have to be kidding me,' " said Davenport. "I knew she was feeling she needed to practice or do something extra. I was already confident by then anyway, but that only added to it. I slept nearly ten hours that night."

On the day of a final, the stands are buzzing but the locker room has the oddly empty feel of a seaside resort after Labor Day. The racket bags and the piles of towels that littered the room have been removed, the buzz is muted, the toilet stalls and showers are vacant, save for a few unrecognized players who remain in the junior draw. The players' lounge, which had 128 main draw players socializing in it just days earlier, is oddly empty, another reminder that the circus has packed its tents and moved on. The two finalists often pretend not to notice each other as they dress in the locker room, though they have the entire place to themselves. Davenport though, ambled in shortly before her match to find Hingis sitting on a couch. "Hey, how's it going, Martina?" Davenport asked. "I'm fine, I guess," answered Hingis.

Her equanimity evaporated once she got on the court. Hingis took the first game of the match with a forehand winner, then Davenport went into steamroller mode. Pounding the ball with a level of pace and depth that was almost ruthless, she reeled off the next six games to win the set in nineteen minutes. Arms raised in helplessness, Hingis looked to her mother as if to say, "What do you expect me do?" Molitor returned her daughter's look blankly.

The second set was more of the same, as Davenport, continuing to show a nose for the lines. As she rushed to a 5–1 lead, the winner's trophy was wheeled hastily onto the court. Hingis, the world's No. 1

ranked player, was so befuddled that she groped for moral victories. "I just kept looking at the clock and tried to keep [the match] over an hour," she said later. "I felt sorry that people were paying for this." Hingis at least achieved her modest goal of pushing the match into a second hour. At 5–1, 30–30, Davenport played a few sloppy points. Hingis smelled blood and eventually pulled even at five games apiece. Even so, there was little sense that Davenport was in any danger. "Oh, I never thought I was going to lose the second set," she said breezily after the match. After taking a deep breath, Davenport held serve at 5–5. Then Hingis played three uncharacteristically loose points, including a double fault. On the first championship point, Hingis drove a routine backhand long, handing Davenport her third career Grand Slam. Davenport performed a typically understated pirouette and then jogged to the net, where she gave Hingis a big-sisterly pat on the back. Hingis, her voiced edged with frustration, blurted out: "I can't play you!"

Davenport's tennis had been extraordinary—"Maybe the best match I've ever seen her play," said Van't Hof. But Hingis's performance was stunning as well. Hingis is blessed with a fiendishly clever game and an uncommon tactical sense, but on this day neither were in evidence. Like a finesse boxer whose knockout power has been ridiculed, Hingis abandoned her skills and foolishly went toe-to-toe with Davenport. Never mistaken for Mercury, Davenport has one glaring weakness: foot speed. But Hingis did little to draw her to the net or move her laterally. And while the 6–3 Davenport, suffering from a sore thigh, would have been vulnerable to shots that forced her to bend, Hingis deployed few slices. Not surprisingly, Hingis got worse than she gave.

Hingis's success has been built on fearlessness and bulletproof confidence that suddenly seemed to be cracking. *I can't play you!* She was still the world's top-ranked player, but she had just admitted—with signature candor—how fragile her psyche had become. For all her wile and guile, she was reaching a grim conclusion: perhaps she was simply too slight to compete against the top guns. On the heels of losing her last Grand Slam final to Serena Williams, Hingis looked across the net at Davenport's towering physique and saw the future of women's tennis. And she understood enough to realize that it might not include her.

Molitor, who had been nervously leaning so far over the rail she could practically kiss the court, seemed to realize it too. She couldn't bring herself to clap after the match's end or register anything resembling a smile during the trophy presentation—even after her daughter, chastened by the previous day's fiasco, graciously accepted defeat and heaped praise on the winner. For the second straight day, Molitor departed for the tunnel between the players' entrance and the locker room to await her daughter. As Hingis spotted her mother in the corridor leading to the locker room, her entire body started to quiver like a hummingbird. As they neared, hot tears started streaming down her cheeks. "Mom, I didn't win," she cried, burying her face in her mother's shoulder.

While Hingis found solace in her mother's familiar embrace, Davenport's mother was 8,000 miles and nineteen time zones away. In fact, Davenport had inadvertently neglected to mention her mother in her victory speech. Mortified, she borrowed a cell phone and called home after the match. The first words out of her mouth were: "Mom, were you watching?" as if somehow her mother might instead have tuned into an episode of *Walker, Texas Ranger*. (For the record, Ann Davenport did watch her youngest daughter win her third Grand Slam.)

Davenport often jokes that she has the most pathetic entourage in tennis. Her section of seats is usually occupied by her coach, her agent Tony Godsick, and . . . "Well, sometimes Mary Joe Fernandez [Godsick's wife] sits with Tony," she says. On this day, she'd asked Lisa Raymond and Rennae Stubbs to sit in her box, since any empty seats would look unsightly on television. Had her parents considered coming? "Oh God no." Davenport laughed. "They have their own lives. Besides, they're kind of over my career."

Nearly two hours after the match, Davenport had completed a round of interviews when she was approached by WTA Tour communications officials and told she needed to pose for the winners' photo shoot. To balance the sweaty on-court images of players, the Tour strongly encourages each new Grand Slam champion to sit for a photograph alongside, say, the Eiffel Tower in Paris or Big Ben in London. For most players it is a chance to play runway model. For Davenport, it was a pain in the ass. Davenport turned to Godsick and pleaded, "Tony, you promised. You said if I won I wouldn't have to do this."

But she did. Bitching all the way, she entered the tournament's beauty salon for the first time during the tournament. An hour or so later, clad in a modest black T-shirt with a plunging neckline, her face uncomfortably covered in assorted cosmetic products, Davenport sat in a gondola making its way down the Yarra River. With the Melbourne skyline behind her, Davenport clutched the winner's trophy and tried not to roll her eyes at the sheer cheesiness of the moment. As the boat neared the scrum of photographers assembled on the banks, the gondolier whispered to Davenport: "Should I stop the boat so they can take more pictures of you?" Teeth clenched behind a smile, the 2000 Australian Open champion replied, "Don't you dare even think about it."

I'M OKAY; YOU'RE IN OKLAHOMA

IT WAS A COLD AFTERNOON IN FEBRUARY, just three days before the IGA Superthrift Tennis Classic in Oklahoma City was set to begin, and the phones in Sara Fornaciari's makeshift office in her Marriott hotel suite were chirping like an electronic symphony. The tournament's chairwoman for the past ten years, Fornaciari relishes what she calls the "organized chaos" of running a Tour event. She fields call after call, batting aside potential crises like so many short balls. *The court surface, laid down over a basketball court, isn't ready for play.* "Well, it damn well better be ready by the time the players get there." *A ballboy has lost his wallet.* "I'll be sure and make an announcement. That's all I can promise you, sir." *Monique Viele, a young, overhyped American to whom Fornaciari gave a wild card into the qualifying draw, was due to play that afternoon, but is nowhere to be seen.* "Are you kidding me? The heck with her."

Fornaciari's intensity and abruptness intimidate some and charm others, but she knows no other gear. Talking, walking, making deals— she does everything at auctioneer speed, and doesn't seem to know what no means. Raised in Baltimore, she recalls signing up to work on the school newspaper her freshman year at the University of Pennsylvania. "They said, 'What do you want to write, news or features?' I said 'sports.' I went to an all-girls high school and it never occurred to me that women weren't sportswriters." Two summers later she was the first female intern in the history of the *Washington Post* sports department.

After graduating from Penn, Fornaciari earned her law degree at night and worked for the Washington-based sports agency ProServ, representing tennis players such as Tracy Austin, Zina Garrison, and Pam Shriver. She also served as the executive director of the WTA Tour's players' association. In her late thirties, Fornaciari decided she wanted to run a women's tournament and set her sites on Oklahoma City, then a struggling event owned by ProServ. She founded her own management agency, Sports+Plus, bought the rights to the event from ProServ, and has been a presence in the heartland ever since. "I had never even *been* to Oklahoma City before this tournament," says Fornaciari, a mother of two who lives in suburban Washington, D.C., ten months a year. "But the timing was right, so I said what the hell."

The tournament is popular in Oklahoma's capital city. In 2000, it had been relocated from a local country club to the more commodious Abe Lemons Arena on the campus of Oklahoma City College. "This event is the Green Bay Packers of tennis tournaments," Fornaciari says. "We may be small, but the community support makes it work."

Just then, a call came in that momentarily left Fornaciari slack-jawed. Stephanie Tolleson, one of the agents for the two-time champion Venus Williams, is calling to say that her client is withdrawing. Venus is willing to fly into town to take part in a few promotions, but the tendinitis in her wrists that prevented her from playing the Australian Open is still bothering her and she "doesn't want to risk anything." Fornaciari had heard the rumors that Venus was either recovering slowly or had lost interest in tennis. But she had still been optimistic that Venus would make her 2000 debut in Oklahoma. Now that it's clear she won't, Fornaciari is screwed. Trying nobly to mask her disappointment, Fornaciari speaks to Venus and says all the right things—"I totally understand," "Your health comes first," "I hope we'll see you next year"—but her teeth are grinding and her mind is racing. Her other headliner, Anna Kournikova, had pulled out a week earlier, proffering the weak excuse that she wanted to curtail her playing schedule. (Kournikova played a lucrative exhibition in Mexico City that week instead.) All of Fornaciari's promotions touting Kournikova and Williams were suddenly worthless. And now, with Venus out, France's Julie Halard-Decugis is the top seed. She's a nice enough player, ranked a career-high No. 7 in the world; but few fans will line up at the box office to see her play. Venus' withdrawal is a particularly devastating blow considering Fornaciari had been planning to petition the Tour to upgrade her event to a Tier II for 2001. Tier II status would mean doling out an additional $365,000 in prize money; the Tour, in turn, would guarantee more top players, which would boost ticket and sponsorship sales and give Fornaciari a shot at a television deal. Fornaciari was banking on robust crowds and outsized buzz in 2000 to help make her case.

She's not ready to roll over quite yet, though. No sooner does she hang up the phone than she is seized by an idea. "I wonder if Monica Seles would want to come," she says out loud. Fornaciari has heard that Seles has been cleared to play after a five-month layoff due to a stress fracture in her foot. Though Seles has never played in Oklahoma City, Fornaciari figures it is worth a shot. She calls Seles's agent, Tony Godsick, and explains her predicament. "What would it take to get Monica to play?" she asks.

Godsick tells her that Seles is eager to return to the Tour. At home in Sarasota, whiling away the second longest hiatus of her career, Seles is going stir crazy. Her ranking has slid to No. 14, the lowest it has been in more than a decade. Seles is excited about working with her new full-time coach, Bobby Banck, anxious to adjust to her new, smaller-faced Yonex racket, and has even been tinkering with a slightly different service motion. Oklahoma would be ideal, Godsick tells Fornaciari. It's exactly what Seles needs: a low-key warm-up event before the outdoor hardcourt season begins. Fornaciari offers to pay for Seles's airfare and hotel, and give her a first round bye, so she won't have to arrive until Sunday or Monday. But what seals the deal is her offer of a "promotional fee."

Unlike the men's game, which permits tournaments to pay players simply for showing up—and, invariably, casts doubt on their efforts when they lose in the early rounds—the WTA Tour technically bans appearance fees. The Tour's Code of Conduct even threatens a $50,000 fine plus the amount of the improper payment on tournaments that lure players with "unauthorized" inducements. Still, it is an open secret that, particularly at smaller events, top players seldom come for free. They casually mention the cash, the jewelry, the laptops, even the Porsches bestowed upon them simply for playing such-and-such event. There are various means of circumventing the ban on appearance fees and assuring that top players still receive financial benefits at events—in addition to prize money. Some management agencies have even been known to reduce a player's fees and commissions if she plays events owned by that agency. In other cases, a tournament sponsor will compensate the player so that, technically, she's not being paid by the event.

At tournaments in Europe and Asia in particular, top players routinely collect a low- to mid-six-figure payout when they attend. Sources both within and outside the Tour say that in February 2001, Martina Hingis garnered a seven-figure windfall in conjunction with playing a weeklong Tier II event in Dubai. Responds Phil de Picciotto, president of Octagon, Hingis's management agency: "We're not going to comment on any of our clients' business opportunities financially, but I can say that we only do things within the rules. . . . Are there other business opportunities we can build around our clients in events where they play? Sure. That's just intelligent business."

At times, even the Tour itself effectively pays players to participate. When the Tour fails to meet its "commitment" and can't deliver the requisite number of top players based on the tier level of the tournament, it must compensate the event. In April, for instance, the Tour paid the Amelia Island tournament organizers $60,000 because it didn't meet its player guarantee. As a Tier II event, Amelia Island had been promised one of the top three players would be in the draw; when Lindsay Davenport, Martina Hingis, and Venus Williams all begged off, the Tour was responsible. According to multiple sources, in an attempt to avoid paying the fee to the promoter, at the eleventh hour the Tour offered the money up front to any of the absent players if they would change their mind and show up.

Another loophole events use to compensate players is to pay them a "promotional fee" to publicize the tournament. A top player can make as much as $25,000 for agreeing to fly to the host city and meet with the local media and sponsors for a few hours in the weeks before the event. In Oklahoma City, Seles agreed to attend various sponsor functions during the week of the tournament as quid pro quo for her bounty. Many promoters, most of whom claim they're barely breaking even, hate to spend the money. But an experienced entrepreneur like Fornaciari understands that it's a cost of doing business. In order to sell sponsorships and put fannies in the seats, she knows that it's vital to lure players of Seles's caliber and cachet. "Fair market value" it's called in polite circles.

Few players grasp the financial realities of the sport better than Seles. She's not greedy and she's hardly ostentatious—in fact she's notoriously thrifty—but Seles is an unregenerate capitalist who, as one veteran on the Tour puts it, "really, really likes getting paid." Seles still has vivid recollections of her modest upbringing in Yugoslavia. She was the most proficient English speaker in her family when they all emigrated to the United States in the mid-eighties, so she was the one who read over the contracts, paid the bills, and developed a keen business sense. Since then, she has won some $12 million in prize money—and earned several times that in endorsements and exhibition fees—but she is ever eager to amass more.

Seles regularly plays exhibitions, makes a mid-six-figure stipend from playing World Team Tennis, and has a multiyear shoe, clothing, and racket deal with the Japanese company Yonex that pays her roughly $3 million annually. It's fitting that one of the few men to whom she has been romantically linked is Paul Allen, the Microsoft

cofounder who *Forbes* estimates to be worth $36 billion, making him
the third wealthiest American.

A former communications manager for the WTA Tour recalls an
event in Japan at which the tournament sponsor was seeking players
for a corporate function that entailed various games of tennis skill.
Desperate to find another player, he asked a veteran American if she'd
be willing to participate. "I can't," said the player, who is one of Seles's
friends. "But ask Monica." The Tour staffer was skeptical that a player
of Seles's stature would be interested. "Just tell Monica how much
money she can win," the player said with a knowing wink. The staffer
shrugged and did as he was told. Half an hour later, Seles was on the
court, smiling broadly as she served tennis balls at an enlarged tic-tac-
toe board. The staffer recalls that Seles earned $9,000 in thirty minutes
and was the happiest anyone had seen her all week.

Fornaciari and Godsick, a former Dartmouth football player, settled on a fee of $70,000. Just like that, OKC had a headliner to replace
Kournikova and Venus Williams. Seles's addition proved to be particularly fortuitous since Julie Halard-Decugis pulled out with an
abdominal strain the day of her first match. Just in case Seles didn't
realize how much her presence was appreciated, Fornaciari managed
to have a handwritten banner draped inside the players' entrance:

**Monica Seles, You are So Zealous, We Love to Watch You Play.
Thanks for Coming to OKC, You Really Saved the Day!**

For all its whistle-stops around the globe, the Tour cuts a surprisingly
narrow swath through the United States. The U.S. is the site of the
Tour's international headquarters as well as home base for the vast
majority of the top players, but in 2001, only eleven of the Tour's sixty-
eight calendar events, including the U.S. Open, will be held on American soil. There are currently no tournaments in Texas, Chicago,
Boston, Philadelphia, or the Pacific Northwest. Aside from Scottsdale,
the only event between the two coasts is this one in Oklahoma City, the
nation's forty-fifth largest media market.

Since Oklahoma is a Tier III event, it offers a measly purse of $170,000, less than a player makes for reaching the semifinals of the U.S. Open. The Tour guarantees that three players among the top twenty will compete in a Tier III tournament, but mostly the events are the preserve of little-known upstarts who play to accumulate points, bolster their rankings, and pay for another week's groceries. Venturing to this board-game flat outpost in the heart of the Dust Bowl is something of a culture shock for players accustomed to visiting the world's most glamorous cities and staying in five-star hotels. But the timing of the Oklahoma event is excellent for players—it's held indoors the last week in February, just prior to a string of North American hardcourt events. The alternative is to play in Europe for a week, then fly back to the U.S.

There is something else endearing about events like OKC. In a sport still derided for its elitist, patrician aura, this is truly a populist event. Tickets are reasonably priced and fans snack on two-dollar chili cheese dogs. Even the name of the event—the IGA Superthrift Classic—conjures up the simple charm and purity of the bush leagues. Playing in a market with no major league sports franchises or major colleges, the players are feted like movie stars. Hundreds of fans will attend a midweek session to watch Erika de Lone and Tatiana Panova—neither ranked anywhere near the top twenty—play two sets of tennis. And the players are genuinely amused by the change of scenery from the usual, sterile resort settings. Rita Grande, a run-of-the-mill player who was born in Naples, Italy, and trains in Rivoli, looks as though she has arrived in the Twilight Zone when she lands at Will Rogers World Airport and is driven past oil rigs, cowboy boot depots, and fields of corn as high as an elephant's eye.

At the same time, this tournament lays bare the essential loneliness and the brutality of the Tour. Even before a deus ex machina plugs Aaron's Furniture—"Home of the $99 pre-owned couch"—over the crackling loudspeaker during changeovers, it is clear that this is as far from the big time as bumper cars are from the Indianapolis 500. The players have to pay their own hotel bills after three nights (four if they remain in the draw); the "interview room" is a closet-sized converted locker room; the "tournament transportation" is the backseat of a local volunteer's station wagon.

Still, for most of the players here an early round match is packed with as much pressure as a Wimbledon final. The top women can afford to lose a few matches and retain their rankings, their endorsement deals, and their comfortable lifestyle. For players one level down on the food chain, playing on a midweek afternoon in front a handful of fans can be a matter of life and death. As a rule, players need to earn at least $50,000 a year to break even. Players can spend upward of $30,000 annually in airfare; coaching generally runs around $1,500 a week—what a coach could otherwise make giving lessons at a club plus expenses; and even string jobs run $20 a racket. Given that a first round loser in Oklahoma City makes only $1,300, it's easy to see how a run of first round defeats at Tier III events is a treadmill to oblivion. "It can be hard to get motivated," says Nicole Pratt. "But if you want to go from being a middle-class player just getting by to living comfortably, these are the matches you *have* to win." Tournaments like Oklahoma City make it clear that, in addition to skill, an indomitable spirit is a prerequiste for success in this sport.

Both Pratt and her first round opponent, Canada's Vanessa Webb, ooze nervous energy as they prepare to take the court for their Tuesday afternoon match. Both are ranked outside the top fifty, both know the importance of winning a match like this. Like two boxers about to enter a ring—albeit with no cutmen, cornermen, and entourage to inflate them with confidence—Pratt and Webb stand stone-faced. They try settling their jitters by taking practice swings or running in place. Players say that the brief, awkward interval before they step onto the court is the most agonizing time on the Tour. One veteran likens it to the feeling she had when a bully threatened to beat her up after school. "It's the same thing, where you try to [muster] hatred for your opponent and at the same time, you live in mortal fear of losing. I don't know if I can explain it better than that."

Once they're on the court, the stress escalates, as both players try to find a delicate balance during warm-up, summoning enough adrenaline to get "pumped up" while remaining loose enough to react to a fast-moving object and make clean contact. And unlike golf, an individual sport that is played without much heed of one's opponent, tennis is truly gladitorial. "You hear players say, 'I just try to play my game,' but you really want to break your opponent down at the same time," says Pratt.

Such an intensely competitive, necessarily self-centered existence hardly makes for a collegial atmosphere off the court. Killing time in Oklahoma, some players cruise through the 50 Penn Place Mall; others bivouac at the Barnes & Noble bookstore adjacent to the tournament hotel or work out in the weight room above the court. Mostly, though, they sit in the modest players' lounge, glassy-eyed and vaguely disconsolate as they fritter away the day, trying to escape the dismal reality with the help of a Discman. The players are colleagues, roughly the same age, from similar social classes, with countless common interests and experiences. Yet their interaction is minimal. When the French player Nathalie Dechy parked herself in front of the lone computer monitor in the lounge and surfed the Web for hours, impatient players stood behind her and muttered; but no one actually confronted her. "It doesn't have to be this way," says American Kim Po. "But I think a lot of players feel that if they are friendly with other players, it will make them less fierce and focused in their matches." Adds Webb: "If you get to know a player too well, the fear is that you end up playing against her personality more than her game."

Some players handle this tension better than others. Lindsay Davenport is social by nature but admits it's tough to engage in deep conversations with the other top players. Her closest friends on the tour—Debbie Graham, Corina Morariu, and Lisa Raymond—are all ranked outside the top twenty. Martina Hingis is gregarious as well but has formed an impenetrable clique with her mother and Mario Widmer, and has few confidantes on the Tour. The Williams sisters have each other as a support group and have no interest in winning any locker room popularity contests. "I don't come to make friends," Venus says. "I come to win matches." On the other hand, Annie Miller, once a top-forty player, quit the Tour at age twenty-one last year and enrolled at the University of Michigan, in part because she missed having a social life. "I just didn't gell with the culture of the Tour," says Miller, now a junior majoring in business. "If you're naturally outgoing, it's hard traveling from week to week and not having real friends."

This tension is less palpable on the ATP. The men go for their opponent's throat on the court, and, sure, there are grudge matches and personality conflicts. But you'll also catch them playing cards in the players' lounge, kicking around a soccer ball, or even simulating WWF moves. At a tournament hotel, it's not unusual to find ten or twelve players and coaches crowded around a table eating dinner. Carlos Moya and Alex Corretja even dined together before they played in the 1998 French Open final. At the 2000 Canadian Open later in the year, Yevgeny Kafelnikov and Wayne Ferreira played a round of golf together an hour after a grueling match. Fifteen minutes after a match, the same players who were locked in combat on the court are playfully snapping towels at each other in the locker room. "Women aren't like that," says Webb. "If someone pumps a fist in your face—or even if they just beat you—that's something you remember for a long, long time."

Some of the differences between male and female pros are practical. In search of the best "hit" possible, men usually work out with other men on the Tour, while women often enlist their male coach or male hitting partner, so there's less socializing among the women on the practice court. And on average, the women are younger and less socially mature than their male counterparts. Also, the top female players make enough money to subsidize an entourage. "My friends ask me 'what's Kournikova like?'" says Webb. "I tell them I barely even see her the whole week."

Others say the differences between the circuits are more subtle. Todd Crosset, a professor of sports management at the University of Massachusetts who researched the LPGA, says: "Guys bond over competition, whereas women think about the relationship. [Women], rather than have a dispute, will literally switch games. Guys will battle it out, solve the problem, and then move on." Julie Anthony, a player on the Tour in the 1970s who is now a psychologist in Aspen, has a slightly different take. "Women tend to personalize competition more. Men can have arguments and then be fine off the court. Men usually have played other sports so they have a healthier attitude about competition. For female players, tennis may be the only sport they've played. When you invest so much time and energy in a sport, it's hard to detach your feelings of self-worth from your results. In one way it's healthy but it makes winning that much more important and losing that much harder."

There are exceptions, of course. Webb is a 1999 Duke graduate who triple-majored in French, economics, and Canadian studies; her maternal grandfather was a member of Pierre Trudeau's cabinet. She is among the Tour's most self-possessed players. After playing sluggishly and losing to Pratt, 6–2, 6–3, she slung her duffel over her left shoulder and trudged to the locker room, disappointed but not devastated. Playing on a team in college for four years, she learned to compartmentalize her emotions. In the locker room, she congratulated Pratt again and wished her luck in her next match. When Pratt asked where she was off to next, Webb flashed an expansive smile. "All I know is that after I lose in doubles, I'm getting on the first plane home and sleeping in my own bed."

As hungry parvenus and upwardly mobile veterans played with a ferocious intensity, wishing they could click their heels and go from the heartland to Wimbledon's Centre Court, Monica Seles's appearance in OKC was freighted with poignancy for other reasons. At age twenty-six, there are fewer and fewer clicks left on her odometer and, still, Seles soldiers on. In her first match of the year, she walked onto the court in Abe Lemons Arena to raucous applause and proceeded to route Francesca Lubiani, a baseliner from Bologna, perhaps best known for posing nude in an Italian tennis magazine. Seles was here alone. Her new coach, Bobby Banck, was in Florida with his ailing father. Her mother, Esther, was home in Sarasota tending to the dogs. There's something vaguely heartbreaking about seeing a former world No. 1, a nine-time Grand Slam champion, play a small event, alone by herself on a Tuesday, before repairing to a room at a Marriott. But Seles was thrilled to be back doing what she loves. Over a late dinner after her opening match, sitting in a lounge overlooking the court, Seles could barely stop smiling. "I just really missed the game when I was away this time," she says between bites. "It just reinforced that this is what I love to do."

Seles makes it tough for journalists to do their job. A bedrock value of the fourth estate is objectivity, the attempt to prevent emotion and partisanship from coloring the facts. Sports journalism even has its own bromide on this point: no cheering in the press box. Yet if tennis reporters are not, at some level, pulling for Monica Seles, they're either sitting on their hands or they have calcified hearts. If karmic justice demands that good things happen to deserving people, Monica Seles wouldn't lose another match for the rest of her career. You can't help wishing that her story finally starts to break like one of those formulaic movies, where the protagonist's faith and hard work get rewarded in the end. And it's not just the fans and observers of the game who feel this way. "A part of me wants to see Monica win," says Lindsay Davenport, one of Seles's few friends on the Tour, "and I'm the one who has to play her."

It's been seven years since Seles went from world-beater to tragic figure. Seven years since Guenther Parche, the deranged German who introduced the term "unemployed lathe operator" into tennis's lexicon, gripped the green handle of a nine-inch boning knife and plunged it into the back of Seles, then nineteen, during a changeover in Hamburg. The game has changed in a million ways since then. The players have gotten bigger, stronger, and, mercifully, older. The equipment and training has become space age. Prize money has nearly doubled. And yet the horror is still fresh, a lingering reminder of sports' dark side. What befell Seles on April 30, 1993, was nothing short of premeditated evil. Never before had a *fan,* acting in the name of a rival—in this case, Steffi Graf—trespassed on the field of play and so profoundly altered the course of a sport's history. "I won't forget it as long as I live," says Rennae Stubbs, who was in the stands that day. "When they carried Monica out we had no idea what her condition was. When we heard she was going to be okay our first reaction was relief. But you knew right away that people don't recover overnight from something like that."

At the time of the stabbing, Seles was as dominant as any player tennis had ever seen. She had won seven of the past eight Grand Slams she had played. Having already unseated Graf as the top player in the game, she was on her way to becoming the best of all time. It wasn't just that she punished the ball, striking it violently with two hands, smacking it on the rise like a cricket batsman; it was how well she played the big points. Seles was at her best when the pressure was ratcheted highest, the acid test of a tennis champion. "I don't know if I've ever seen a player as mentally strong as Monica," says Pam Shriver. "When the going got tough, she just got you in a death grip and wouldn't let you out."

The knife missed her spine by millimeters and the incision on the right shoulder blade was a half an inch or so wide. Seles endured more than two years convalescing in her Sarasota mansion after several months of rehab at the Steadman-Hawkins clinic in Colorado. Before she returned to the court, she summoned Jackie Joyner-Kersee and her husband, Bobby, to help her regain her fitness. Barring the occasional peek in a mirror, she thought little of the wound itself. The psychic scar tissue, on the other hand, has never completely faded.

Though her house in a gated community was secured by an orchestra of alarms, Seles was unable to sleep during the night. She has said that hearing her own scream is what haunts her the most. Seles, who pointedly never mentions Parche by name, had nightmares of seeing her tormentor's twisted, sadistic grin—he had apparently stalked her at her hotel a few days earlier. (At his trial, Parche told a German court that he had originally planned to give Seles a bouquet of flowers and then sever her hands.) She was treated for post-traumatic stress disorder and turned increasingly inward, unable to face the world. She was in the Atlanta airport on her way to back to Florida when she heard that Parche had been given a suspended sentence. She collapsed in her mother's arms. As she wrote in her autobiography, *From Fear to Victory,* "I would spend two years in the jail he was supposed to inhabit."

For all of her banshee screams and stone-cold winners, Seles has always been nonconfrontational, gentle to the core. Even today, the grunts have been largely muted and she is a player who prefers practicing to playing because there is no loser on the practice court. She also claims that she prefers exhibitions to tournaments because everyone is on their best behavior. With years of detachment, she still has trouble making some sense—any sense—of what befell her. Seles's friend, Mary Joe Fernandez, a devout Catholic, has tried to impress upon her that "everything happens for a reason." But Seles hasn't quite been able to convince herself of that. "I'm definitely not happy with the situation, but I'm happy with how I've dealt with it and tried to move on," she says. "I'm still not at the point where I can accept it and maybe I'll never get there. It's hard when you feel there was no justice done."

When Seles finally returned to the Tour in late summer 1995, she had some success, winning her first tournament in Toronto and then reaching the finals of the U.S. Open, where she lost to Graf. Four months later, with Graf out of commission tending to an assortment of injuries and her tax bill, Seles won the 1996 Australian Open, her ninth—and, barring a Touched by an Angel miracle, last—Grand Slam. Not unlike a woman in corporate America who returns from a maternity leave only to find that underlings have replaced her, Seles never truly regained her foothold. In her glory days, Seles never had to think much on the court; she simply pounded her opponents into submission with heavy balls and confounding angles. Suddenly, she had to scout the field, incubate a strategy, cook up a game plan. The avatar of power tennis, she was suddenly being outslugged by a younger, bigger, faster generation that wasn't in awe of her. Also, Seles's body had changed during her 820-day hiatus; flaps and bulges emerged where there was once natural adolescent tone. She continued to struggle with the new contours of her body, which included an added inch of height as well as twenty pounds of extra cargo she picked up from junk food binges.

Seles had just begun to find her form, lose the convex curvatures, and regain her timing, when she suffered another setback. On New Year's Eve 1996, she learned that her father's stomach cancer had metastasized. Karolj Seles, a cartoonist by trade, first introduced his daughter to the game by drawing cartoon figures of Mickey Mouse and Tom and Jerry on tennis balls, stringing a net between cars in a Novi Sad parking lot and feeding her balls. Karolj could be dominating, but at heart, he was both a gentleman and a gentle man who remembered names, graciously congratulated opponents, and had a ready smile for everyone. He never treated his daughter like a meal ticket; in fact, he was more concerned that Monica liked tennis *too much* and might not mature into a well-adjusted adult. As his health deteriorated, Karolj encouraged his daughter to continue playing. It was an excruciating dilemma: Monica hated not being at his side, but she knew that nothing gave him as much gratification as seeing her play well.

Shortly after Karolj passed away in the spring of 1998, Monica, clad in black, wearing her father's wedding ring on a chain around her neck, reached the finals of the 1998 French Open. Finally, it seemed, fate had gotten the script right. But Seles played an uneven match and lost to Arantxa Sanchez Vicario. Her morale slipped and she has not seriously challenged for a Grand Slam since.

Seles's past is now like a foreign country she doesn't care to visit. Her mantra has become: "I'm about the present." Yet the reminders of her history are everywhere. At an event in Japan last year, Seles appeared at a sponsor function where the security was particularly lax. When she was mobbed for photos and autographs by well-dressed Japanese businessmen, one former WTA Tour employee recalls that she "started freaking out." Seles pleaded, "Get me out of here," to Tour officials, who sneaked her out a back door. She dissolved in tears. She still registers at hotels under a pseudonym. Any tournament director who wants Seles in their draw knows to hire guards to hover around her chair. "When Monica plays Fed Cup for me," says Billie Jean King, "one of the first things I do is ask whether she's okay with the security arrangement." In one of the more eerie and sadly touching scenes in tennis, Seles sometimes takes the court and promptly pivots her chair 90 degrees. Instead of facing the court during changeovers as her opponents do, she will sit at an angle, keeping as many spectators as possible within her line of vision.

Another painful reminder was Graf's success. Seles won't admit it publicly, but what makes her ordeal particularly devastating is that Parche succeeded in his goal to alter the course of women's tennis history. While Graf won just one Grand Slam a year during Seles's heyday of 1990–92, she opportunistically won six during Seles's absence, burnishing her claim as the greatest player of all time. Seles, meanwhile, was transformed into the personification of "what if."

As Seles struggled to regain her form, something funny happened: she became enormously popular, far more so than she ever had been when she was scooping up Grand Slam trophies like they were complimentary mints. She became transformed from a celebrity to one of us. Seles can't go into a Starbucks, browse at Barnes & Noble, or pick up cereal at the local supermarket without being approached by sympathetic strangers. Even in Oklahoma City, as Seles had finished beating Lubiani and was dutifully signing autographs on the court, a woman said to her: "I admire you so much and I know what you're having to go through because my husband's brother Eddie . . ." Rather than walk away or nod vacantly, Seles looked the woman in the eye, listened to the sad tale of a stranger she would never see again.

Seles has always been what she calls "a pleaser." In Oklahoma City, she needed ten minutes to get off the court after her matches, accommodating every autograph request and letting kids pet the miniature stuffed tiger affixed to her Yonex racket bag. With no fanfare or self-congratulatory press release, Seles makes a hefty annual donation to Andrea Jaeger's foundation for terminally ill children. At the Sydney Olympics, Rulon Gardner, the American heavyweight wrestler, recognized Seles and wanted to meet her. They talked for twenty minutes and she waited patiently for him to get his camera and take a picture with her. That was before Gardner won his gold medal. He was just an anonymous lug from Wyoming, but she couldn't say no. "I'm trying to live more for me, but it's hard to change who you are at heart," she says. "Sometimes you have to put yourself first because no one else will." As if on cue, a tournament volunteer interrupted Seles as she was swigging her iced tea. "We're so happy you came to Oklahoma City. Can I have your autograph?" Naturally, Seles obliged.

The irony is that at a time when fans feel an intimate connection with her, Seles has never been more guarded with her privacy. As a giggly, innocent teenager, she was a quote machine—her interviews were disarming, discursive filibusters peppered with her trademark Woody Woodpecker giggle. A question about an opponent might end with Seles talking about her latest shopping trip or her propensity for slathering her french fries with butter. Today, she is tennis's Greta Garbo. Even in mandatory press conferences—one of the few times she has to put on a public front—she is as circumspect as a presidential candidate. She begins answers with a reflexive response of, "Oh definitely," and then segues into a polished, and often vague response. A few days prior to Oklahoma City, the WTA Tour held a media teleconference heralding Seles's return to the Tour. One caller asked Seles a fluffy question about her favorite American sports team. Seles shot back: "Why do you need to know that?" When the caller responded that he was merely curious, Seles responded, "I hate to do that."

She also keeps to herself in the locker room and players' lounge, more likely to socialize or go out to dinner with Mark McCormack, the septuagenarian head of her management agency, IMG, and his wife, Betsy, than with any other players. Seles's routine at tournaments is simple: she hits with her coach, plays her matches, and returns to the hotel. If the Tour staff need to find her in the afternoon, odds are she's in her suite, reading magazines or watching television.

Seles laughs when reminded that she was a precursor of the glamour culture pervasive on today's Tour. In another life, it was a carefree Seles who once spoke of her fascination with Marilyn Monroe, who had an endorsement with No Excuses jeans, who at times appeared as interested in being a celebrity as she was in winning matches. "Remember how I got criticized for that." She laughs. "I was growing up, I was enjoying myself, and people used to criticize me for it. Now the celebrity and personality is such a big selling point for some of these girls. It's good for the game, but we shouldn't lose sight of what happens on the court. Sometimes I worry that it's a lot of gossip and no one cares about the tennis. But what do I know?"

It's not that Seles lacks opinions. At a World Team Tennis event in the summer, Seles was rightfully appalled when her opponent, fifteen-year-old Monique Viele, strode onto the court wearing heels and a slinky dress to sing the national anthem before changing into her tennis clothes. Seles turned to Paul Assaiante, the coach of Seles's Hartford WTT team, and said, "I'm. Going. To. Kick. Her. Ass." (And she did.) She also seethed to her friends that the Tour's decision to move the year-end Chase Championships from New York to Germany—where she has vowed never to play again—was callous and insulting. But in public, Seles recoils from controversy. She knows what it's like to be the object of attention, to be vulnerable, to have enemies, to be attacked. She would just as soon never again put herself in that position.

It turns out that Karolj Seles's worries about tennis stunting his daughter's life were unfounded. Secluded as she has become, she is also perceptive and thoughtful, with an uncanny knack for reading people. Her interests and curiosities transcend the fuzzy yellow ball. With more perspective on the human condition than she ever wanted, she is, ironically, better prepared than most of her colleagues for life after tennis. Yet she's still out there traveling the globe, sleeping in strange beds in strange towns, trying to regain at least some semblance of her former dominance. When she lets slip that she still receives death threats and notes from stalkers, the obvious question is: why does she still play? It can't simply be for the money.

The answer is simple: Seles is still hanging around a converted basketball venue in Oklahoma City on a rainy Tuesday night because, for all the millions she's won, she is still tennis's equivalent of a gym rat. She is still intoxicated by the game, the sensation of cracking the ball past her opponent, the surge she gets from hitting a crosscourt, two-fisted winner or an untouchable serve down the middle. Her psyche has a hard time accommodating the losses, but she takes solace in knowing that she still plays tennis better than all but four or five women on the planet. The tennis court was the site of Seles's most horrifying moment; but it is also one of the few places she feels most secure.

Seles wasn't the only player trying to resurrect her moribund game under the low-intensity lighting of Abe Lemons Arena. On a bleak Tuesday morning, Samantha Stevenson hovered over a washing machine in a dingy closet near the players' locker room. Her daughter, Alexandra, was playing her first round match that night and Samantha was washing a duffel bag full of her daughter's sweaty socks, bras, and T-shirts. Clad in a baby blue warm-up suit, Samantha winced when a tournament employee handed her a box of Snuggle fabric softener. "Don't you have anything else?" she asked. "This smells too perfumey."

Just eight months earlier, the Stevensons' dirty laundry had been aired before the world. At Wimbledon in 1999, Alexandra became the first player to go from the Wimbledon qualifying draw to the semifinals since John McEnroe in 1977. But for reasons having little to do with her tennis, she became an overnight cause célèbre—a titillating new character in the WTA Tour soap opera. Alexandra had come to Wimbledon as a giggly, somewhat loopy, doe-eyed eighteen-year-old who had planned to play tennis for Pete Sampras's sister, Stella, at UCLA in the fall. She had just graduated with honors from La Jolla Country Day School near San Diego and still had the songs from *Grease*, the school's spring musical, playing in her head. Weeks later, she would leave the All England Club as a professional player with her life thrown irretrievably into the public domain. When she returned home to California, she was a celebrity. "It was like, okay world, heeeeeeere's Alexandra," she said.

In two weeks, the mother-daughter team provided enough gossip to satiate the maw of the Fleet Street tabloids. First there was Samantha, a former sportswriter, threatening to sue the WTA Tour if it failed to recognize her daughter's professional status and withheld her prize money. Then, in what Samantha admits was an attempt—albeit a clumsy one—to emulate Richard Williams and redirect the spotlight on herself and away from her daughter, she complained about the

Tour's "rampant lesbianism" (she later claimed to have been misquoted) and threw around flabby allegations of racism. There was also
the salacious sidebar about Alexandra's coach, Pete Fischer, an eccentric pediatrician who also nurtured Sampras, who was in prison,
charged with molesting young patients. Then the pièce de résistance.
In a well-timed story, the *Ft. Lauderdale Sun Sentinel* confirmed years
of rumor and suspicion and revealed that Alexandra's biological father
was basketball icon Julius "Dr. J." Erving. When Alexandra returned
home, she had an agent, a Nike deal, and an invitation to tell the world
her story on Barbara Walters's TV couch.

Against insurmountable odds, Samantha tried to protect her
daughter from the storm. She claims that she didn't even let Alexandra
read newspaper accounts from Wimbledon. Alexandra couldn't really
understand all the fuss, anyway. She had no interest in cultivating a
relationship with her father, whom she had met only twice. "My mom
is my mother and my father," she insisted repeatedly. The revelation
did nothing to change her sense of self or her racial identity, as Alexandra had known about her father since she was a small child. (Her
mother is white; her father is black; Alexandra jokingly calls herself a
"Half-rican.") She was even unfazed when her mother told reporters
she initially considered an abortion when she learned she was pregnant. "People need to get over it," Alexandra said. Her thoughts on the
entire sensational episode were reduced to a solitary SoCal catchphrase: "What. Ever."

While Alexandra aroused both pity and praise while keeping her
composure and charm amid tabloid hell, Samantha has been pilloried.
Former colleagues painted a nasty and unsparing portrait of her as a
temptress who, as Philadelphia columnist Bill Conlin recalled, wore
"minis, short-shorts, and no bra with semi-opaque blouses and halter
tops" while working locker rooms in the seventies. Another wrote that
Samantha always had a thing for black athletes.

Whatever her flaws as a coach or publicist, Samantha loves her
daughter and there's no doubt that she is immensely proud of her own
success as a single mother. Sharing a one-bedroom apartment, subsist-

ing on a limited income, Samantha instilled in her daughter an "us-against-the-world" ethic. "When Alexandra was born, I walked away from the life I had at the time," Samantha says. "I've been in a bubble raising her and I'm damn proud of that."

An unfortunate manifestation of Samantha's zeal is that she is the mother of all stage mothers. She's so involved in her daughter's life that she phones Alexandra during a date just to see how everything is going. In Oklahoma City, Alexandra competed against local "person-alities" in a shopping spree to benefit the tournament's sponsor, IGA. Samantha scouted out the supermarket in advance so Alexandra could make a beeline to the most expensive groceries and win the competi-tion. On the Tour, Samantha is omnipresent, by her daughter's side on the practice court, in the interview room, and, until a rule was passed banning nonplayers, in the locker room. When Belgium's Kim Clij-sters was given the Tour's Most Impressive Newcomer Award for 1999, Samantha demanded—and got—a revote on the grounds that Alexandra's credentials received short shrift on the ballot. (Clijsters allegedly won by a wider margin the second time). Later in the year in Rome, players complained that Samantha was loitering in the locker room. "Why don't you tell Lindsay Davenport's mom to stay out too then," Samantha snapped when confronted by a Tour representative. A Tour staffer recounts that when Davenport was told that her mother couldn't be in the locker room either, she just smiled and shook her head. "Sure," Davenport is said to have responded. "That shouldn't be a problem since my mom is in California."

Alexandra would employ a conga line of coaches in 2000, but in Oklahoma City, Samantha was filling the job. "I need to have the coaching badge," Samantha explained. "Otherwise they won't even let me back here." Asked when she planned to stop traveling with her daughter, she replied: "I don't think I'll ever stop. Look at Mrs. Sanchez. She still travels with Arantxa after all these years. You have to have family and a support group close. You don't understand how difficult a life this is."

In the wake of Dr. J–gate, Samantha has postponed her work as a tennis journalist, but she continues to cast a critical eye on the sport. Although she claims her antigay remarks at Wimbledon were misconstrued, when a veteran player passed in the hallway of Oklahoma City, Samantha stops midsentence and whispers, "Talk about your angry lesbians. . . ." The real problem with the Tour, she asserts, is the way women compete. "A few understand that you play the game on the court and off the court you get on with your life," she says. "Ninety percent don't understand that and they're so catty." Needless to say, extemporaneous riffs like these have made Samantha bête noire for players and the Tour personnel. "She is meddlesome and calculating and usually doesn't know what she's talking about," says one American player. "I don't think she realizes it but she brings hostility on her daughter. It's sad because Alexandra's not a bad kid."

Indeed, Alexandra is conscientious about promoting the sport and being a role model for young girls. Trained by her mother, who conducted mock press conferences as they drove from San Diego to tennis lessons in L.A. five days a week for years, Alexandra is refreshingly open with the media. Regardless of how she plays, she'll engage fans and sign autographs until there are no more requests. She is also chirpily affable.

At other times, Alexandra, like her mother, shows little regard for discretion. She angered many veteran players when she complained to *Sports Illustrated for Women* that in the locker room "Conchita [Martinez] just plops herself down naked, which is disgusting, walks around butt naked." Likewise she told ESPN's magazine that she had nicknamed Martina Hingis "Martin." Why? "She's a dork. She's a nerd. She tries to be cool." She gleefully ticks off the names of players whom she suspects have eating disorders and she says that she hates the French players. "They are really mean."

Most teenagers would be overwhelmed by the attention, but Alexandra can't get enough of it. "Do you know I made *Teen People*'s Most Intriguing list?" she asks out of the blue. Owing as much to her lineage as her tennis skills, she has her own Nike deal, which pays for her training. She also made the WTA Tour's Commitment List in

2000, which gives special financial dispensation to the twenty most marketable players. And she routinely plays her matches on show courts. In fact, despite not being seeded, she was the second biggest draw in Oklahoma City behind Seles.

Now if she could only back up the hype with some winning tennis. Like so many of Stevenson's matches since her star turn at Wimbledon, her first round match in Oklahoma City was a disappointment. The line on Stevenson is that in spite of her superior genes, she isn't particularly athletic. At six–one, she hits a booming serve and her one-handed backhand, similar to the one Fischer taught to Pete Sampras, is a potential weapon. But Stevenson moves poorly, her strokes break down under pressure, and she tires easily. In an unsightly match, Stevenson sprayed balls all over the court and lost to Austria's Sylvia Plischke 6–1, 6–3, yet another early defeat since her Wimbledon breakthrough. (Even Nike acknowledges they don't have a winner on their hands yet. The slogan of Stevenson's 2000 ad campaign—"You beat me, I learn. I beat you, I learn. It's a good system"—doesn't exactly scream world domination.)

After the match, Alexandra, eyes rimmed in red, wailed, "This is so frrrrrrustrating." By her daughter's side—as always—Samantha tried to offer good cheer. "It's okay, you'll do better next week," she said solicitously. "She's a good player, and you hit some really nice shots, Alexandra. You looked good." After a pause she added. "At least your clothes smelled clean." With that, the mother-daughter team laughed and bounded out of the room, arm in arm.

By the second round, the IGA Superthrift Classic has become the Monica Seles Invitational. After blitzing Lubiani in the first round, Seles faced Sarah Pitkowski, a twenty-four-year-old flame-haired Frenchwoman ranked thirty-fifth in the world. In a match that reveals the wide gap between the top players and everybody else, Seles delivered the dreaded double-bagel, drubbing Pitkowski, 6–0, 6–0 in 42 minutes. The match would have been even more abbreviated had Seles not stopped her service motion to say "Bless you" to one sneezing fan.

In the semis, Seles played the indefatigable South African, Amanda Coetzer, perhaps the fittest player on the Tour and the second highest ranked in the draw. Seles never gave her a chance. Overpowering Coetzer with her signature crosscourt groundstrokes that kissed the sidelines, Seles yielded just three games and prevailed in less than an hour. The following day, Seles had a tougher match against Nathalie Dechy, who celebrated her twenty-first birthday earlier in the week and was playing in her first WTA Tour final. Dechy, a self-assured Frenchwoman, who has the elegant strokes and mature carriage that could eventually land her in the top ten, dropped the first set 6–1, but then calmed her nerves and answered Seles's firepower. After scoring a break of serve in the second set, Dechy held a 5–2 lead. That, though, seemed only to make Seles angry. Summoning her "A" game Seles held her serve, broke Dechy at love, then held at love. She closed out the match in a tiebreaker, winning 6–1, 7–6. Grand Slam titles may be a distant memory, but even with a five-month layoff, a new racket, an absent coach, and a sore foot, Seles still cruised through the draw without dropping a set.

When the final match ended, Seles smiled sweetly and acknowledged the sponsors. The consummate pro, Seles knew that Fornaciari had ambitions of moving her event up a tier for 2001, so she took pains to praise the facilities and call Oklahoma City her favorite indoor court in the world. Seles then held a quick press conference but it was clear that she was antsy to catch a plane to the next event in Scottsdale. A volunteer asked: "What airline are you flying, Monica? I'll call ahead so they know you're on your way."

"Southwest," Seles responded.

"Southwest?" the volunteer asked. "That can't be right. That's like the Greyhound bus in the sky. They don't even have first class."

Monica Seles—a $33,000 winner's check in her pocket, forty-five singles titles on her record, $11,783,858 in career earnings, and some five times that in off-court lucre in the bank—shrugged. "It was the best deal we could find."

Fornaciari, meanwhile, was beaming. Ten days before, Venus Williams had pulled out of her tournament and the IGA Superthrift

Tennis Classic was in danger of having no buzz beyond Tulsa. But thanks to Fornaciari's deft behind-the-scenes footwork at the eleventh hour, the tournament was a smashing success. The triumphant return of Monica Seles made international news, and in keeping with the unwritten rule, she would likely return in 2001 to defend her title. Fornaciari's hopes of upgrading Oklahoma City to a Tier II event were still alive. "It just goes to show," she said, grinning. "You always know to expect the unexpected. But in the end, it all works out."

THE SISTERS OF NO MERCY

ONE WOULD BE HARD-PUT TO FIND A MORE picturesque backdrop for a tennis tournament than the Indian Wells Tennis Garden outside Palm Springs, California. Framed by stately mountains and an unremitting canopy of blue sky that sprawls to the horizon and tints the desert hues of rust and gold, the complex looks like an artist's rendering. The crown jewel of the complex, completed just in time for the 2000 event, is a $77 million stucco stadium that seats 16,000 spectators.

It's a crystalline March day at the complex and Richard Williams is blowing smoke in all directions. He has come to this paradise in the middle of the California desert with his youngest daughter, Serena, who hopes to defend her title in the high-stakes tournament. His next oldest daughter, Venus, is still at home in Florida, recovering from the wrist injury that, he alleges, prevents her from hitting balls. According to Richard, she is seriously considering a year sabbatical from the Tour. That would be big news for the WTA Tour, but Richard has little interest in talking about tennis at the moment.

Sucking on his trademark cigarillo and turning his head to puff cumulus clouds of nicotine soot, the man who has said he was looking into buying Rockefeller Center for $3.9 billion is updating an acquaintance on his latest business ventures. He says he just launched a website "for fucked-up girls," called homegirls.com, that he expects will net him more than $100 million by year's end. He claims to have purchased the air rights over India and "will make millions" charging a fee to planes that traverse this space. "It's based on the weight of their cargo," he explains. He also purports to have recently purchased a seat on the "Shanghai Stock Exchange." Then there's his fledgling career as a vocalist. He says that a Bahamian casino—he can't recall the name—has offered him $250,000 a night to sing and another $250,000 if he can coax Venus into backing him up on drums.

He cuts off this litany of his prospects when Irina Spirlea happens by on her way to the practice court. It was, of course, Spirlea who made headlines—and more than a few friends on Tour—when she chest-bumped Venus in the semifinals of the 1997 U.S. Open. At the time, Richard called her "a big, tall white turkey." Spirlea was never the same player after that match, and now, at age twenty-six, is pondering retirement. But apparently she and Richard have made some sort of peace.

"Hey, Spirlea," Richard bellows. "Congratulations."

"Thanks," the Romanian says with a smile, clearly bracing herself for a detour into Fantasyland. "What for?"

"I heard you got married."

"Nope. Not me," she says.

"No? I thought I heard that. Well, congratulations anyway. Nice to see you."

"Nice to see you too," she says, shaking her head.

Now where were we? Oh right. "Yesterday," Richard says, "I went to L.A. to try and get a bus contract from the Bush campaign." It's a curious claim, since many saw him in Indian Wells throughout the previous day. Suddenly, he interrupts himself again.

"Well if it isn't Debbie Graham!" Richard howls, jumping out of the golf cart to give Graham, a veteran player, a warm peck on the cheek. "How you doing?"

"Hi, Richard. How are you?"

"Great. Now, Debbie, I wanted to talk to you. Do you want to make $250,000?"

"Sure," sputters Graham, who earned just $57,000 in prize money in 1999. "What do I have to do?"

"All you have to do is stay in a Marriott hotel."

"Richard, for $250,000, I'll stay wherever you want me to stay." She laughs.

"Great, so I'm counting on you," he says, abruptly ending the exchange.

By now, the unlikely story of the Williams family has been repeated so often that it has the ring of an urban legend—which, one might argue, it essentially is. Richard Dove Williams was born on February 16, 1942, in Shreveport, Louisiana, to a single mother, Julia May, who was nicknamed "Miss Knee." Richard likes to tell the story of how his mother was a sharecropper and picked cotton. Those who knew Richard as a child say the story is absurd. "He said he was the son of a sharecropper?" says Arthur (Turd) Bryant, one of Richard's childhood friends who still lives in Shreveport. "He ain't no fucking son of a sharecropper. Only thing I ever saw him raise was his fork to eat the vegetables someone else raised."

Richard also says that he was a star athlete in high school, the best football player in the state this side of Heisman Trophy winner Billy Cannon, a basketball talent so gifted he was offered a tryout with the Knicks, and "the greatest golfer in the state of Louisiana." However, Leonard Barnes, the football, basketball, and track coach from 1949 to 1967 at Booker T. Washington, Shreveport's predominantly black high school, reports he never heard of Richard before his daughters became successful. Neither had Jim McClain, who has covered high school sports at the *Shreveport Times* since 1962. "If he says he played football and basketball, he's lying," says Leddell Lattier, 60, who still lives behind Richard's 30-by-30-foot boyhood home on 78th Street in Shreveport. "I was a forward in basketball and a back in football and I never saw him. I would remember if I did."

Williams dropped out of high school at sixteen, he says, and moved to Chicago to work construction. From there, he landed in Los Angeles and eventually started his own company, Samson Security. In a little-known phase of his life, he married Betty J. Johnson, on December 7, 1965. He was twenty-three and she was thirty-one and the couple had five children, two daughters and three sons. According to Richard and Betty's oldest daughter, Sabrina, now age thirty-seven, the marriage was stormy and volatile. It ended when Richard filed a notice of dissolution on March 22, 1973. A few years later, Richard met a college-educated Los Angeles nurse, Oracene Price, who had three daughters from a previous relationship. Venus was born to Oracene and Richard in 1980; Serena was born barely a year later. Despite published reports that they married in 1972, Oracene says that they did not marry until 1980, after Venus's birth.

In the late 1970s, Richard was flipping channels on his television set when he watched Virginia Ruzici, a Romanian tennis player, receive a cartoonishly large cardboard check for $35,000 for winning a tennis tournament. He says that inspiration struck: if this player could win all that money for a measly four or five days of work, why not conceive a few more daughters and raise them to be millionaire tennis players? As he told a dumbstruck Matt Lauer on NBC's *Today Show* in 1999: "I went to my wife and I said, 'We have to make two more kids.' And she didn't want to do it. So I used to take her out on dates and I'd hide her birth control pills. That's how Venus came. With Serena, what I'd do with my wife when I'd take her out is make sure that she had her birth control pills. I'd tell my buddy—you know we're from the ghetto, right?—'you just act like the worst Crip and take her purse.' And I'd calm her down and that's how Serena came."

The story, even if it were believable, doesn't make much sense. Richard and Oracene Williams already had three young daughters at the time. If Richard were so eager to raise a tennis star, what was wrong with daughter Lyndrea, who was only a year old when Venus was conceived? But Richard has Don King's mastery of publicity—the more outrageous, the better. If someone punches holes in your story or debunks your tale, just give them another one.

When Venus and Serena reached two years of age, Richard says that he put them to work delivering phone books, which built their muscles. (In a 1997 interview with Linda Robertson of the *Miami Herald,* Richard asserted that he had delivered phone books at the same age himself. "Man, they were heavy!") When Venus was old enough to grip a racket, the proud progenitor, who had since taught himself tennis through instructional videos and books, took her to the pocked, weed-infested local courts. Richard stood on one side of the net and patiently fed his daughter the 550 balls he kept in a shopping cart. When they were done, they would pick up the balls, load the cart into a Volkswagen van, and drive home. Then they would do it again the next day.

It didn't take long for Venus to show promise. At age ten, she was five-four and had won nearly twenty junior tournaments in California. By age eleven, she could hit the ball monstrously hard, serve close to 100 mph, and covered the court with the loping strides of an impala. At that point, Richard removed her from the junior tennis establishment that he criticized for chewing up players and spitting them out. In retrospect, it was a shrewd move, one of many that would follow. The curiosity of the tennis world was piqued by this young, mysterious African-American whose name—Venus Ebony Starr Williams—was straight out of pulp fiction. Richard fed the ravenous hype machine, declaring his daughter was "the Cinderella of the Ghetto" and calling Compton, "the worst neighborhood in the world." Richard likened their practice court in South Central, L.A., to a war zone, painting a picture of his daughters ducking the AK-47 crossfire of rival gangs and sweeping empty crack vials off the court before practice each day.

In 1993, the family moved across the country to a rustic, ten-acre estate outside West Palm Beach, Florida. There was speculation that the family had moved so that the sisters could start training at one of the many tennis academies in south Florida, but Richard scoffed at the idea. He retained Rick Macci, a coach and notorious publicity hound, to work with his daughters; although Richard would oversee every-thing. His daughters lived at home, were assigned chores, went to school, and steered clear of the "freak show" (Richard's pet phrase) of junior tennis. On the court, Richard instilled in his daughters an unblinking confidence and mental toughness. They were the queen bees and all other players were drones. Mercy is for the weak. Intimidation can crush an opponent before the first ball is put in play. "From day one, it was like being at Muhammad Ali's camp," says Macci. "The mental part of the game was stressed every bit as deeply as skill-building."

Venus made her professional debut at a tournament in Oakland, California, in the fall of 1994. She was fourteen and all elbows and knees. Finally, many hoped, the Williams myth would combust, Richard would be exposed as a fraud and the profiteering management groups, shoe companies, and tournament directors that had been hot on the Williamses' trail would have to walk away disappointed. After all, how could a player with no junior tennis experience be match tough? How could a player succeed when her father, who had no formal tennis expertise, was her coach?

Richard's own debut was characteristically contrarian. To emphasize the point that tennis wasn't the be-all, end-all, Richard took Venus to Disneyland before the tournament. He also told Venus' opponents that he hoped they would beat his daughter. In her first match, Venus dusted Shaun Stafford, a former NCAA singles champion ranked in the top sixty. In her next match, she held a 6–2, 3–1 lead over Arantxa Sanchez-Vicario, then the world's second-ranked player, before losing in three sets. "Everyone who saw Venus was thinking the same thing," recalls Macci. "This crazy guy Richard Williams isn't full of it after all." tennis's most unlikely story was no fairy tale.

Then Richard threw the tennis world another curveball—or maybe it was a brushback pitch. He announced that, good as Venus was, she wasn't even going to be the best player in the family. His younger daughter Serena had the build of an Olympic swimmer and she was every bit as athletic as Venus. Plus, he said gleefully, she was meaner.

One day soon, Richard predicted, his daughters would rally the top ranking back and forth and play each other in Grand Slam finals. The tennis world laughed. This wasn't a tennis father from hell. This was a tennis father from outer space.

A few years later, Richard Williams was vindicated. Venus and Serena proved to be as good as advertised. Even more confounding, though, was the fact that they were clearly wired differently from their colleagues, sidestepping the emotional land mines that claim so many talented players. Terms like "choking," "pressure," and "big points" are lost on them. When they step onto the court, they expect to dominate. They have little use for tennis's politesse and stand on ceremony for no one. You won't catch them holding up a hand in faux apology when they hit a net-cord winner—the single least sincere gesture in the sport—or clap their rackets in praise when their opponent slugs a shot past them. Put simply, they wield authority like no other players. Were they male, we would applaud their "intensity," their "competitive streak," their "ferocity." Because they are women—black women, no less—they are "catty," and they are "trash talkers." To quote John McEnroe, "they lack humility."

Is Richard Williams crazy? Is he crazy like a fox? Is he a benevolent despot, who slyly makes outrageous pronouncements in order to divert pressure (and attention) from his daughters? Or is he just another overbearing, self-aggrandizing tennis father whose unique background and eccentricities mask his fierce ambition? Getting a grip on the man can be like trying to grab a handful of cigarillo smoke. Just as you're about to dismiss him as a kook who happened to have hit the genetic Pick Six with his daughters, he offers a perceptive analysis of the flaws of the WTA Tour's business model. ("They provide the players and the Grand Slams get all the money.") He is also keenly aware of the leverage he lords over the Tour when he sets his daughters' playing schedules. Spurred by Richard and the sway he holds over his daughters' business interests and playing schedule, the Williams family topped *Tennis Magazine*'s list of the most powerful people in the sport.

Just as Richard starts to sound like he's within a lob of sanity and is playing the world for a fool, he says with a straight face that his father-in-law was once the CEO of General Motors. "My father did work for GM in Michigan," admits Oracene Williams with an uneasy chuckle. "But it was on an assembly line. You should know by now to take [Richard] with a grain of salt."

And it's not as though Richard is bizarre only when he's in public and the cameras are on. Beyond his on-again, off-again relationship with the truth, he has an ugly habit of making virulently anti-Semitic remarks. He's claimed, for example, that he could have afforded to raise his family in a more upscale neighborhood but chose to settle in Compton because he wanted "to give the Jews"—who, he asserts were buying all of the homes in the area—"a little competition." He also claims to have an employee whose job "is to collect money from the Jews." He eagerly and unapologetically tells of giving his daughters "ass-whippings" when they disobeyed him. He has suggested that Lindsay Davenport "be taken to the junkyard" and that "Little Martina Hingis is a crybaby."

Even the outgoing messages on his answering machine are news-worthy. One message several years ago said: "There are those that ask me what I think of intermarriage. Anyone that's marrying outside of this race that's black should be hung by their necks at sundown. Please leave a message." For most of 2000, callers to Richard's cell phone received this confounding greeting: "I will be going through some tough times in the next months. Some of my best friends and acquaintances will have the opportunity to judge me. I hope you will judge me according to my acts and deeds and my heart. Richard Williams." Beep.

Apparently his penchant for tall tales is nothing new. Sabrina DeVille, Richard's oldest daughter from his first marriage, says that as far back as she can remember, her father drew little distinction between fact and fiction. "He was always telling us that he studied law at Yale, he went to UCLA, he played for the Lakers," recalls DeVille, now thirty-seven, who cleans houses in Southern California and is pursuing a second bachelor's degree. "Imagine being a little girl telling your friends your father played for the Lakers and then having their fathers telling you that it's not true. That broke my heart. Richard—I don't call him my dad—is a manipulator. He likes to think that he can make people believe what he wants them to."

"There's a method to all his madness," assures Leland Hardy, the baritone-voiced, self-described "business adviser" to the family. Hardy, in fact, fits neatly into the Williamses' outside-the-box leitmotif. A former professional boxer who regularly wears a bow tie and baseball cap, Hardy claims to speak five languages, including Mandarin, and says he has acted in a dozen feature films. As the agent for New Orleans Saints football star Ricky Williams, Hardy negotiated what is regarded as the worst contract in the history of professional sports. Yet Hardy is a regular fixture in the Williams entourage. "Richard likes messing with people and keeping them guessing," Hardy says. "That's just his way of having fun." A few years ago, for instance, Richard accompanied his daughters to an event. When he met the tournament director, Richard draped an arm around him. "So," Richard said. "How does it feel to have a couple of niggers in your draw?" The startled director nearly choked, then smiled and said: "I don't care if they're pink, blue, or purple, as long as they can hit the shit out of the ball like that." Richard laughed out loud and Venus or Serena has played the event every year since. Just Richard's way of having fun.

But there is also plenty of madness *in* his methods. Richard's daughter, Sabrina, says that when her father left her now-deceased mother, Betty, he also abandoned the family. While Richard moved on to start a new life with Oracene, Betty worked two jobs to support the family; and yet the household still required public assistance. In Richard's absence, two of his sons spent time in prison in California. According to California Department of Corrections records, Richard Jr. received a thirty-two-month sentence for a firearms offense and Ronner Williams received a sixty-eight-month sentence for second-degree robbery. Sabrina claims another sibling lived briefly in a homeless shelter. Sabrina says she's gotten over her anger for her father but wonders whether Venus and Serena would have been so successful had Richard not been an abstentee dad to his "first" family. "The bottom line is that he left us," Sabrina says. "[Venus and Serena] know they walked right over our backs. All that money Richard should have been sending to us, my mother had to work for that. Indirectly, they are where they are because of my mother's sacrifices." (Richard did not return calls seeking comment.)

Richard's conduct with his "second" family hasn't always been exemplary either. Rick Macci recalls an incident when Richard angrily accused Venus and Serena, then perhaps fourteen and twelve, of running away from the ball. To correct the problem, Richard positioned each daughter three feet from the net on opposite sides of the court and told Macci to feed them short balls. Richard demanded one sister hit the ball at the other's head. "Richard said to the girls, 'I want you to take her eye out,'" Macci recalls. "They just whacked balls at each other." According to Macci, after a few near-misses, Venus pelted Serena in the chest. As Serena tried to stifle tears, Richard nodded approvingly. "That's it," Macci recollects Richard saying. "Keep moving forward. I want your middle name to be Forward."

Richard has also been suspected of spousal abuse. On February 7, 1999, Oracene Williams went to Columbia Hospital in West Palm Beach for treatment of three broken ribs. According to sheriff's reports, asked how she sustained the injury, Oracene first told hospital workers that she ran into a door handle. Pressed by a deputy from the sheriff's office, Oracene said, "I know you know what happened but I am fearful for my daughters' careers." In a report filed with the domestic violence unit, the deputy wrote that he suspected Oracene was assaulted by her husband or another family member. A sheriff's deputy asserts that the office followed up, leaving domestic violence pamphlets at the front door of the family's house. Richard claims that he was in Chicago assisting underprivileged children at the time of the incident. He alleges he thought she had injured herself jet skiing and was too embarrassed to tell him. No charges were filed. (Asked if she wished to comment on the alleged incident, Oracene responded: "It happened. I can't deny that. I would like to deny that but I can't because it's the truth. The police report speaks for itself." Richard Williams declined to comment.)

It wasn't Richard and Oracene's first interaction with the local sheriff's office. Two years earlier, deputies received an emergency call that, according to reports, came from Oracene, who said that she was being threatened with a gun. When authorities arrived, she told them that the conflict had been resolved. The police report states: "I then talked to the suspect Richard Williams and he told me that he was playing around with a pellet pistol and that Oracene had thought he was going to shoot himself with it." Richard claimed that he was merely acting out a screenplay he was trying to write and his wife and daughters had been confused. As he told the reporters, "It looked so good, they thought it was real."

Despite conduct that ranges from bizarre to deeply troubling, Richard is rarely accused of anything more than being a few games short of a set. Why? "With Richard, the proof is in the proverbial pudding," says Macci. Question his methods, question his behavior, and question his sanity, but the man has done—twice!—what countless tennis parents before him have not been able to do: nurture a prodigiously talented, well-adjusted champion without making sacrifices at the altar of junior tennis. In short, he has done right by Venus and Serena. Virtually everything he prophesized for his daughters has come to pass. And he did it all without making tennis the focal point in their lives. Venus and Serena's horizons extend far beyond the baseline. Their priorities are God, Family, and Education. If tennis is fourth, it's a distant fourth. "With some of the things he says, you wonder if there isn't a screw missing," says the broadcaster and former player Mary Carillo. "But look at the girls. They've turned out great. He has the Midas touch with them."

Both sisters are fiercely—almost pathologically—loyal to their father. Even as they've become young adults, they've shown few signs of moving beyond his considerable sphere of influence and authority, much as Tiger Woods did with his eccentric father, Earl. Further,

Venus and Serena show no signs of embarrassment for their father's rantings and antisocial behavior. Questioned about Richard's outrageous statements, his quixotic venture or bizarre antics, Venus and Serena unfailingly shrug and reply: "You have to ask him about that." When Richard is not at events, Tour staffers say that he and his daughters speak by cell phone as often as once an hour. "I think a lot people are waiting for [Venus and Serena] to put some distance between themselves and Richard," says Pam Shriver, who is paired with Venus in the WTA Tour's mentoring program. "Well it hasn't happened yet and it may never happen. They still worship the ground he walks on."

But Richard didn't do it alone. Obscured by her husband's larger-than-life presence, Oracene Williams is the fulcrum of the family. A graduate of Eastern Michigan University, she worked as a nurse before assuming the full-time job of raising five daughters, and she is her husband's polar opposite. While he is full of exuberance, she is often spotted stifling yawns and even nodding off during her daughters' matches. She is as soft-spoken and dignified as her husband is coarse and bombastic; as honest and direct and he is slippery and vague. And like most tennis fans and administrators, she often rolls her eyes at his self-aggrandizing antics. Once asked if she would ever hold up self-congratulatory signs in the stands the way her husband does, she replied: "Never. Let's just say I'm more secure with who I am."

Observe not just Serena and Venus but any of the five Williams girls walking, talking, laughing, interacting with strangers, and Oracene's powerful influence is undeniable. "My father's the arms and legs of the family, but my mother is the spine," Serena told a group of adolescent girls during an October visit to a Harlem school. "Imagine a body without a spine. It would just be a blob."

It is because of Oracene that the five Williams daughters are Jehovah's Witnesses, a sect of Christianity that forbids traditional celebrations such as Christmas, believes that government is the work of Satan, and espouses a strict code of modesty and morality. It's hard to see how the last tenet squares with Venus and Serena's skintight dresses and their unflinching bravado, but it's immediately evident off the court, where they both are impossibly virtuous, even prudish. Never mind drinking, smoking, or staying out late. Neither one of them even curses. The sisters recently described to a friend a locker room exchange in which one player allegedly called another a "b."

"A what?" the friend asked.

"You know," Serena said. "A 'b.' "

"A bee?"

"No," they said, exasperated. "A b-i-t-c-h."

In many ways, the sisters act their age. They watch Generation Y shows on the WB network, they think Enrique Iglesias can melt polar ice caps, they listen to the punk band Rancid, devour Harry Potter, and love shopping for clothes, particularly blouses "that show some belly." But there is startlingly little talk of typical celebrity self-indulgences, or even boyfriends. During the U.S. Open, the press linked Serena to Washington Redskins linebacker LaVar Arrington—she was even caught watching him play on the television in the players' lounge. But Serena is adamant that there's no romance. "I don't have time for a relationship," Serena says.

Venus agrees. Several years ago, she called Justin Gimelstob and asked if he wanted to be her mixed doubles partner. "Being a guy, naturally I figured she was into me," says Gimelstob. "Either that, or she was doing it to make Martina jealous." (Gimelstob had a brief romantic dalliance with Hingis). Venus quickly disabused him of both notions. She simply thought he'd make for a good partner. Period. Not long after their first match together, the two spoke late into the night. "It was a really interesting talk," recalls Gimelstob. "She's an intelligent person who obviously doesn't come from your typical tennis player mold. But there was no sexual vibe there at all."

The same rectitude manifests itself in their attitude about knowledge and education. To them, there's nothing cooler than being smart. In addition to their coursework in fashion school, they are voracious readers, and they try, with varying degrees of success, to teach themselves foreign languages. They love learning new words. In her 2000 WTA Tour media guide entry, Serena—the defending U.S. Open champion—lists her most memorable achievement as "receiving an 'A' in geometry." Venus lists her passions as Russian history, French furniture, and Chinese culture. "If I'm not enhancing myself," says Venus, "I feel like I'm wasting my time."

Two years ago, Venus and Serena decided that tennis coverage in the media was excessively negative, so they reported and wrote a four-page newsletter, printed five-hundred copies, and distributed it in the locker rooms at big tournaments. The *Tennis Monthly Recap* contained charming articles such as "Tommy Haas: Der German King," a tribute to Steffi Graf, and a gossip page called "What's the 411?" The two-person masthead listed both Serena J. and Venus Ebony Starr Williams as "Editor Chief" [sic]. "We just wanted to do it for ourselves and get the word out," said Venus with a shrug, as if all star athletes snuggle up with a laptop and compose essays for their peers. Some players thought the whole thing was bizarre, further evidence that the Williams family is "too weird," a refrain one hears countless times around the Tour. But it's precisely the kind of thing you do when you've been told there's nothing in life you can't achieve.

The publication of the newsletter was also surprising since the sisters take pains to steer clear of the "scene" in the locker room and are often criticized for being aloof. A well-circulated story on Tour has it that Venus came off the courts after a grueling win and another player congratulated her by lightly putting her hand on Venus's shoulder. Venus scowled and snapped "Don't touch me ever again" before walking off. (Tellingly, no one seems to know which player Venus allegedly spurned, much less where the incident occurred.) Other players say that the sisters are so detached that they don't even shower in the locker room after their matches.

Venus and Serena admit that they keep to themselves, but can't understand what all the fuss is over. Both express antipathy for "hanging out" and Serena raises a fair point when she wonders why Pete Sampras, Monica Seles, or Steffi Graf, none of whom are known for their mingling, haven't been chastised for being antisocial.

Besides, who needs to be in the running for Miss Congeniality when your best friend in the world is already on Tour with you? When Oracene likens her two youngest daughters to a husband and wife, she's not exaggerating. Venus and Serena finish each other's sentences, need to know the other's whereabouts at all times, and even have mushy pet names for each other. Serena answers to both "Cutie" and "Mama Smash"; Venus to "Beauty" and "Ace." At Grand Slams, they usually share a hotel room. At the smaller events, which they alternate playing in order to avoid facing off against each other, they are in constant contact, each instant messaging or calling the other's cell phone as often as ten times a day. "They say they're sisters," says Richard. "I think there was a mix-up at the hospital and they're really twins."

Their preternatural closeness is just one more reason that the sisters are conflated as a monolith. They aren't Venus and/or Serena; invariably they are "the Williamses," "the sister act," or as Hingis calls them, "a two-headed monster." In fact, they are as different in personality as they are in physique. While Venus reveals a large palette of moods, Serena is usually either upbeat or don't-come-near-me pissed off. While Serena is more outgoing and has ambitions of being a movie star, Venus, the aspiring veterinarian/architect/entrepreneur, is more likely to spend an afternoon reading or sitting quietly in her hotel room. It was Serena who once yelled, "Hey, Lover Boy" to Australian heartthrob Patrick Rafter while a mortified Venus ran away giggling. "I would say Venus is much more conservative in every way," says their sister, Lyndrea, twenty-three, a 2000 graduate of Howard University now working in L.A. "Not that Venus isn't hip, but Serena is more daring." Serena is the one with the navel ring.

At the Driftwood Academy in Lake Park, Florida, a small private school "emphasizing individualization" from which both sisters received their high school diplomas, founder Sandra McManus says Venus was a gifted poet and strong English student, Serena the harder worker. "If a subject came easy to Venus, it came easy. If it didn't, it didn't. But Serena would plug away until she got it. Once she got her teeth into something she wasn't going to give up."

As one might expect from the more muscular sister, Serena is also more prone to confrontation. Rick Macci recalls that when Serena was ten years old, he would have her play against men. "She'd be out there against some guy who just got off the satellite tour and when she started losing, she would start making bad calls, and getting pissed off," Macci says. "It was beyond her comprehension that *anyone* was a better player." Serena once told a group of reporters that the word "ghetto" derived from Nazi Germany. When it was suggested that the word traced much earlier to the Middle Ages, Serena shot back, "You have your information and I have mine." Venus says that as a kid, Serena would flex her muscles at other kids at school and in the neighborhood to scare them. On the court, Serena will occasionally crack a racket, kick a bag in disgust, or even rifle a "message ball" perilously close to her opponent's head. As Richard said after the infamous Spirlea chest bump incident: "She ought to be glad it wasn't Serena she knocked into. She would have been decked."

Venus, on the other hand, is more contemplative, more sensitive, more passive-aggressive. Instead of smacking a ball when she gets angry with herself, she'll bite her lip in silent fury and become so intense she'll forget to blink for minutes. "With Serena, if something's bothering her, you know it, and when she loses she gets mad at herself," Oracene says tellingly. "With Venus it's more subtle and it can be months before she gets it out of her system. When she loses she gets mad at the world." At this point in the year, she was seething.

One of the benefits of attending a tournament in person is the opportunity to watch players practice. Few fans take advantage of their access to it, but the practice court is the best place to appreciate the confluence of skills required to be a pro. There's something almost mesmerizing about watching players strike ball after ball after ball with tidal consistency, tracing perfect rainbows with their rackets as the light *pfffft* of a backswing and the *ping* of the ball serve as background music. The vast differences among players, both technically and temperamentally, are most pronounced on the practice courts. While Lindsay Davenport strikes balls in earnest silence, Anna Kournikova, believe it or not, an intense practice player, slugs them with an exaggerated grunt. While some pros merely grab a partner and hit around for an hour, a player like Martina Hingis will hit every ball with a purpose in a Byzantine system of drills methodically planned by her mother.

Then there's Serena Williams. Unlike her sister, Serena is a morning person. At seven A.M. on the first Saturday of the Indian Wells tournament, before the sun had crept above the stands, she strode onto the stadium court with her father and her hitting partner. ("I don't want to feel like anyone is beating me to the courts," she says.) Before she removed her Wilson racket from her bag, Serena tethered her Jack Russell terrier, Jackie, to the umpire's chair. Wearing a collared shirt, tight shorts without pockets, and cross-trainers, Richard stuck a toothpick in his mouth, popped open a can of balls, and grabbed a racket. He tried to rally with Serena only to have her pace-laced shots careen off his racket and into the photographers' pit. He eventually ceded to the hitting partner, former ATP pro Todd Nelson, but often halted the session to whisper words of encouragement in his daughter's ear.

At 8:40, Richard's cell phone beeped. He glanced at the caller ID. As his daughter was winding up to serve, he yelled: "Serena, what's the number of that guy in Atlanta?"

"What guy, Daddy?"

"That guy we was going to do business with?"

"Uh. I don't know, 404 something, Daddy."

"Oh, this isn't him then."

A few minutes later, Richard, clearly bored, flicked on his cell again. "I'm calling Venus," he announced to no one in particular. Ten minutes later, he signaled an end to practice. Richard untied the dog, Serena packed up her bag, Richard hugged the hitting partner and the coterie walked off the court. The conventional wisdom is that until the Williams sisters retain a "real" coach, who will structure a practice and give them legitimate instruction, they're only scratching the surface of their potential. But perhaps by making practice fun and lighthearted, father knows best. "Venus and Serena know how to hit a tennis ball already," he says. "Actually, I'd like to see them practice less and spend that time on education."

That afternoon, Serena played a torpid match on the stadium court of the Tennis Garden but beat Alexandra Stevenson in three sets. The next day she dropped the first set before rallying to beat seventy-eighth-ranked Rita Grande. Three days later, she met Mary Pierce in the quarterfinals. Moving sluggishly and splattering balls all over the court, Serena was blitzed 6–2, 6–1. After characterizing Pierce's play as "pretty much nearly impeccable" and assessing her own play at "10 percent" of her potential, she angrily stormed out of the press conference.

To the untrained eye, it was a low point for the House of Williams. Serena bore only a faint resemblance to the athletic dynamo that had won the U.S. Open six months prior. Venus was a cipher, home in Florida nursing her wrists, still weeks removed from playing her first match of the year. Naturally, the all-knowing paterfamilias couldn't have been happier. "I think one of my girls will win Wimbledon, yes sir, I'm very confident of that," he said. "You can print that and take it to the bank." He was happy to be leaving the California desert, though. You see, there was this "big Internet deal" on the table and if he didn't return home to Florida soon, he "could lose millions, maybe even billions."

MONEY FOR NOTHING

FROM ITS HUMBLE BEGINNINGS AS A MOM-and-pop tournament hosted at the courts of a nearby resort hotel, Indian Wells has evolved into a Grand Slam–quality event. The tournament's unchecked growth is a testament to the vision, persistence, and deal-making savvy of its director, former pro Charlie Pasarell. But it also attests to the wisdom of combining men's and women's events. Each circuit bristles at comparisons to the other—"It's apples and oranges" is the dronelike response of administrators from both tours. But so long as both the ATP and WTA Tours are in the business of selling professional tennis, it makes sense for them to combine assets. As Pasarell is fond of saying, "With pro tennis, one plus one equals much more than two." And the numbers support his fuzzy math. Prior to 1997, the men's and women's events were held separately and, in their best years, drew crowds of 100,000 combined. In 2000, more than 200,000 fans attended the matches.

The sticking point keeping both circuits from holding more combined events is, not surprisingly, money. Indian Wells marked the inaugural event in the ATP's Masters Series, a streamlined collection of the Tour's ten most prestigious tournaments outside the Grand Slams. In exchange for sponsorship, marketing, and television rights to these events, the Swiss marketing firm ISL agreed to pay the ATP a staggering $1.2 billion over the next ten years. By the end of 2000, the deal was collapsing under its own weight and an overextended ISL was desperately trying to renegotiate more favorable terms. Nevertheless, contrast the ATP figures with those of the WTA Tour, which, despite comparable ratings and fan support, reaps roughly $7 million apiece—for perspective, it's no more than Venus Williams is paid to endorse Reebok—from its television and sponsorship revenues. The men are reluctant to share this windfall with the women, whose tour is worth a great deal less on paper. Meanwhile the women are reluctant to accept an inferior wage, given that it is their more colorful field that makes the turnstiles click and drives television dollars.

The Solomonic Pasarell appeased both sides. He paid the men the standard Masters Series purse of $2.45 million, and he bumped the women's share up by more than 50 percent, from $1.3 million in 1999 to $2 million in 2000. It was another reminder that equal work (and equal ratings) still doesn't yield commensurate pay in professional tennis. But given that the WTA Tour's highest-tier tournament disburses only $1.08 million, Pasarell's offer was too good to refuse.

Ask any female player to assess their Tour, and the paucity of prize money invariably tops the list of complaints. It's understandably frustrating that a mediocrity like Wayne Ferreira made more in 2000 ($1,237,864) than all but the top three women. Or that the fortieth-ranked WTA Tour singles player, Tatiana Garbin, took home $201,925 in singles and doubles while her male counterpart, fortieth-ranked Max Mirnyi, amassed $760,368.

But over the past generation, the financial gains in women's tennis have been staggering. In 2000, the WTA Tour put $47 million in prize money up for grabs, spread among sixty-two events held in twenty-eight countries. Six players would earn more than $1 million and another dozen would bank more than $500,000. Even the fiftieth-ranked player, Sabine Appelmans, would take home $243,748. When Martina Hingis won the year-end Chase Championships, she made $500,000 for four matches, double the *purse* for the entire Tour thirty

years ago. "The money keeps getting crazier and crazier," says Irina
Spirlea. "You catch yourself saying things like, 'I had a shitty week, I
only made $5,000.' You don't realize how ridiculous it sounds because
you've gotten used to it."

The purses have come a long way, baby. In 1970, Margaret Court
won the U.S. Open and received scarcely one-third of the prize money
awarded the men's champion, Ken Rosewall. A few weeks later, the
top female players threw down the gauntlet. On September 23, 1970,
the "original nine" (ringleader Billie Jean King along with Rosie
Casals, Judy Dalton, Julie Heldman, Kerry Melville, Peaches
Bartkowicz, Kristy Pigeon, Nancy Richey, and Valerie Ziegenfuss)
boycotted the Pacific Southwest tournament in Los Angeles when
tournament director Jack Kramer refused to amend the purse: $12,500
for the men, $1,500 for the women. The nine rebels instead signed
symbolic $1 contracts with Gladys Heldman, the abrasive founder of
World Tennis Magazine. Heldman put up $5,000 and the women staged
a separate event in Houston that week.

That tournament was a success and chaos ensued. The incumbent
organization governing women's tennis, the USLTA, moved to sus-
pend the nine insurrectionists, precluding them from playing Wimbledon or the U.S. Open. "You'll never work in this sport again," they
were told. But the women didn't budge. Heldman recruited a friend,
Philip Morris executive Joe Cullman, to help subsidize the fledgling
tour. Philip Morris, it turned out, was about to market a cigarette for
women, and Cullman thought women's tennis might be the ideal
sponsorship vehicle. By 1971, the Virginia Slims Circuit had nineteen
events offering a total of $250,000 in prize money. King would amass
$117,000 that year—more than any other pro, man or woman—making
her the first female athlete in history to earn a six-figure income in a
year. "We laugh now," says King. "But it was a heck of a lot better than
what we were getting."

The rebels tirelessly promoted their breakaway tour. Every player
from that era has a compendium of war stories—the time she took a
cab to the local newspaper so she could personally plead with the sports
editor for coverage, or all the mornings she set her alarm for an

ungodly hour so she could be interviewed on AM radio, or the afternoons she passed out women's tennis fliers on a street corner. King often wonders how many more matches she could have won had she trained properly and left the endless promotion to professionals. "There were nights when I'd get to the arena half an hour before my match and barely have time to stretch," she says. "I would have just come back from spending the day giving interviews or trying to set up meetings with potential sponsors. That was just the reality of what we thought we had to do to survive."

Eventually, the USLTA realized it was fighting a losing battle and dropped the sanctions. By 1973, not only did the USLTA merge its existing tour—which featured loyalists such as Chris Evert and Virginia Wade, who had refused to join the new Tour—with the Virginia Slims circuit, but it agreed to compensate the men and women with equal prize money at the U.S. Open. Under the aegis of the USLTA and International Tennis Federation, with the continued financial backing of Philip Morris, the consolidated women's tour grew rapidly and by the following year prize money had topped $1 million. By 1983, it would surpass $10 million. By the early nineties, players competed for more than $25 million. "Now," says King, "players make more in a year than I did in my career."

The person in charge of making sure the purses continue to swell is Bart McGuire. The Tour's genial, avuncular fifty-nine-year-old CEO is an unlikely figure to be overseeing the leading women's sport. A bespectacled, buttoned-down lawyer, McGuire speaks in the slow, rolling cadences of Walter Cronkite and chooses his words with painstaking precision. He played tennis at Princeton in the early sixties, was a legal adviser to the Tour from 1987 to 1997, and helped craft the Age Eligibility Rules in the mid-nineties. But he is the consummate tennis outsider, never having run a tournament or worked for a management agency. When McGuire accepted the chief executive's position in early 1998—only after another candidate, Ric Clarson, an executive at the PGA Tour, agreed to the post and then turned it down the following day—he was teaching at Lewis and Clark Law School in Oregon, where he and his wife, Cindy, own a seventy-acre ranch.

Two experiences helped shape McGuire's vision for the Tour and his leadership philosophy. In 1999, he visited the Sistine Chapel with Pam Shriver and was amazed when autograph-seeking fans mobbed her. "That reinforced to me how popular the game had become on a global level," he says. Second, he recalls his own elation when his daughter, Jil, signed a contract to play professional volleyball in the mid-nineties and how crestfallen he was when the league folded soon thereafter for lack of financial support. He is also an unapologetic feminist who recognizes the somewhat delicate position he's in running a women's sport. "There are places in this world where it's easier for a man to sell a woman's agenda," acknowledges McGuire. "But women's tennis is part of a cultural evolution that's taking away that sense."

The position of Tour CEO is, inherently, a political high-wire act. A mediator and consensus builder by nature, McGuire is continually trying to mollify tennis's various fiefdoms: players of all levels, management groups, promoters, and board members, whose interests are often adverse. Consider the opposition he faces in augmenting the purses at Tour events. Tournament directors vigorously oppose it as it cuts into their profits. Rank-and-file players are concerned that the spoils won't be distributed evenly and that the tournaments will cut draw sizes and playing opportunities in order to defray costs. While management groups like IMG and Octagon would reap more in player commission from bigger purses, they own and operate Tour events as well, so they're ambivalent about prize money increases.

As a result, McGuire is constantly embattled. Tournament directors complain that he doesn't do enough to encourage the players to promote the game and their particular events. The players perceive him largely as an ineffectual leader who kowtows to promoters and management groups and retreats when confronted. IMG personnel think he accords Octagon favorable treatment. Octagon contends the opposite. "Bart McGuire is bright, he's decent, and he's a glutton for punishment taking this job," says Octagon's head, Phil de Picciotto.

McGuire has also failed to rally the support of the top players, who have nicknamed him "Bart Simpson." Davenport is particularly vocal in her disapproval, but she is not alone. According to Nicole Pratt, the Tour's players' council—composed of seven players in the top hundred including herself—recommended to the board during Wimbledon that it not renew McGuire's contract. "We keep hearing how well the Tour is doing, but where's the money?" asks Pratt. "We're supposedly this hot sport, but why don't we have a better television contract? Why do Tour events still get away with paying so little in prize money?"

In truth, the Tour's failure to parlay the sport's popularity into even bigger financial gains is largely beyond McGuire's control. The fundamental problem with the Tour is in its structure. Set up as a nonprofit organization, the Tour serves as a governing body for players and promoters. The events pay a fee to the Tour, but they operate independently, cutting their own television deals and finding their own sponsors. With little streamlining, promoters often put their own financial interests—and self-preservation—ahead of the good of women's tennis.

The other overarching obstacle facing the Tour is its failure to reap significant financial gains from the Grand Slams, the four premiere events on the calendar. The Slams are all wildly profitable, flush with luxury boxes, monstrous television contracts, and pricey sponsorships. They pay a smaller percentage of their revenue in prize money than any other events and are so prestigious that they don't have to pay appearance fees to lure players. Yet the windfall goes to the International Tennis Federation and the four host countries' tennis associations. Consider that the USTA cleared a profit from the U.S. Open—due in no small part to the popularity of WTA Tour players—that greatly exceeded the entire annual *revenues* for the Tour. With negligible domestic television revenues (tournaments, in fact, must often *buy* time from networks like ESPN to put their event on the air) the Tour must rely on sponsorship dollars to offset most of its operating expenses, which exceeded $15 million in 1999.

The quest for a sponsor has been an ongoing challenge for the Tour since it parted ways with Virginia Slims in the mid-nineties, unsure how to reconcile a vibrant, health-conscious sport with funding from tobacco sales. Several years ago, a potential alliance with Tampax was

scotched after the WTA Tour board deemed the product "too femi-
nine." Also, tennis's global marketplace can work against the sport.
Insiders say an American brokerage firm was interested in a major
sponsorship until it realized how few of the Tour's events are held in
the United States. After a four-year agreement with Philip Morris sub-
sidiary Kraft ended in 1994, the Tour needed two years before it signed
a deal with Corel, a little-known Canadian software firm. That deal
was impressive at the time, $12 million over three years, but the mar-
riage was short-lived. The players had little knowledge of the product,
the company did little else to support the sport—there was no synergy,
to use the tired word of the decade—and the partnership ended in
1998.

Sponsorless for 1999, the Tour enlisted IMG—another potential
conflict of interest—to help with the search for corporate dollars. The
sport may have been burgeoning in popularity, but many companies
expressed sticker shock at a sponsorship asking price that hovered
around $10 million annually. Finally, during the Chase Champi-
onships in November of 1999, the Tour announced a deal with the
European skin care company Sanex, a division of Sara Lee, worth $34
million over five years. The deal requires that Sanex provide at least an
additional $34 million for promotions and marketing. It was far and
away the biggest sponsorship in the history of women's sports. And it
did wonders for McGuire's job security.

Aside from the bigger purses, there's another reason female players
look forward to mixed events. A coed field at a tournament like Indian
Wells means plenty of men. Rich, handsome, athletic, age-appropriate
men. Some players circle the coed events on their calendars. "If it were
up to us," says Jennifer Capriati, "we'd put all the tournaments together."

On the men's tour, there is plenty of "action"—or at least plenty of
stories of groupies hanging out in lobbies, women slipping players
room keys, and a hopping pickup scene in the bar of the tournament
hotel. Broach the subjects of casual sex, dating, and romance with
players on the women's circuit, though, and they respond with wistful

smiles. The standard response: *What casual sex? What dating? And Lord only knows, what romance?* "The guys have these crazy rock star stories," says one American woman player with a laugh. "I'm thinking, what did I do last night? Oh yeah, I went out to dinner with friends, I watched some TV, played around on the Internet, and went to bed. And I know I wasn't the only one."

The radically different men's and women's social scenes stem from a familiar double standard. Even the empowered, attractive, hyperconfident women on the WTA Tour aren't comfortable in the role of pursuers, and groupie culture doesn't carry over much to women's sports. Also, the average age in the women's tour is younger than the men's and the players are often traveling with a coach who moonlights as a chaperone. The upshot is that the absence of companionship adds to monotony and social displacement of life on the Tour. As Laxmi Poruri, a Stanford graduate who quit the Tour after two years, wrote in a *New York Times* essay: "In the end losses don't put you over the edge, for your young mind can straighten that out. But dinner for one, that's what breaks your heart."

So, like a college mixer, a joint event with the ATP affords women a chance to mingle with men who have similar experiences and goals. At the Indian Wells tournament in 2000, many trysts developed between players—which, for whatever reason, seemed to involve a disproportionate number of Argentine men. The nocturnal activities of one couple in the hotel room next door were so loud that veteran French player Fabrice Santoro blamed his next day's loss on lack of sleep. ("It was finally quiet," he told the French press. "Then it starts up again. Unbelievable.") A number of longer-term relationships also flourished or took root in the desert, including those of Martina Hingis and Magnus Norman, Kim Clijsters and Lleyton Hewitt, and Jennifer Capriati and Xavier Malisse.

"When you're home, a lot of times with guys you think 'Why do they like me? Is it for me? Or is it my money or because I am a tennis player?' With [male players] they know what you're going through, they understand the travel and the training," says Hingis. "You start out already with a lot in common." Athletes in other sports are also kindred spirits. Anna Kournikova dates a hockey player (Sergei Fedorov and/or Pavel Bure), Hingis had a brief fling with one too (the Tampa Bay Lightning's Pavel Kubina), Mary Pierce and Amanda Coetzer were dating baseball players (former Baltimore Orioles teammates Roberto Alomar and Brady Anderson), and before Andre Agassi won her heart, Steffi Graf kept the company of a race car driver (Michael Bartels). "Roberto understands the pressure of performing and what you go through when you compete," says Pierce. "That kind of stuff can be hard to explain to someone who doesn't do it for a living."

Perhaps for the same reasons, more than a dozen players on the circuit in 2000 were married to or in a serious relationship with their coach. In many respects, it's a natural match. Players and coaches travel the world together, spend upward of sixteen hours a day together, and have an emotional bond from navigating life on tour. "Remember, if there weren't some degree of personal chemistry, the relationship wouldn't work in the first place," says Pam Shriver. "For every one that's acted upon, I bet there are sexual feelings in 99 percent of the other player-coach relationships that never surface."

Having your boyfriend or husband or lover as your coach presents an additional challenge. How do you avoid personalizing losses? How do you have your coach exhibit the requisite toughness and intensity but show tenderness away from tennis? What do you do when it's time for a coaching change but not a divorce? "You just have to try to keep the two [roles] apart," says Austrian Barbara Schett, whose former fiancé, Thomas Prerovsky, was also her coach. "Just because he gets upset with me for something on the court or in a match, doesn't mean he doesn't love me." (Still, sometimes, the lines blur. Schett recalls a match against Jana Novotna several years ago during which Prerovsky grew upset with her play and began furiously shaking his head. Schett then became so irate that she took a ball from her skirt pocket and whizzed it at Prerovsky. Indeed, she and Prerovsky split, both romantically and professionally, by year's end.)

This coach-athlete relationship often requires that the man sublimate his ego, check machismo at the door and accept a subordinate role. It's the wife who is the breadwinner, the celebrity. "I have no problem when the attention is on Julie," said Arnaud Decugis, who coached his wife Julie Halard-Decugis, a top ten player. "To me I am living a dream. I get to be with my wife, travel around the world and be around tennis." Halard-Decugis, who retired at the end of 2000, attributed the success that came late in her career to the stability and the support that her husband provided.

Not all coach-player romantic entanglements are healthy—or consensual. In his controversial book *Ladies of the Court,* Michael Mewshaw laid bare the issue. "Parents and tennis officials are so irrationally anxious about lesbians in the locker room, they have ignored far more pressing problems caused by . . . male coaches," he wrote. A decade later, women's tennis remains rife with stories of coaches who exploit their power and the insularity of life on the Tour to forge sexual relationships with their charges. In recent years, two coaches were dismissed by the French Tennis Federation for allegedly sleeping with junior girls. Another high-ranking official at the Federation was relieved of his duties as well for allegedly conducting an affair with a teenage player, now on the WTA Tour. The official was fifty at the time. In 1998, the WTA Tour investigated widespread allegations that a former Grand Slam champion was molested by her coach starting at the age of eleven. (According to a source close to the investigation, the player declined to cooperate and no action was taken against the coach, who still has a presence on the Tour.) Another coach on the WTA Tour was once dismissed by the USTA for allegedly having an inappropriate sexual relationship with a junior girl.

Coaches having sex with young athletes is hardly unique to tennis—or, for that matter, to women's sports. A study by University of Winnipeg professor Sandy Kirby revealed that prior to the 1996 Olympic Games in Atlanta nearly 20 percent of the 266 female Canadian athletes interviewed had engaged in sexual intercourse with a coach. Derry O'Rourke, the former Irish Olympic team coach, was sentenced to eleven years in prison for sexually abusing eleven girls between 1976 and 1992. In 1998, National Hockey League player Sheldon Kennedy recounted being systematically abused sexually by his junior coach,

Graham Jones, who is now serving a prison sentence. Any sort of mentor/student relationship is complex and fraught with tension to begin with. Add in the physical component of athletics—the body is at the essence of what an athlete does—and, in the any sport, the cocktail can become explosive

Women's tennis, however, is particularly ripe for sexual abuse. In many countries, the coaches for the national tennis federations have immense, if not absolute, power, because they decide which players do and don't receive funding to train and travel. Men provide "a better hit" during practice than women do, so the vast majority of players are coached by physically fit males, ages twenty-five to thirty-five. And because the sport is so transitory and many parents can't afford to accompany their child full-time, coaches are often deputized as guardians. In *Ladies of the Court* Mewshaw recounts a South American player telling him: "My father sent me out on the circuit when I was sixteen. He told me to do whatever the coach said. So when he said we were staying in the same hotel room and then he moved over to my bed, I didn't know how to say no."

The WTA recently issued a code of conduct for coaches. At the risk of incurring penalties ranging from "monetary sanctions" to a ban, coaches must attend an annual orientation meeting and abide by rules including a prohibition of having sexual contact with a player under seventeen. The Tour also takes measures to educate players on how to rebuff unwanted sexual advances by a coach. "Players need to realize that you're not meek, and you're not helpless to put the brakes on," says Pam Shriver. "If you don't want to go back to his hotel room after a match to discuss how you played, don't. If you don't want him to give you a massage, don't. And if you think a coach is violating the code of ethics, report it."

But the Tour can only do so much. Take the case of Patty Schnyder. A crafty lefty from Switzerland, Schnyder cracked the top ten at age nineteen in 1998 and seemed destined for greatness. But prior to the 1999 Australian Open she met Rainer Harnecker, a forty-two-year-old self-styled "guru." Under investigation in Germany at the time, for the unlicensed practice of alternative medicine, Harnecker claimed he could cure AIDS and cancer patients. He had no background in tennis, but as he explained his alternative practices to Schnyder, she was flattered by the attention, happy for the companionship.

A few weeks later, she fired her coach, Eric Van Harpen, broke up with her longtime boyfriend, severed contact with her family, and embarked on a romantic relationship with Harnecker, who was still married. She also embraced his unorthodox training methods. At his behest, she consumed two liters of orange juice each day and submitted to *baumscheidtism,* a "blood cleansing therapy." In front of horrified onlookers at a tournament, Harnecker perforated Schnyder's skin with a wheel covered in needles and then rubbed Oriental herbs onto the wounds. As Schnyder fell deeper under Harnecker's spell, her parents retained an expert on cults to try to deprogram their daughter. Other players and Tour administrators grew profoundly concerned, but there was little they could do. Because Harnecker was technically a trainer and not a coach, he wasn't subject to the code of conduct for coaches. Because Schnyder was past the age of consent, there was no legal recourse. There were philosophical issues as well. What sort of a feminist message would the Tour be conveying had it intervened to end a disturbing, yes, but otherwise consensual relationship? And what is the threshold test for when the Tour should step in on behalf of a player and when matters should stay personal? Tour personnel breathed a deep sigh of relief when Schnyder terminated the relationship with Harnecker after a few months and reconnected with her parents, but not before falling out of the top twenty and losing a number of lucrative endorsement deals.

Nearly a year after breaking off the relationship with Harnecker, Schnyder hadn't come close to replicating the success she had before she met him. At Indian Wells, she got her clock cleaned 6–0, 6–3 by Monica Seles. She lunged halfheartedly for easily retrievable balls, batted careless forehands three feet outside the court, and shrugged when winners off Seles's racket sailed past her. She may not have her mojo back, but she did have a new boyfriend—reportedly he was one of the detectives hired to investigate Harnecker on her behalf. Watching Schnyder slog through a desultory match, a shadow of her former self at age twenty, one recalls her own haunting explanation for why she became involved with Harnecker: "I wanted someone who could understand me and who I could have fun with. I just wanted someone to talk to."

Frittering away idle time before facing Martina Hingis in the Indian Wells final, Lindsay Davenport and coach Robert Van't Hof chatted outside the women's locker room. Intimately familiar with Hingis's game, Davenport needed little advice from her coach. As an afterthought, Van't Hof instructed Davenport that if she fell in an early hole, "just hang in there until you can turn a corner. Sometimes a key point or two can turn everything around." Davenport listened, but the notion of falling behind seemed like a remote possibility. It had, after all, been only a few weeks since Hingis's astonishing admission in Australia that Davenport had pitched a tent inside Martina's psyche.

An hour into the match, under an azure sky, Hingis was on cruise control. Playing meticulous tennis and varying the pace, location, and height of her balls to keep Davenport off balance, Hingis held a 6–4, 4–2 lead. Then, on a point that validated all of Davenport's extra sessions in the gym, all those mornings when she'd rather have been sleeping or at the beach, she turned the corner, as her coach had prophesied. After Hingis hit what she was sure was a forehand winner, she watched in amazement as Davenport sprinted beyond the doubles alley and flagged it down. Hingis coldly directed Davenport's ball to the opposite corner, seemingly annoyed that she had been forced to play another shot. In full sprint, Davenport reached the ball and spanked a crosscourt screamer that tattooed the line.

Hingis reacted as if she'd been slapped in the face. As often happens in tennis, a game with the slimmest of margins for error, one player's focus blurred while the other found her groove. Davenport banged winner after winner that landed within six inches of the lines, and won the next ten games to close out the match 4–6, 6–4, 6–0. Hingis, who ate the business end of more than fifty winners, was so dispirited that she double-faulted on match point. After shaking Davenport's hand, she glanced at her mother, with a look that again said: "What else can I do?"

With the Williams sisters ailing or flailing, and no other players near them in the rankings, Davenport and Hingis were being hailed as the great rivalry in women's tennis. But at the time, it was no rivalry— it was a mugging. Davenport had won seven of their previous eight matches, including five straight, and, more important, had perforated Hingis's confidence. Even the usually modest Davenport said that if she and Hingis were at their best, she's the superior player. "I will win. I have more weapons." Hingis admitted that in spite of Davenport's No. 2 ranking, she was "an unstoppable force." No one that day would have imagined that the "unstoppable force" would go seven months without winning another tournament.

RUMORS DU JOUR, SCANDALS D'AMOUR

I F THERE'S AN UNDERSIDE TO THE VIVIDNESS of the WTA's cast of characters, it's that their tennis is too easily rendered a sideshow to rumors du jour and scandals d'amour. The Ericsson Open (née Lipton Championships) in Key Biscayne, Florida, is the next stop on tennis's road show after Indian Wells. Another mixed event that offers monstrous prize money—$3.2 million for the men and $2.525 million for the women—the Ericsson is so big that it bills itself as the "Fifth Grand Slam." Yet most of the tournament's buzz in 2000 was generated not by the matches but by two riveting rumors: the engagement of Anna Kournikova to hockey star Pavel Bure and the retirement of Venus Williams.

Tennis's very own rock star, Anna Kournikova has a magnetic force field that can pull grown men out of their orbit and push boys into a frenzy. The world's most photographed/downloaded/Internet-searched woman is particularly popular in pink-and-blue Miami, which she has adopted as her home base. So rather than tout Pete Sampras or Lindsay Davenport, an ad campaign for the Ericsson featured a picture of Kournikova and the catchphrase "Come See Anna's Serves and Curves." The list of rules for the tournament's ballboys included this all-important—and all but impossible to follow—directive: Do Not Stare at Kournikova. Her practice sessions in Miami were mobbed by men in the narrow twelve-to-seventy-five demographic who panted like puppies as she hit balls. All the while she feigned obliviousness to the salivating masses as only she can. As a local columnist observed, Kournikova single-handedly "turned a charming venue into a construction site."

As is the case at many of the events she enters, Kournikova supplemented her tennis with glamour-pussing during the first week of the tournament, including a photo shoot for the cover of *Sports Illustrated for Women*. After arriving late to the shoot, Kournikova told the photographer, Nesti Mendoza, to make it snappy. Five minutes into the shoot, Mendoza frantically changed lenses on his camera. As he reached into his bag, he absentmindedly said to Kournikova, "Just hold on one second and we'll make you beautiful." Arms akimbo, Kournikova shot back, "I already *am* beautiful. Just take the picture." A New York fashion photographer who rarely shoots athletes, Mendoza later tried to engage Kournikova in small talk. "So," he asked. "Do you have a boyfriend?" Kournikova gave him a "What planet are you from?" look and said: "You don't know who my boyfriend is?"

Mendoza's question wasn't completely off the wall. Kournikova has an uncanny ability to keep any of a half dozen suitors on the down end of her yo-yo. She is the first female athlete to treat men the way most male celebrities treat women. Trying to sort out Kournikova's romantic life was the parlor game of choice for fans, the media, and players at the Ericsson. A month before the tournament, Kournikova had supposedly accepted a marriage proposal from NHL superstar Pavel Bure, who plays for the Florida Panthers, over dinner and a $3,000 bottle of champagne at Bure's favorite Miami Beach restaurant, the Forge. Though unexpected, the announcement wasn't altogether implausible. Bure and Kournikova lived in the same apartment complex in Miami and were often spotted cruising South Beach in his silver Ferrari. At a Panthers charity auction in Boca Raton in the winter of 2000, bidding on a dinner for six with Bure had reached $6,500 when suddenly Kournikova, in attendance as Bure's date,

hopped onto the stage and promised to go along. The price of the dinner doubled.

The person most surprised by Kournikova's engagement had to be
another Russian hockey star, Sergei Fedorov. The Detroit Red Wings
center had been romantically linked to Kournikova since she was sixteen and she attended the Red Wings Stanley Cup celebration in 1997
wearing a typically understated outfit: a hot pink top and leopard-skin
miniskirt. According to Miami-Dade County property records,
Fedorov had purchased Kournikova's 4,100-square-foot Miami pent-
house for $1.6 million and signed the deed over to her for $100. Reading in *Pravda* that Anna was going to get married that summer made
Fedorov see red.

Kournikova was playing an event in Scottsdale the first week of
March when Fedorov asked his crusty coach, Scottie Bowman—who
often refers to Kournikova as "that girl"—for a day off. With blessings
from Bowman, Fedorov jetted to Arizona and, armed with twenty
dozen roses, walked into the players' lounge and tried to win back his
girl. "I read she got engaged to Bure and then I walked into the locker
room and I was like 'wait, that's Fedorov!' " says Lindsay Davenport.
"I just about died, the whole thing was so funny. I think she doesn't
know what she wants and it went too far. I'm not sure she's quite ready
to walk down the aisle."

Fedorov apparently knows what he wants and he returned to his
team a happy man. According to teammates he and Kournikova
reached "an understanding" and it was clear that Kournikova would
not be playing her home version of "Who Wants to Marry a Multi-
Millionaire?" anytime soon. At least not with Bure. Three weeks,
later, it was Fedorov, not Bure, who came to see Kournikova play at
the Ericsson. If the situation weren't already dizzying enough, a Ft.
Lauderdale gossip columnist reported spotting Kournikova at an Ericsson player party at the South Beach club, perched on six-inch heels,
wearing a tight dress and an ill-concealed leopard-skin bra—and
escorted by the Ecuadorian pro Nicolas Lapentti, with whom she has
allegedly had an on-again, off-again fling.

Rather than talk tennis, most players and fans at Ericsson were try-

ing to guess the real story behind the Kournikova-Bure on/off nup-
tials. *Bure couldn't handle Kournikova's notoriously overbearing mother,
Alla, "the stage mother from hell"*—to quote the *New York Post.
Kournikova was merely trying to manipulate Fedorov and test his loyalty.*
Or perhaps most preposterously: *The marriage was orchestrated by the
Russian Mafia, which hopes to install the popular Bure in Soviet politics
but needed to dispel the rumor that he was gay.*

The truth, alas, was nothing so sexy. Like nature, Kournikova
abhors a vacuum; and with little noteworthy on-court success, things
were simply getting a bit stale in Anna-land. She figured it was her cue
to drum up some news as only she can. Months later, Bure would roll
his eyes when hockey writers asked about the engagement. "It's postponed indefinitely," he said with a sardonic smile. Regardless, it was a
brilliant publicity stunt by Kournikova, enough to divert attention
from her match results. In fact, nobody seemed to notice when the
tournament's headliner and star attraction lost in the fourth round—
6–0 in the final set—a full five days before the final.

Kournikova may have been raising eyebrows by being everywhere,
but Venus Williams was doing the same by being nowhere. At the
1999 Key Biscayne event, Venus had made history by beating Serena in
the final. It was a ragged, discordant three-setter, but it was the first
time sisters had played in a final in more than one hundred years. A
match less about the past than the future, it seemed to augur what their
father humbly called "the era of Worldwide Williams Domination."
But a year later, Serena was still a work in progress, if not regress. As
for Venus, the hot rumor at Ericsson was that she was about to retire.

Speculation of Venus bidding the game farewell at the ripe age of
nineteen had been building steadily since the Australian Open. By the
time she pulled out of the Ericsson—her sixth withdrawal of the
year—the murmurs had reached an audible chorus. The popular
explanation was that she was so severely wounded by her sister's U.S.
Open title that she couldn't play tennis again. What's more, her five-
year, $12 million deal with Reebok was set to expire in a few weeks
and there was no indication they were going to re-sign her. "Is the

Williams Dynasty Dead Before It Started?" asked one headline. "Venus is taking a long break and it seems she isn't interested in coming back anytime soon," said Davenport. "One year, two years, six months—who knows?"

Were it any other nineteen-year-old on the cusp of greatness, the notion of a premature retirement would have been dismissed as quickly as a "Man Births Ostrich" tabloid headline. But in a family that always seems to be enjoying an inside joke at the rest of the world's expense, it sounded plausible. Both Williams sisters had already cultivated a reputation for regarding the game as something of a lark. Their propensity for skipping tournaments and their dubious last-minute withdrawals had become such a concern that Bart McGuire had recently requested a meeting with Richard Williams to emphasize the importance of his daughters being full-time tennis players and competing in more events.

A pro-forma, one-sentence statement from a publicist would have quickly doused the rampant speculation. But that would have been a marked departure from the Williams MO. At the Ericsson, Venus watched her sister's matches from the IMG corporate box and sought refuge from the media. Serena was no help, coyly saying, "I have inside information." As is his wont, Richard Williams only dumped lighter fluid on the the flames. "I would like to see her retire now," he announced. "What I'm trying to get Venus to do is not play any more this year and go to school. Tennis is only a temporary job. I'd hate to see her have to get a job as an announcer or as a coach." What would Venus do for her next career? Join Dad in the business world, of course. "Venus is very good when it comes to understanding the Internet—web sites, web development, web pages. Venus could end up making a ton of money." By the end of the tournament, he rated the odds of Venus' retirement at "seven out of ten."

It was all a ruse. Venus said later that she had been as surprised as anyone when she first learned about the retirement rumors—where else?—on the Internet. She often states that she wants nothing to do with tennis when her playing days end, but at the same time, she says that she never considered quitting. It was maddening, sitting at home waiting for her wrists to heal from the tendenitis, unable to endure the lightest of hitting sessions without pain coursing up her arms. But retire? "Can you believe how many people thought that was for real," she said later in the summer, shaking her head. "What a sport." Still, that the rumor had legs speaks plenty about how off balance the House of Williams, Richard in particular, manages to keep the tennis world. And it lent credence to the perception that the psychic wounds Venus had been suffering over the past six months were more than skin-deep. Clearly, she was vulnerable; her aura as the most feared player on the Tour had vaporized.

Meanwhile, in the real world, Serena continued to struggle. With Venus looking on from the players' box, Serena played a ghastly fourth round match against Jennifer Capriati. On the windswept Stadium Court, the players showed all the subtlety of construction workers wielding sledgehammers and combined to commit 142 unforced errors. Capriati prevailed 7–6, 1–6, 6–3, in her biggest win of the year, but not before mis-hitting one serve four rows into the stands behind the baseline. "That was kinda cool," she said later. "I've never done that." Serena was once again disgusted with her play and admitted she missed having her sister around. And not just for the companionship. "I know she would knock off some of those top players. I have to do all the work now."

Energized by her win in Oklahoma City in February, Monica Seles was playing inspired tennis. She still wasn't in optimal shape and the lingering pain in her foot was restricting her movement and hindering her training. But she was back in the top ten, hitting the ball cleanly and happy overall with the direction her game was heading under her coach Bobby Banck. At the Ericsson, she breezed through her first four matches, beating Kournikova, to the promoters' dismay, in the fourth round and ceding just three games to Amy Frazier in the quarters. Few gave her much of a chance in the semifinals against Hingis, a player to whom she had lost four straight matches including a 6–3, 6–1 waxing two weeks prior in Indian Wells.

Playing in unseasonably hot conditions, Hingis needed only seven minutes to jump to a 3–0 lead. Sensing that Seles was moving as if she had cinder blocks tethered to her ankles, the crowd screamed encouragement. "Wake up, Monica" was one of the exhortations. She never did. Her timing badly off, her serve unraveling like a ball of yarn, and the sticky conditions cruelly exposing her lack of stamina, she quickly lost the first set 6–0. In the ESPN broadcast booth, Pam Shriver and Mary Joe Fernandez, both friends of Seles, exchanged nervous, incredulous glances. Given Seles's history, many players have a hard time summoning full-throttle aggression when they play her. Hingis, though, has no such problem. Opponents don't take pity on her modest size and limited strength. Why should she make allowances for other players' weaknesses and fragile psyches? Hingis surgically exploited Seles's conditioning with drop shots and forced her to run from side to side all match.

Asked whether she felt any compassion for her opponent, Hingis fired back, "What is compassion?" But Seles didn't give her a chance to exhibit mercy. Her face already etched in embarrassment, playing at a clipped pace that suggested she wanted only to get the hell off the court, Seles appropriately concluded a dog day afternoon by throwing in two double faults. For the first time in 535 career matches, Seles had been "double-bageled," the ultimate ignominy for a tennis player at any level. As derisive whistles and boos cascaded from the stadium, her entire body sagged as she left the court.

At 0–6, 0–5, dozens of fans hooted Seles, convinced that she was tanking—purposefully throwing a match. While suspicions of tanking continue to dog the men's tour, it is virtually unheard of on the women's circuit, where the players are too competitive and proud to lose intentionally. In this case, Seles had turned her ankle a few days before the match, tripping on a ball while playing with her miniature terrier, Ariel. Even the most simple lateral movement was painful. Many players on the Tour would have skipped the match altogether, rather than compete on a gimpy ankle. But Seles, the consummate professional, played to the abject end. Questioned about the ankle after the match, she said only that it was "a slight problem."

While the tennis press unfailingly plays it straight when it questions ATP players, no topic seems to be off limits to women in the interview room. "What's the status of your love life?" "What did you think of your opponent's outfit?" "Did you go shopping yesterday?" are all questions the likes of Pete Sampras and Pat Rafter would never have to address. Yet they're de rigeur when Martina Hingis or Serena Williams sits in front of a microphone. The Tour is complicit in this; restricting questions to forehand grips and break points hardly furthers women's tennis's goal of transcending the sports pages. At its best, the "anything goes" atmosphere personalizes the competitors, supplements their on-court persona. It is what helps make them "stars," rather than jocks, and it keeps them from being as insipid as most of their ATP counterparts. At its worst, these free-for-alls trespass the bounds of journalistic integrity, trivialize the sport, and put the players in awkward positions. At the French Open, Russian teenager Lina Krasnoroutskaya was asked by a journalist: "The way you behave here, you look very innocent. Are you innocent in your private life?"

When Seles walked sheepishly into her press conference, the interrogators peppered her without restraint. After several legitimate questions, it was open season. "Is there a constant thing that's defined [Hingis's] dominance over you?" "Are you embarrassed?" "Should you retire?" When Seles was asked, "Do you feel old?" she finally abandoned her obliging, mild-mannered nature and shot back sarcastically: "What a great question." When her media inquisition ended and she was back in the sanctuary of the locker room, the strongest woman on the tour broke down and sobbed.

Seles hardly needed another reminder that there are many things worse than a 6–0, 6–0 defeat. But as she was crying in the locker room, stadium police were busy arresting a forty-five-year-old Croatian man, Durayko Rajcezic, who had been stalking Hingis. While Seles's plight is the most famous and salient example, stalkers are still a constant menace on the WTA Tour and represent an ugly appurtenance of being an internationally famous female athlete. The previous day, Rajcezic had been ejected from the complex and told to stay away from Hingis, whom he had been following all over the world and sending faxes and letters. When Rajcezic ignored the order and returned for Hingis's semifinal match, he was detained at the Metro-Dade jail on $1,000 bail. "I'm not stalking Martina; I believe she feeds off my positive energy," he told a Miami television station. "I am ready to go to jail for Martina because my love is big."

Winston Churchill once described democracy as "the worst form of government—except for all the others." The same could be said of the WTA Tour's ranking system, which in 2000 was based on a player's eighteen best tournament results from the previous fifty-two weeks and adds ranking points accordingly. For a workaholic like Elena Likhovtseva, who thinks little of playing thirty events a year, it works out splendidly, because she can lose a dozen first round matches without paying a price. For Serena Williams, who may be as powerful and as talented as they come, but only played eleven events in 2000—the fewest of any player in the top fifty except for her sister—it is anathema.

Still, ranking players is an imperfect science and the WTA Tour's system can yield goofy results that leave even inveterate fans scratching their heads. To wit: hours after Hingis's whitewash of Seles, she surrendered the top ranking to Lindsay Davenport. Why? While Davenport only reached the quarterfinals of the 1999 Key Biscayne event, Hingis reached the semifinals. So this year, Davenport had fewer points "to defend." By reaching the semifinals in 2000, Davenport actually added points to her total, while Hingis had merely matched her output from the previous year.

Davenport's top ranking made even less sense after she lost to Hingis in a one-sided final at Ericsson. In windy conditions that wreaked havoc on her groundstrokes, Davenport missed routine balls and showed the effects of a bruised left foot. In a trend that would dog her for the rest of the year, she served poorly in a big match, converting just 50 percent of her first balls. Holding set point at 5–3, Hingis waited patiently for her opponent to miss. When Davenport smacked a forehand clearly wide, Hingis strutted to her chair. She froze theatrically when the call was overruled. "That was out by a foot," she protested to the chair umpire. Chastened by her experience at the French Open and more conscientious about not coming off like a brat, Hingis shut up and retreated to the baseline, smiled an insouciant "dems-da-breaks smile," and closed out the set a moment later.

When Hingis wrapped up this stinker of a match 6–3, 6–2, in under an hour, she was as overjoyed as she had been since her last Grand Slam title more than a year ago. Beyond winning a big-ticket event, she had finally broken free of Davenport's stranglehold after five demoralizing matches. Never mind what the rankings said. Hingis was back, as she likes to say, to being "the hunted." She was too elated to react to the news that Rajcezic had returned to the facility and been arrested yet again.

Meanwhile, some eighty miles north of Key Biscayne up Interstate 95, Venus Williams didn't bother to tune into the match on television to see who would replace her as champion. It would have been one more painful reminder that she and the top two players were at vastly different coordinates.

CHUCKY, THE KILLER DOLL

THE COUNTRY HAS A DIFFERENT NAME NOW. The political climate has changed as dramatically as she has. Even the smells and sounds aren't quite as she remembers them. But as the Slovakian countryside hurtles by the window of her car, Martina Hingis is pulled along by a powerful undertow of childhood memories. It is mid-May and she has just lost a semifinal match to Conchita Martinez in Berlin. In years past, she would have headed to Rome for the Italian Open, then to Paris to say a good luck prayer at Sacre Coeur and, since she's an unrepentant optimist, shopped for a Dolce & Gabbana dress to wear to the 2000 French Open winner's celebration. But that regimen served her poorly last year, so she's trying something new. Like a boxer who retreats to the isolation of the Poconos before a big fight, Hingis and her retinue are taking a break and returning to her motherland. Out of the public eye and into a stress-free, rustic environment where she doesn't have to worry about sponsor appearances, media obligations, and fans besieging her for autographs, she hopes to "recharge her battery" as she puts it, and concentrate on improving her clay court play before the French Open, the only Grand Slam she's never won.

During the drive to the house she keeps in Roznov pod Radhostem, a quiet burg not far from Kosice, where she was born, Hingis recalls her childhood collection of matchbox cars—"I never really played with dolls." She remembers when she was six years old, sitting in a plodding van during cold winters, as she and other precocious Czech athletes were driven ninety minutes to the nearest indoor tennis facility. She recalls coming back home to her mother, Melanie, who would be exhausted from working odd jobs—cleaning schoolrooms and assembling television sets—in order to pay for Martina's tennis training. "Martina, tell me how you played today," Melanie would say, and the two would launch into a discussion about strategy and positioning. Sometimes the mother would even grab a racket and hit a ball against the wall of their small apartment to demonstrate a point.

Martina Hingis was born to be a tennis star. It's burned into her DNA. Her father, Karol, was ranked among the top twenty-five Czech players in the late 1970s and still plays competitively. Her mother was more accomplished still. Melanie moved to Kosice in 1975 to play professionally for a team sponsored by a local steelworks plant. A consistent baseliner with a wicked backhand, she held a top twenty national ranking. "She worked like a horse, but her results somehow didn't match up," Josef Slajs, an administrator with the Czech Tennis Association recently told Jan Stojaspal, a Prague-based journalist. "At that time it was unheard of to work out five or six hours a day." But that's what Melanie did. She won a tournament while she was six months pregnant with Martina. She was back on the court within a month of giving birth. Born on September 30, 1980, her daughter was named in honor of Martina Navratilova, a heroine of Melanie's. By age two, Martina was wielding a racket with a sawed-off grip, and was soon able to hit the ball consistently over the net, even though it was taller than she was. At four, she entered her first tournament and lost 6–0, 6–0 to what she says was a ruthless nine-year-old.

It was around this time that the marriage between Melanie and Karol Hingis disintegrated. In keeping with Martina's request that he not submit to interviews, Karol doesn't speak publicly, but friends say the marriage failed because he and Melanie clashed over how to raise their daughter. As soon as Melanie realized that motherhood was the end of her tennis career, she turned her attention and ambitions to training Martina. "With Melanie," says a friend, "it was always train, train, train." Karol wanted his daughter to play with her friends and have a more normal childhood.

Not so, says Melanie. Martina played merely for fun. "Tennis wasn't life or death," she says. "It was a game children played. No one thought about getting rich doing it. No one thought tennis would be what you live. People always said I pushed her to play tennis when she was small. I did not push her. She wanted to do this." But some people who watched Melanie endlessly drilling Martina on local courts give a different account. "[Melanie] was very ambitious and she wanted to make a tennis star out of Martina," says a family friend. Even Martina agrees: "I think my mom saw tennis as a way to a better life."

In 1988, Martina and Melanie moved to Switzerland, where Melanie married a computer salesman, Andreas Zogg. Before they could emigrate, Karol had to sign a document giving his consent. He signed but says that he neglected to read the fine print and when he granted permission, he also inadvertently waived his visitation rights. From that point on, if he wanted to see his daughter, he had to rely on the goodwill of the custodial parent. Meanwhile, Melanie's marriage meant that she and Martina were able to sidestep a long line for Swiss citizenship. A few years later, that marriage too ended in divorce.

In Switzerland, Melanie threw herself into her daughter's training more than ever. She didn't merely feed hundreds of balls to Martina; she taught her about tennis's nuances, about how to transform the court into a chessboard. There were lessons about how to use the ten-minute warm-up before a match to assess an opponent's strengths and weaknesses; how to deploy which spins in which situations; how to disguise shots so your strokes become harder to read than James Joyce. The overriding message: guile can compensate for a lack of size and strength.

As a result of Melanie's tutorials, Hingis learned to play the tennis equivalent of jazz. That is, tennis for the soul. When she's on, Hingis plays with a synchronicity that eludes other players. She uses nooks and crannies of the court that her colleagues scarcely know exist. She knows intuitively when to junk up exchanges with exaggerated topspin, when to unleash a humiliating drop shot, when to "wrong-foot" opponents. At twelve, she became the youngest player ever to win a junior Grand Slam when she cruised through the French Open girls' draw. When she made her pro debut at fourteen, other players were in awe of her cunning and her strategy. "I remember thinking, 'where did she learn *that?*,' " recalls Chris Evert, Hingis's WTA Tour mentor. "You expect young kids to cream the ball, but to have no idea where it's going. Martina was doing things and making plays that girls who had been on Tour for ten years wouldn't think of doing."

Befitting a player able to conduct interviews in five languages, Hingis has a savantlike memory for players, opponents' tendencies, scores and rankings. Make an offhand reference to a match Hingis played four years ago and, with stunning exactitude, she will recount the key points. She also has an uncommon level of intellectual discipline. Shortly after Hingis achieved the top ranking in the spring of 1997, Debbie Edwards, a former WTA Tour media relations officer, took her to dinner at a Cracker Barrel restaurant in South Carolina. Hingis noticed a wooden triangle filled with pegs on her table. It was a brain teaser meant to occupy patrons as they wait for their grits and ham hocks. Hingis was transfixed. "For the entire meal, she played the game, trying to jump [the pegs] until there was one left," recalls Edwards. "I mean she didn't even look up. When she finally figured it out, she had the hugest smile on her face."

She regards each point on the court much the same way, taking great satisfaction in solving the riddles of tennis. Most players know a few basic gambits but win because they hit the ball harder and closer to the lines than their opponent. Hingis has a singular gift for thinking multiple shots ahead, for anticipating, for hitting the right shot at the right time. Hingis gets a rush from blasting a winner; but what's more intoxicating is outthinking her adversary: poaching at the right instant in doubles, faking a drive and unfurling a drop shot, guessing right on a passing shot. As she coldly and clinically dispatched older opponents, a Cheshire cat smirk welded itself to her face. Mary Carillo is credited for dubbing Hingis "Chucky" after the impish doll in the movie *Child's Play* that smiles sardonically as it murders.

At sixteen, Hingis was the world's No. 1 ranked player, reeling off thirty-seven straight matches. Then she hurt her knee falling off one of her horses. Slowed by arthroscopic surgery, she lost in the 1997 French Open final to Iva Majoli of Croatia. Had Hingis prevailed in that match, she would have claimed all four Majors in 1997. "Everything was coming so easy," Hingis recalls. "It was like, I was number one in the juniors and I'm number one in the pros. It's no big deal. You don't appreciate it. You think that's just the way it's supposed to be."

In addition to the solitude, another benefit of returning to her homeland is that Martina would have a rare chance to see her father. At forty-nine, Karol is trim and athletic looking and still plays tennis avidly. He, like his daughter, has striking green eyes and high cheekbones, and friends say they even betray the same mannerisms and facial expressions on the court. But beyond the physical similarities, it is clear they have little in common. Karol Hingis is scarcely involved in his daughter's life, much less her tennis career.

Karol's friends say he wishes desperately that he had more contact with Martina. He speaks to her by phone several times a month but almost never sees her play in person. Karol lives with his octogenarian mother on the ground floor of an apartment building in Kosice, where he works for $250 a month—a living wage—tending to a few clay courts. While his daughter has a garageful of Porsches, Karol shuttles to his job in a Fiat Punto. He wears a pair of shopworn Nikes around town. His daughter has an endorsement deal with Adidas that reportedly pays her $3 million a year. Still, thanks to the satellite dish outside his apartment, Karol follows Martina's career religiously. He watches her matches and often records them on a VCR to discuss later with friends. "When Martina was little, she absolutely loved Karol," says a friend of the family. "They drifted apart and he has a hard time dealing with it."

On a rainy day during this spring visit, Martina had to cancel a hitting session because the courts were too wet, so she called Karol, who drove to Roznov and went for a jog with his daughter. "It made his year," says a friend. "He thinks maybe now she'll start inviting him to tournaments." Martina, though, shakes her head when asked about that. "It was great to see him, but no . . . ," she says, her voice trailing off. "I don't want him to travel. He wouldn't understand everything about the Tour and I don't want to take a year explaining how everything works here. The fewer people around you, the fewer people to take care of, the better."

There are just two members of Hingis's entourage: Molitor, and Mario Widmer, a former sports editor at the Swiss newspaper *Blick*. Austere but decent, Widmer met Molitor while covering Hingis's fledgling career. At the 1996 Summer Olympics, he and Molitor hit it off and a year later he quit *Blick* to become the companion/translator for Molitor and her daughter. By all accounts, it was Widmer who schooled Martina and Melanie in the sport's realpolitik—that they could ask for two hotel suites at a tournament. Or that as a top seed at an event, Hingis could often play her matches and practice when she pleased. Before long, Martina had embraced Widmer as a surrogate father, regularly acknowledging "my mom and Mario" in interviews and victory speeches. "We are like a family," says Widmer in flawless English. "We have fights, like any family, but we resolve everything in the end." That's essentially what happened in the summer of 1999.

After Hingis's disastrous French Open that year, the trio repaired to their home in Switzerland, where Martina exhibited little interest in playing. "Everything was 'boring,' " says Melanie. "She wasn't sleeping enough. She was up late watching TV, always on the telephone, phone calls at 2:00 A.M. With boys? With girls? Maybe with her horse. How can you play tennis like that?"

Melanie tolerated this behavior for a while. She is filled with ambition and intensity—so much that she is regularly warned for on-court caoching, and she has been known to dress down not only Martina but also Marina's doubles partners after bad matches. But ultimately, Molitor is benign and knows when to slacken the reins. A former top-flight player, she is one of the few coaching parents who understands fully the technical, strategic, and psychological sides of the game.

Several years ago, Martina worked briefly with Brad Gilbert, the former pro who is now Andre Agassi's coach. "Everything he told

me," Martina recalls, "my mother had already said to me years ago."
Melanie has always acknowledged that her daughter is not a machine.
From the start, she encouraged Martina to pursue other passions outside
tennis—rollerblading, ski trips, horseback riding. "At age seventeen,
eighteen, nineteen, you have other interests and you have problems
focusing on other things," says Molitor. "No sense trying to change
nature."

But if her prize pupil—daughter or not—was going to be profli-
gate with her biggest gifts, she didn't want to waste her own time overseeing a halfhearted effort. Melanie and Widmer rented Martina a
house for Wimbledon and then returned to Switzerland without her.
You want independence? You're on your own, kid. "She called her mother
two or three times a day from there," recalls Widmer, chuckling.
When Hingis lost in the first round to Jelena Dokic, a match she all but
tanked 6–2, 6–0, she immediately called home from the players'
lounge. "Mom, I need you."

When Hingis returned to Switzerland, Melanie had a speech prepared. "Martina, our relationship is the most important thing to me, not
your tennis," she said. "If you want me to stay away, I'll stay away. It's
your life. If you want to do other things, fine, but do it without me as
your coach, because I won't stay around and watch you lose. I can't coach
you if you're not going to be more serious about tennis. Go away and
think about it. When you've made up your mind, tell me." Hingis said
little and went to Cyprus with her boyfriend at the time, Ivo Heuberger,
a lightly regarded Swiss player. She returned to her mother four days
later. "You feel like you're missing something, you miss having freedom
and you like having no one tell you what to do," says Hingis. "But without my mom and without tennis, my life was very empty." She and
Melanie redefined the contours of their relationship and resumed their
mother-daughter, coach-player, best friend-best friend arrangement.
"At the time, I got pissed because I felt like she was criticizing everything," says Hingis. "Now I feel like maybe she wasn't strict enough."

As if to mark this new chapter in their lives, the Melanie-Mario-
Martina troika purchased a 4,300-square-foot, wood and marble lake-

side home in Saddlebrook, a resort community outside of Tampa. Popular with many players, Saddlebrook is a slightly sterile self-contained world with golf courses, first-class fitness centers, and a spa food restaurant on the premises. Hingis can pump iron with her strength trainer, practice with other residents such as Jennifer Capriati, Jelena Dokic, and Ai Sugiyama, and grab a pasta primavera salad for lunch without going outside the gates.

As Martina spent more and more time at Saddlebrook, something funny happened: she started to become an American teenager. Even her speech was suddenly flavored with phrases such as, "It's like, whatever." She listens to Bon Jovi and eats at the Outback Steakhouse and Chili's. She went to Tampa Bay Buccaneers games—"They even showed my face on the big television screen and people recognized me!"—and darted out of her house to catch Tina Turner's concert at Tampa's Ice Palace arena.

She loves the "unbelievable freedom" she has in America—to exceed the speed limit, to choose from hundreds of restaurants, to go largely unrecognized when she tugs her black Bucs hat down over her not insignificant forehead—and she is also enamored of America's attitude toward athletes. As she braced herself for the booing she knew she'd get at the French Open, that point was particularly opposite. "In the U.S., if you win, great. If not and if you tried hard, it's okay. They say, 'Get 'em next time, Martina.' In Europe you're afraid of losing because fans are so critical. You lose and it's 'booooo.' They just want me to lose every time. The U.S. is the only country in the world left where kids can play sports naturally. In Europe, it's money, money, money."

Another reason Hingis finds the United States so appealing is that she lustily embraces the culture of celebrity. (This, after all, is an athlete who, when asked about the most famous person whom she has met, answers without hesitating: "Donald Trump. It doesn't get much bigger than that.") Two years after the fact, she still talks excitedly about being the first female athlete to grace the cover of *GQ* (tagline: The Champ is a Vamp) as she does about winning Wimbledon. Asked where she lies on the continuum between Lindsay Davenport, who wants simply to be a jock, and Anna Kournikova, who wants to be a star, Hingis grabs a pen and makes a little line drawing:

LD————————————————MH————AK

"I like being recognized," says Hingis. "You feel it's respect. I used to be a little bit shy. Now I like going on TV. I like getting my picture taken. I don't think I'm so ugly, do you?" she asks, laughing. "Look, we're entertainers and part of my job is to put on a show."

Because of Hingis's fondness for the spotlight, an off-court rivalry between her and Kournikova has taken root. Even when the two reunited as a doubles team later in 2000, there was palpable friction. Each wants what the other has. Kournikova can achieve legitimacy only if she can make like Hingis and breeze through a tournament. Hingis, it seems, would gladly relinquish a Slam or two for Kournikova's transcendent popularity off the court. Kournikova once said that Hingis will never be as good looking as she is, and that Hingis is jealous of her endorsement portfolio. Hingis's response: "I don't do so badly myself. If you gave Anna the choice between her [endorsements] or my Grand Slams and the No. 1 ranking, I think I know what she'd say. . . . You have to make money somehow and she's not going to do it with prize money, but I don't think she's happy. I'm sure she wants to be more successful."

The first week of the French Open, Hingis sat in the second story of the refurbished players' lounge. Spotting an American reporter, she immediately sought confirmation of the rumor that *Sports Illustrated* had just printed a long piece on Kournikova.

"I heard she was on the cover and the story was like eleven pages long," she said.

"Maybe when you win your first tournament, they'll do a big story on you," a reporter said teasingly.

"Ooooooh. Win one tournament," she said sarcastically. "That's a tough one. Think I can do it?"

Five minutes later, Hingis was discussing the pressure of playing in Paris when, apropos of nothing, she interjected, "I did an autograph session and they said it was the biggest crowd so far, even bigger than Anna's. Ask anyone."

Kournikova goes months without granting a one-on-one interview, but Hingis wants to be heard as well as seen. Join her for a lunch of sushi and salad and no topic is off-limits. In the course of an hour, she'll peregrinate from her "big butt" to her spring fling with Tampa Bay Lightning hockey player Pavel Kubina. The two were young millionaire athletes, born in Eastern Europe, now driving Porsches to the hotspots of central Florida. Hingis had high hopes, but they were ultimately dashed by the travel demands and time apart. "I thought it could be a dream relationship," she says wistfully. "I have to get him out of my system."

She moved on. Her next squeeze in 2000 was Swedish pro Magnus Norman, who ranks among the ATP's top five players. Hingis was practicing with Richard Bergh, a former Swedish pro, at the Scottsdale tournament in March when Norman happened by. True to form, Hingis not only remembered Norman from the juniors but was able to remind him of various wins and losses. "You lost to [Nicolas] Escude and then you disappeared for years!," she told him. "What were you doing?" With a smile, he said: "I didn't disappear. I'm just not like you who becomes number one at age sixteen. I was working hard and building my ranking." At the next tournament at Indian Wells they had their first date, and by the French Open they were watching each other's matches. By Wimbledon, to the tabloids' glee, each had deemed the other "shaggable" and Norman referred to Hingis as "my rock." By October, they were splitsville and she was actively exploring other options.

At the tournament in Filderstadt, players are given a sizable discount at a nearby Hugo Boss clothing outlet. The catch is that most of the available clothes are for men. Kournikova, according to lore, still managed to spend more than $25,000, enough to prompt the shopkeepers to reduce the discount soon thereafter. The ever practical Hingis bought only a few men's T-shirts, several in extra large, several in large, several in medium. Why? Laughing, she explains that she wasn't sure what size her next boyfriend would need so she wanted to keep her options open.

If it's endearing that Hingis lets down her guard so easily, so too does it reveal a central contradiction of her personality. How can a player so coy and so viperously clever on the court leave herself so vulnerable and reveal her most intimate thoughts so freely in public? Why does a tennis savant who chooses her shots so meticulously allow herself to be provoked into so many unforced errors—loose points, so to speak—when she opens her mouth? She sees no conflict or cause for confusion. Her frankness is an extension of the confidence-bordering-on-cockiness she betrays on the court. Just as she doesn't duck opponents, she doesn't duck questions. Just as she makes no concessions in her matches, she isn't going to resort to spin control and politesse. "I know I don't always say maybe the perfect things," she concedes. "But I have to be myself, you know?"

Without losing sight of who she is, Hingis has become increasingly self-possessed. And she's begun to channel her candor and her extroverted nature to more productive ends than trashing other players. She plans on being more active in Tour politics and is running for a spot on the players' board. She signed on as a goodwill ambassador for polio eradication for the World Health Organization. No mere PR gimmick, she went to Bogotá in midsummer to publicize the plight of street children. Above all, she gained a new outlook on her career. "In the past, success may have come too easily," she says. "Right now, I want to do better and to make my mark, but I also want people to respect me as a person, not just as a tennis player. I've learned not to just live in the moment. I sound like I'm over the hill, but I step back and say, win or lose at the French Open or wherever, I have a great life."

HAIL MARY

PLAYERS HAVE STRONG FEELINGS ABOUT
the French Open. Some are mesmerized by the red clay and mystique
of Roland Garros. They relish the protracted rallies, the slow motion
of the points, and they see the dust that gradually cakes their bodies
during a match as an honorable token of trench warfare.

Others despise everything about it, from the austere stadium to the
language barrier to the glacial pace of clay-court tennis. Preferences
tend to break down by nationality. Europeans and South Americans
weaned on clay regard the French Open with the esteem and rever-
ence they have for any Major. American players tend to perceive it
much as they do Europe in general: quaint and different, but, finally,
agonizingly slow and inefficient. "I'll admit it, it's my least favorite
Slam," says Lindsay Davenport. "The people are never that friendly.
They have attitudes. The food isn't that great and I get homesick. If I
went to Europe weeks in advance to prepare for the French, I swear
I'd just want to lose in the first round so I could go home."

It's somehow fitting that Mary Pierce, the WTA Tour's version of
J. Everett Hale's "Man Without a Country," is one of the few players
who has mixed feelings about the French Open. A self-proclaimed
"citizen of the world," Pierce was born in Montreal, raised in Florida,

spent time in Paris, and shares a home in Cleveland with her Puerto Rican fiancé, baseball star Roberto Alomar. By virtue of her mother's French citizenship, she keeps a French passport and lists French as her nationality. In truth, though, she is about as French as the Cadillac D'Elegance her father drives. Mary lives full-time in the United States; she has, for years, declined to represent France in the Fed Cup or the Olympics, and she doesn't speak in Français unless she has to. Even she seems confused about the overlapping nationality issues. Asked whether she is the most American of the French players or the most French of the Americans, she says: "A little of both."

The French fans are just as ambivalent about her. When she wins, she is the belle of the fuzzy ball, a statuesque blond they gleefully embrace as their own. When she loses, she is just another American poseur whose shortcomings are seen as an act of national sedition. Time and again Pierce has lost matches in her "homeland" and walked off to a chorus of boos. "No question," she says, "they're fickle about me."

The contradiction is thrown in particularly sharp relief at Roland Garros. Pierce's first memories of being there are so painful, she swallows hard as she recalls them. When Mary was thirteen, her famously ill-behaved father, Jim, antagonized the United States Tennis Association to the point that it withdrew her funding. Because of her mother's heritage, Mary was invited by the French Tennis Federation to train in Paris, so Jim pulled Mary out of school in Treasure Island, Florida, and off she went. A young, scared stranger in a strange land, her French barely passable, she hit balls by day on the amber clay of Roland Garros. At night, she retreated to the nearby dormitories and cried herself to sleep. Within a month, she was back in Florida.

"For all sorts of reasons," she says, "it has always been difficult emotionally for me to play here." It was also at Roland Garros in 1993 that security personnel ejected Jim for harassing fans and choking one of Mary's cousins. (Witnesses say that Jim was irate that the cousin was talking to Mary and distracting her from scouting her next opponent.) That outburst earned him a ban from women's tennis.

Yet for all of the sour memories, Roland Garros still holds undeni-

able allure. The colors, Pierce thinks, have something to do with it—
the noonday sun reflecting off the red clay, with an unblemished sky
overhead, creates a near-hypnotic tableau. When she's playing well,
Pierce—the highest ranked French player, male or female—receives
fan support like she gets nowhere else. When she reached the French
Open finals in 1994, the entire country watched with rapt attention. So
nervous about the prospect of giving a victory speech in French that
she was unable to sleep the night before the match, she was waxed by
Arantxa Sanchez Vicario. Still, she never forgot the feeling of being so
popular, of feeling so appreciated. "I have been through so much at
Roland Garros, but I still look forward to playing there. In a weird
way, this place has become part of who I am. It's like I always feel like
I belong here."

Now, at age twenty-five, she arrived at Roland Garros in the midst of
her strangest year on Tour. At the Australian Open earlier in the
year—the site of her only Grand Slam title (1995)—Pierce lost a fourth
round match to Japanese baseliner Ai Sugiyama. A few weeks later in
Japan, she fell to American baseliner Lilia Osterloh. Sitting in her drab
hotel room after the match, confused and frustrated, she took a deep
breath, picked up the phone, and dialed a familiar number in south
Florida. "Dad," she said quietly. "I'm not playing well. I think I need
to work with you again."

   Jim Pierce had been waiting for this call for nearly seven years. Jim
surfaced from time to time once his ban lapsed—once for a stint coaching the American Vince Spadea. But Mary had never asked the Tour
to relax the rule requiring that he submit written notice before attending a women's event. Still, the man whose physical abuse of his daughter has been well-documented, who had once exhorted her to "kill the
bitch" during a match, and who bragged about the stab wounds he
received from one of Mary's bodyguards, had apparently changed little
since his exile. Around the time of Mary's call, a reporter from the
London Observer interviewed Jim for a lengthy "where is he now?"
story. In addition to boasts of sleeping with other players' mothers, Jim

brought to the interview a female companion who was someone other than his wife. (When the reporter phoned for a follow-up interview a few weeks later, Jim's wife answered the phone, claiming he had left her for another woman, taking $225,000 with him.)

When Mary flew home to Bradenton from Japan in February, Jim packed up his Cadillac and made the four-hour drive from his modest home outside Ft. Lauderdale to practice with her. For two hours a day, he and Mary worked out on a public court not far from Nick Bolletieri's Academy, where she once trained. They mostly did footwork drills and conditioning. After a week, Jim drove Mary to the airport, where she flew to an exhibition in Mexico. Says one friend: "You have to remember that he's still her father and she doesn't want to cut him off. She decided that the relationship is going to have to be on her terms."

On February 25, a few days after leaving for Mexico, Pierce made another long-distance call. This time she phoned her younger brother, David, in London and asked if he would be her full-time coach. The two had discussed such an arrangement for years. "Originally, my dad was supposed to be the coach and David was supposed to be my hitting partner," Mary says. "Obviously that didn't quite work out." A laidback, unassuming, coffeehouse type, David was giving tennis lessons at the David Lloyd Club in a London suburb and welcomed a change of scenery. Three days after Mary's call, he joined her in Scottsdale, warming her up, scouting opponents, and charting her matches.

David took his duties seriously. A week after Scottsdale, in Indian Wells, Mary won her first match against Canada's Sonya Jeyaseelan, 6–1, 6–3, but David was so displeased with his sister's sluggish footwork and her sloppy shotmaking that he ordered her back on the court for an additional hitting session. The extra work and discipline paid off. She had always hit one of the bigger balls on Tour, but rarely supplemented her power with much strategy. David helped her improve her movement, her ability to caress a point, and even boosted her usually mercurial confidence. Mary's results picked up dramatically. At Hilton Head in April, she won the fourteenth title of her career, dropping just twelve games in five matches, and waxing Arantxa Sanchez Vicario 6–1, 6–0 in the final. "More than anything," says Pierce, "David makes tennis fun, which I can't say that it always is."

It doesn't take a Freudian analyst to see the toll Mary's hellish childhood—which included living out of a car while the entire family traveled from one junior tournament to the next—has taken on her. She is notoriously fragile and high-strung, and talks incessantly about getting stressed out. She is chronically late, famously, and has a self-dramatizing streak. Before big matches, she madly paces the locker room. Her weight fluctuates wildly and her eating habits and late-night fast-food runs are legendary on the Tour. On the court, a point can't start until Pierce completes a ritual more elaborate than the flashing of signs by a third base coach. She slaps her Nikes with her racket, fingers her ponytail, adjusts her headband, tucks her necklace into her dress, and towels off. "Babe-ing and re-babe-ing herself," commentator Mary Carillo calls it. (Mercifully, her habit of adjusting her contact lenses ceased when she had laser surgery on her eyes in February.) Earlier in the year, Pierce watched herself on tape and was mortified by her own routine. Roberto Alomar good-naturedly told his fiancée that if a baseball player took that much time in the batter's box, he'd get beaned. "Just get the ball and play," he told her. "I told myself I had to stop," Pierce says. "I think all the fidgeting makes me more nervous."

A shrink might also link Mary's use of Creatine, the controversial muscle enhancing supplement, to her relationships with her father. For years, Jim allegedly physically abused his gaunt, introverted, bespectacled daughter. Now nicknamed "The Body," the hulked-up, bulked-up Pierce has made it abundantly clear that only a fool would try to lay a hand on her.

Given her history, however, it's a minor miracle she's not more of a psychological train wreck. Plenty of players who grew up in far more stable homes are bigger head cases. Pierce may be a first-rate drama queen, but she is generally well liked by other players. "When Mary first came on Tour, a lot of us didn't talk to her because of the whole family situation. We had heard all the horror stories and sometimes saw it for ourselves," says Kim Po. "Since her father was banned, a lot of us got to know her better, and she's such a nice girl. For her to come out on top after all that, it's really a credit to her." In her tenth year on the circuit, Pierce has been a fixture in the top ten for the better part of a decade and has won more than $6 million in prize money.

Pierce generally refuses to talk about her father, but in a rare unguarded moment, she says that, if anything, having such a volatile parental figure made her a stronger person. "He made me the player I am today." On one level, she's probably right. Despite his craziness and the dysfunction, Jim was able to motivate Mary like no other coach she's had. But one suspects that what really instilled confidence was finally standing up to him. "He was this dominating guy who could make her life miserable," says a friend of Pierce. "Now, all of a sudden, he's begging her to let him train her for a few hours. That's empowering and that gives her confidence."

Heading into the French Open Pierce had lost her previous match in Madrid to a little known Italian, Germana di Natale, a player so far down in the rankings she had never even qualified for a Grand Slam. Earlier in Pierce's career, an embarrassing loss like that would have savaged her self-assurance. But now, with her brother beside her, she chalked it up as a fluke—one of the four or five egregious off-days every top player must endure each year—and was sanguine about her chances in Paris.

In fact, Pierce radiated calm. The serenity to accept what she could not change had come in part from her newfound spirituality. She has always been a devout Catholic, she asserted. But her faith had intensified after ushering in the new millennium at Roberto Alomar's home in Puerto Rico by lighting a candle and saying a prayer. "Too many good things have been happening in my life for it to be a coincidence," said Pierce, who wears around her neck a large crucifix she purchased with Alomar during a trip to the Dominican Republic. "My relationship with God is basically very simple. I put everything in His hands and I don't worry. Whatever happens, happens, and it's made a huge difference with my tennis, as it has in my life."

Alomar has also been a godsend. Baltimore Orioles slugger Brady

Anderson, who now dates Amanda Coetzer, introduced Pierce and Alomar during spring training in 1997. They hit it off immediately. Their bonds went far beyond sports and their shared experiences as professional athletes. The product of a close-knit family, Alomar has helped give Pierce some of the stability and support that she was denied in her transient childhood. Though they're often apart—the big drawback of their relationship—they share a mansion in the quiet Cleveland suburb of Westlake. If the Indians have the night off, a typical evening out for the couple consists of dinner and a Blockbuster movie. Roberto, who once turned down more money from other teams for the chance to play alongside his brother, Sandy, in Cleveland, strongly encouraged Mary to take on David as her coach. He also urged her to reconcile with her father. Even Jim Pierce says, "Roberto Alomar is the best thing that's happened to my daughter."

Pierce's fiancé, seven years older than she is, also doubles as "my role model." She recounts a story of asking Alomar why he insisted on playing winter ball in Puerto Rico after slogging through a grueling 162-game regular season with the Indians. "Because I never want to look back on my career and say, 'I should have done more,' " he told her. She took the advice to heart. "We talk a lot about the mental part of being a sports figure, of what goes through your head," says Alomar, who travels with Pierce to some of her winter events, including the Australian Open, and scouts her opponents. "Even after she wins, I'll tell her things she needs to do like be more aggressive." He even drills with her, tossing balls to different areas of the court.

Sitting in her hotel room the weekend before the 2000 French Open, Pierce told herself, *I can win this thing. I can't be stressed out. I have to make this feel like any other tournament*. A few hours later, she phoned her French relatives and told them all the same thing: "I love you guys and I want you to come watch my matches, but I have a job to do. We'll have to wait to get together until I'm out of the tournament." They had to wait two weeks for that reunion.

Lindsay Davenport's distaste for Europe was about to become a self-

fulfilling prophecy. During a practice after her first round match at the
Italian Open, she stooped to hit a forehand and felt her back seize up.
"My first thought was 'I really don't need this,' " she says. Barely able
to move without wincing in pain, she pulled out of the tournament
and consulted several doctors. She hoped that a combination of rest,
muscle relaxants, and massages would loosen her back enough to play
in the French Open. After spending a miserable ten days virtually
immobile, she decided she was well enough to play.

Her first round opponent at the French was Dominique Van
Roost, a solid top twenty player with a doelike face and stylishly
cropped hair. In December 1999, Van Roost had learned that her
mother, Louise Anne, had ovarian cancer. She curtailed her schedule
to spend as much time as possible at home in Belgium and often
skipped workouts to be at her mother's side. When Louise Anne's
health deteriorated, Dominique withdrew from the Ericsson Open in
late March and flew home. She made it just in time to see her mother
before she passed away. "It was like her mother waited for her," says
Van Roost's husband, Bart. Coming into this match with Davenport,
Dominique was in poor shape to play, dispirited, and pondering
retirement.

Neither player was at her best; Davenport won the first set in a
tense tiebreaker. In the second game of the second set, Davenport con-
torted to hit a serve and her back went into spasms again. Van Roost
then took advantage of her opponent's limited movement and closed
out the match 6–7, 6–4, 6–3. She had barely shaken Davenport's hand
when her emotions gushed forth. Alternately crying and laughing, she
clutched her husband and buried her face in his shoulder. Van Roost
lost her next match, but her spirits were lifted; she played out the summer and competed in the Sydney Olympics before retiring.

Being the first No. 2 seed to lose in the first round of the French
Open in nearly thirty years hardly crushed Davenport's spirits; she was
happy to be headed home to California, where new boyfriend
Jonathan Leach—a San Francisco investment banker and the younger
brother of American doubles standout Rick Leach—was waiting. A

day later, she was "back to normal," cruising the freeways in her SUV, hanging out with her friends and her family, and going to a Lakers playoff game. She could scarcely have been happier.

With the spotlight on the top remaining seeds—Hingis, Williams, Seles, and Pierce—few noticed a Paraguayan named Rossana de los Rios, who blazed through four rounds of qualifying and steadily advanced in the main draw. Playing in her first Grand Slam since 1993, de los Rios was such an unknown quantity that WTA Tour administrators were unsure about the spelling of her name, much less her history. When de los Rios walked off the court following her second round win over Germany's Marlene Weingartner, even she began to shake her head in disbelief and giggle about her improbable journey.

When Christopher Brown first got an e-mail from de los Rios, he figured it was a gag, probably one of his buddies' idea of a practical joke. In October of 1999, the thirty-year-old Texan has just opened Lakes Tennis Academy outside of Dallas and he was in the market to train a player with pro potential. He hadn't been in business for more than a few weeks when he received an intriguing correspondence. A woman from Asunción, Paraguay, who claimed to be the 1992 French Open girls champ and then spent a few unremarkable years on Tour, wanted to make a comeback. Her husband, she explained, was vying to make the roster of the Dallas Burn of Major League Soccer (MLS) and she was looking for a place to train in the area. Could she practice at his facility? Brown suppressed his skepticism and did some research. After combing the record books and searching the Internet, he realized de los Rios was for real, so he invited her to his complex. "After about four balls, I was like 'whoa,' " he recalls. "I didn't know her from Adam, but it was pretty easy to see her potential."

Though Brown speaks little Spanish and de los Rios speaks only halting English, he pieced together her story. Eight years earlier she had beaten Paola Suarez—now a top fifty pro—in the finals to win the French Open junior title. She had left the circuit in 1994 to marry Gustavo Neffa, a soccer player from the legendary Boca Juniors in

Argentina. In 1997, de los Rios gave birth to a daughter, Ana Paula, and stopped playing tennis altogether. "I was very happy with my life," she says. "But I was also missing tennis."

In the spring of 1999 she woke up one morning and decided to give tennis one last shot. After Neffa helped her get back into shape, the family moved from Paraguay to Dallas. She had scarcely touched a racket during her hiatus, but it didn't take long for her flat strokes to resurface, for her touch to return. Brown provided her with lodging and subsidized her training expenses. Within a few days she was serving close to one hundred miles an hour. Brown communicated with her by using his racket to demonstrate points and he taught her a few choice English words like "topspin" and "patience." "It wasn't your conventional arrangement," Brown recalls. "But we made it work."

At the beginning of 2000, de los Rios launched her comeback in earnest. While most of the players on Tour were preparing for the French Open in Hilton Head, Hamburg, or Rome, de los Rios was in slightly less exotic precincts. In hopes of earning enough points to get into the qualifying draw in Paris, de los Rios spent the spring of 2000 on the challenger circuit, playing in small tournaments in Sarasota, Florida; Norcross, Georgia; and La Canada, California. She, Neffa, and Ana Paula shared a motel room. They often shopped in the local grocery store and made sandwiches in their room for dinner. If they were lucky, de los Rios made enough money to cover her expenses for the week. "All those cities blend together," says Neffa.

By the time de los Rios took the court for her third round match against ninth-seeded Amanda Coetzer on Court Suzanne Lenglen, she was a week removed from the qualifying draw and a million miles from Norcross, Georgia. With Ana Paula perched on Neffa's lap, alternately sleeping and sucking her thumb while her back faced the court, de los Rios played superior tennis, looking nothing like a player coming off a five-year layoff. Her biggest weapon was a penetrating forehand that registered thirty winners; but she also leavened her power with fiendishly clever drop shots that seemed to burrow into Roland Garros's red clay.

As word of the brewing upset spread, fans and other players

flocked to the court. When de los Rios served out the match, 7–6, 6–7, 6–4, the packed stadium was roaring. Steely all afternoon, she burst into tears when she saw Neffa and her daughter in the tunnel underneath the stadium. Soon Rossana was greeted by a legion of players including Laura Montalvo and Suarez, who remembered her from the juniors and assumed they'd never see her on Tour again. Wiping away tears, Suarez said, "All of us remember how good she was. We were wondering, 'How good could she have been?' Now we know."

De los Rios played again less than twenty-four hours later. Emotionally drained, she fell to Marta Marrero of Spain, 4–6, 6–0, 6–4. Still, she was beaming as she left the court. She had earned enough money to support her family for the rest of the summer; she had garnered enough ranking points to earn automatic main draw berths; and, above all, she had made it back. "It is still so unbelievable to me," she said. "Now I'm not satisfied just being here. I want to win."

Her dramatic comeback made her the only mother currently playing full-time on the Tour. In the past, a handful of players have taken time off to have children, but today the increased level of competition and training, compounded by heightened travel demands, makes motherhood virtually impossible for most full-time players. "I'm dying to have kids one day," says Lindsay Davenport. "But I can't even imagine it now. It's hard enough just having a relationship with a guy. Can you picture calling your child and saying, 'Mommy can't come home now because she has matches in Philadelphia or Zurich or wherever.' No way."

De los Rios quickly realized the challenges confronting working mothers, but claims that she wouldn't have it any other way. "In some ways it's hard," she says. "But when I look in the crowd during my matches and see Gustavo and Ana Paula, I feel like I'm playing for three people, not just for myself."

There are few sights in sports more pathetic than an adulation-starved athlete coming out of retirement to stage an ill-fated comeback. Why can't legends go gracefully into the night, we wonder, without humiliating themselves by succumbing to middle-age hubris? When Martina

Navratilova announced in April that she was rejoining the Tour—at age forty-three!—to play doubles a full decade after she had won her last Grand Slam singles title, she did so to a chorus of disapproving clucks. Though Navratilova means "she who returns" in Czech, even Martina's father, Mirek, was skeptical when his daughter told him of her plans. "Martina," he said, "What if you fail?" Even if she succeeded it would be double-edged: if Navratilova, just seven years away from AARP membership, could hold her own on the WTA Tour, what would that say about the level of play in women's tennis?

Navratilova was an unlikely choice for un-retirement. As she did with everything in her life, she had charged full-bore into retirement. In her six years away from tennis, she had earned her pilot's license, written three mystery novels, traveled to Africa numerous times, and played on a state championship hockey team in Aspen called the Mother Puckers. She was learning how to make furniture, she was trying to master Swahili, and in April of 2000 she was a keynote speaker at the Millennium March for Equality in Washington. What void was there for tennis to fill?

Initial speculation was that Navratilova was returning so that she could win one more title and tie Billie Jean King's mark of twenty Wimbledon trophies. When Navratilova played her last match at the All-England Club in 1994, she acted like a horticulturist and removed a clump of grass—many suspected the place held such deep meaning that she wouldn't be able to stay away. Even Navratilova's publicist, Linda Dozoretz, said, "I think she's always had her eye on that [record]." Others posited that Martina's return was somehow tied to sponsor obligations. There was even the flabby suggestion that, unlike Chris Evert, who segued fairly seamlessly from tennis to mothering three boys, the societal roles for middle-aged homosexuals are less defined. So without 2.5 kids to raise in Boca and load into a minivan, Navratilova was necessarily floundering. None was true, as it turned out. "I'm playing because I can," she said with conviction. "People say, 'Why, Martina?' and I say 'why not?' "

Navratilova made no bold pronouncements about playing singles— "My heart doesn't want to work that hard," she said and laughed. She hardly pilfered the spotlight from the full-time players, and while she wanted desperately to win she was careful not to take herself too seriously. Navratilova wanted a doubles partner faster and more powerful than she. After an e-mail exchange, she settled for the latter and paired with the plodding but potent Mariaan de Swardt, a veteran player from South Africa. When they entered the wondrous asphalt bowl that is Court 1 for their first match against Belgian Sabine Appelmans and Rita Grande of Italy, the crowd serenaded them. So Navratilova thought, anyway. Later, she learned that the singing was, in fact, directed at Appelmans, an emerging sex symbol recently voted the most desirable female in her country. Welcome to women's tennis circa 2000, kid.

Navratilova and de Swardt won the match, and the oldest player in the draw by nearly a decade was seized by euphoria. Sounding like a Gen X teenager who had just completed her first bungee jump, Navratilova gushed: "I still managed to get the juices going and have fun at the same time. It was a blast to be out there, a total blast." Far from embarrassing herself, as her father had feared, Navratilova impressed everyone. The serve may have lost a little pop—"Jeez, that's pathetic," she once barked to herself after a 71-mph meatball—and the reflexes may have diminished a tad, but otherwise there was little indication that her game had been in mothballs for years. She still had those famously striated muscles, and, as she was overheard bragging the next day, "Do I have a flat tummy, or what?" Thanks to Pilates training, she was more flexible than she had been since the mideighties. She covered her half of the court just fine (far better than the twenty-nine-year-old de Swardt), her wonderfully efficient volleys still packed a mean punch, and her timing was superb. She also retained her doubles craftiness, hitting the majority of her winners not on angles but on balls that split her two opponents.

If Navratilova's game seemed familiar so too were her off-court pronouncements. Be it anti-tobacco, gay rights, or the ethical treatment of animals, Navratilova had lustily embraced more causes than an Oberlin College freshman. It seemed fitting, then, that she walked into the interview room for her first match cradling her two-legged

fox terrier, Bina. "It's a thalidomide puppy," she explained. "Some people don't know how to take care of their pets. She still hops around like
nothing is going on." It was also no surprise that a few weeks later at
Wimbledon she reportedly refused to provide television commentary
with Marv Albert, who had pleaded guilty three years earlier after facing sexual assault charges against a former girlfriend. Characteristi-
cally open with opinions, she decried the "sexualization" of fin de
siècle women's tennis and lamented that runaway technology appears
to have sounded the death rattle for serve-and-volley tennis. Like
many former players, she worries about "isolationism" that exists on
the Tour. "Everyone has their own coach," she says, "so players don't
hang together and there isn't the interaction."

Her other overarching observation about the game is that players
have grown appreciably. "I'm walking around the locker room, just
looking around, it's like, 'Whoa, these women are big.' I used to be big.
I'm like a little pipsqueak compared to them." When asked earlier that
day if she had seen Navratilova walking around, Venus Williams
began giggling. In the kind of exaggerated baby voice one usually
deploys to describe cute puppies, Venus said: "She's very small. I
passed her by and I barely even saw her!"

When Navratilova emigrated to the U.S. at age eighteen she fell in
love with the International House of Pancakes, hamburgers, fries and
steak. A pudgy player with middling results, she finally took her physical training seriously in her mid-twenties. Within a few years, she was
unapologetically buff and, not coincidentally, winning truckloads of
trophies. By the time she retired, sweat and biceps had become a prerequisite for success. Now, you see fourteen-years-olds from the juniors draw running wind sprints outside the courts and in the main
stadium's tunnels after their matches. You see half the players in the
field pumping iron at 7:00 A.M. in the hotel gym. You see players in the
tournament cafeteria asking how many grams of fat are contained in
the baked ziti. "No one went to the gym in the beginning," says Chris
Evert. "Martina did it first, then the rest of us were like 'we'd better
too.' Now you look at the Williams sisters and Pierce and Mauresmo
and everyone else and you can see how far we've come."

For Navratilova, there was another gratifying sign of progress. When she was winning her nine Wimbledon titles, she was anathema to Madison Avenue. Part of this was her role as Chris Evert's muscle-bound foil, born on the wrong side of the Iron Curtain. But the chief reason was her sexual orientation. "My agent used to say that when he brought up my name, people went silent," she says. "At events, everyone would clap for Chris and when they would announce me, the crowd would hold back. I knew damn well the reason and it hurt. If I had been quiet about [being gay] I would have had ads. That's just fact."

In the winter of 2000, before her return was anything more than a rumor, she signed her first deal to endorse a product not related to tennis. Subaru made her the centerpiece of a campaign that not only had a feminist bent but was unabashedly pitched to homosexuals. One ad, featuring Navratilova and golfers Julie Inkster and Meg Mallon, ends with them saying sarcastically: "But what do we know? We're just girls." Another spot advertised a minivan with the cheeky catchphrase: "It's not a choice, it's the way we're built." "Martina is the consummate professional," said Tim Bennett, Subaru's marketing programs director. "We view her as an active-lifestyle woman and the other stuff as nobody's business." That was essentially the sentiment of Lucy.com, the on-line apparel company that signed Navratilova to a clothing contract in the weeks before her return. "Women identify with Martina and what she's doing more than they do with a nineteen-year-old with a killer body," says Sue Levin, CEO of Lucy.com, which also signed on in 2000 as the presenting sponsor of women's tennis in North America. "Anyone who would say having Martina is bad for your brand name because she is gay is insane."

Still, there are some pockets of intolerance on the Tour. Alexandra Stevenson claims that she refers to her lesbian colleagues as the "gone girls," as in they've gone to the other side. Her mother, Samantha, told Tour administrators that "predatory" lesbians were behind the edict banning nonplayers from the locker room. Even Oracene Williams readily admits that when Venus and Serena first joined the Tour she warned them about lesbianism. "I'm not embarrassed to say it," says

Oracene. "The women are there undressed and they, some of them, are lesbians. Young kids see that and think 'maybe that's me' when it's not. So, yes, I taught Venus and Serena about that."

Overall, though, the circuit is accepting of gay players and there is little sense—as there is in many women's sports trying to capture the public's imagination and the corporate world's dollars—that lesbianism is bad for business. When Amelia Mauresmo summoned reporters to her Melbourne hotel and "came out" at the 1999 Australian Open, the repercussions were minimal. Not only did she retain all of her sponsors but they contacted her to applaud her courage. When Martina Hingis referred to Mauresmo as "half a man" during the tournament, the remark was met with outrage and disapproval by players and fans. "I'm [closeted] because that's a choice I've made," says one gay player in the top fifty. "But I don't feel any pressure from the Tour, the sponsors, or the other players. The simple fact is that it's not a big deal out here."

No one appreciated this cultural shift more than the comeback player of the year in women's tennis. As Navratilova observed about her new colleagues: "They can express themselves without having to apologize for who they are. We weren't brought up like that."

Venus Williams spent the spring bored out of her mind. Cursed with a short attention span to begin with, she was home alone, whiling away the days until the tendinitis in her wrists healed. She couldn't sew, she couldn't drive, she could barely type on her computer. Time and again, she would try to practice, only to pack up her gear a few minutes later when she felt twinges of pain. Hitting a forehand was no problem. But when she served or rolled over her two-handed backhand, the pain was like a needle jabbed in her wrists. She considered switching rackets, but then decided against it. She experimented with a one-handed backhand, slicing the ball as if whacking weeds with a sickle, but that didn't work. "Not my game at all," Venus said later.

She took courses at the Art Institute of Ft. Lauderdale for a few hours a day and filled her days reading Amy Tan books, *Memoirs of a*

Geisha, and Harry Potter. But there was also a lot of time sacrificed on the altar of the television or falling asleep watching bad movies late into the night before her father would herd her to bed. "She was pretty low," says Oracene. "She wanted to play and assumed she'd be able to a lot earlier than she was. Venus doesn't like being in a situation she can't control."

It was during a drawing class at the Art Institute that Venus had a mini-epiphany. As part of a lesson on shading and texture, she and her classmates were given an assignment to draw their shoe. The kid next to her, a surfer with a tattoo, produced a picture-perfect replica. Venus drew a few lines, ripped up the paper, and started anew. "It wasn't fair," she says. "But I realized, people have natural talents for different things."

Hers, of course, is for hitting the felt off a tennis ball. Venus has said that tennis needs her more than she need tennis, but down deep, she likes the sport—and cares about it—more than she lets on. She follows results, she's as up on the Tour gossip as anyone. At home, she watched matches on her dish and looked on helplessly during the winter as points dropped from her ranking. She tracked tennis results on the Internet and looked on forlornly as Martina Hingis and Lindsay Davenport distanced themselves from the pack. "I wanted to return so bad," she says. "But it hurt too much. I didn't want to rush back and have it cost me years of my career."

With Serena home in Florida convalescing from a knee injury she suffered at the Amelia Island event in April, Venus finally returned to the Tour in May in Hamburg, aware that she was rusty but elated to be back in the mix. With her wrists heavily taped, looking even more lithe than usual, and having lost some of her considerable muscle definition, she prevailed in an ugly match against her old nemesis, Irina Spirlea. In her next outing, she fell to Amanda Coetzer, an opponent she was used to beating handily. From there, Venus went on to Rome to defend her title at the Italian Open. She survived two rounds but suffered a 6–1, 6–2 loss to Jelena Dokic that reduced her to tears as she left the court. "It was bitter crying," recalls Oracene, who accompanied

Venus to Europe. "That's as upset as I've seen her on a tennis court. I told her that her wrists were sore, she had been out half the year, and everything would be fine. But she didn't want to hear it."

Next was the French Open, held on her most challenging surface. Unlike the way it is for most other Americans, clay isn't alien to the Williamses—one of the courts at their home in Palm Beach Gardens is Har-Tru. But Venus has never played well on the dirt. It blunts her power and prolongs points, increasing the likelihood of an unforced error. The previous year, she didn't even make it out of the fourth round at the French Open, falling to an Austrian qualifier, Barbara Schwartz, after holding three match points. Upon arriving in Paris this time, though, she told her mother that she was ready to win. She started out auspiciously enough, dusting her first four opponents—including Anke Huber, the eleventh seed—in straight sets.

Venus is notorious for displaying a kaleidoscope of moods, but in Paris she was filled with unbridled joie de vivre. She even walked around Roland Garros wearing a Miss Piggy T-shirt festooned with a protruding plastic snout. Asked about it, she showed a persona totally different from the intense competitor who had stalked the court an hour earlier. "Oink, oink, oink," she said, laughing and squeezing the snout. "Isn't it so cute?" A few days later, leaning back in a chair in a small, low-ceilinged room above the players' lounge, Venus was still smiling. "School seemed too much like a job," she said. "I was procrastinating on my homework, sometimes getting up early in the morning the day it was due. And I'd get bored in an office, just sitting around, eating donuts. Tennis, I know, is what I do for a living, but when you're happy with how you're playing, it can be so much fun."

Her run stopped when she faced Arantxa Sanchez Vicario in the quarterfinals. The conditions for this match on Court Suzanne Lenglen were more befitting Lambeau Field than Paris in the spring. A whipping wind made the temperature in the low fifties seem much chillier, yet Venus emerged from the locker room in a Tweetie Bird yellow skirt/bikini top combo better suited for Florida in August. The running joke in the women's locker room was that if Venus won the match, Reebok would give her the rest of her outfit. (Venus was wearing the Reebok apparel gratis, as the company still hadn't renegotiated her contract that had lapsed in April.)

Sanchez Vicario took the court wearing a sensible sweatsuit she later shed to reveal a plain white T-shirt and plain white skirt. Her regard for style is so minimal that she once committed the fashion sin of wearing a plastic ball holder attached to her belt. Sanchez Vicario's game is as short on glamour as her appearance. In an era that puts a premium on pace and power, she relies on patience and percentages. She is a junk ball pitcher in a fastball league. The quintessential indefatigable counterpuncher, she retrieves every ball like a loyal dog and exasperates opponents by goading them into errors, rather than blasting them into submission. Not for nothing did Bud Collins nickname her "The Barcelona Bumblebee." She has an insect's knack for stinging, biting, and vexing opponents until they surrender. In her previous French Open match against Austrian Barbara Schett, Sanchez Vicario was trailing 0–6, 1–4 but exasperated the mentally shaky Schett by hitting scads of drop shots, which elicited boos from the crowd. Schett came unraveled and the Bumblebee won the match.

The twenty-eight-year-old Spaniard has won more prize money (in excess of $15 million) and more singles matches (approaching seven hundred) than any player in the game. This, amazingly, was her thirteenth French Open quarterfinal in fourteen appearances. There is no exchange of birthday cards between Sanchez Vicario and the House of Williams, the ill will stemming from a 1998 match in which the Spaniard thought Serena purposefully rifled a ball at her head. "They have no respect," she sniffed. On this day, she was perhaps the worst possible opponent for Venus, particularly on clay. After splitting the first two sets, the Bumblebee snared Williams into her web—to mix entomological metaphors—and tortured her with interminable baseline rallies.

After clinching the match, 6–0, 1–6, 6–2, Sanchez Vicario turned to her mother, brother, and coach, Emilio, in the stands and pumped her fist. "Today I beat Venus on the same court I beat her sister on two years ago from a set and 5–2 down," she crowed afterward. "I think I'm winning this tournament." For Venus, the match marked yet

another Grand Slam disappointment—thirteen and counting, now—
another squandered opportunity. The whispers started up again. *She
can't win big matches. She's wasteful with her talent. She lacks her sister's
valor.* Dispirited about the state of her game, Venus left Paris for two
weeks of grass-court preparation at home in Florida. No one—not
even her bombastic father—would have predicted that five months
would elapse before Venus Williams would lose another match.

In the quarterfinal that followed on Court Suzanne Lenglen, Martina
Hingis methodically dissected the soft-spoken African-American
Chanda Rubin. Hingis couldn't escape the wrath of the crowd,
though. Late in the second set, Hingis argued about a line call. She
summoned the chair umpire, circled a mark beyond the baseline with
her racket, and put on a pouting grimace. She didn't win that argu-
ment and the French fans seemed to appreciate the opportunity to boo
her again. They had, after all, waited a year for this. In another quarterfinal match, Conchita Martinez faced the bronzed, liberally jeweled
seventeen-year-old Marta Marrero, who had gotten here from the
qualifying draw and was being swarmed by agents. Prior to the match,
Marrero betrayed a hip-to-the-times parvenu attitude and matter-of-
factly predicted that she would beat her countrywoman. She didn't.
But she served notice that she's worth watching in the future.

After her embarrassment in Key Biscayne, Monica Seles contacted her
friend Bobby Kersee, husband of Olympic gold heptathlete Jackie
Joyner-Kersee, to work on her conditioning. Within a month, she had
dropped nearly fifteen pounds. Seles captured the clay court title at
Amelia Island and then the Italian Open at Foro Italico, a tournament
she had last won in 1990, when she was sixteen. Her early results in
Paris were encouraging as well, as she breezed through her first three
matches. In the fourth round, amid a partisan atmosphere she likened
to that of a soccer match, she subdued the powerful but erratic Frenchwoman Amelie Mauresmo, in straight sets. That put her in the quarterfinals against Pierce.

On cue, the clouds cleared for the first time in days when Pierce and Seles took the court for their match in the late afternoon. Though this was clearly the match du jour, pitting a three-time champion seeded third against the highest-ranking French player, it was scheduled for the secondary, 10,000-seat Court Suzanne Lenglen. Meanwhile a fairly pedestrian men's match between Alex Corretja and Juan Carlos Ferrero played on the main stage of Court Central. Regardless of the venue, Seles and Pierce played the best match of the year to that point. The crowd was in a lather before the first ball was struck. Pierce took off her warm-up to reveal a black piece of Nike lycra into which she had somehow, against all prevailing laws of physics, squeezed her body. As the crowd shrieked in appreciation, Pierce tried to smother a smile. Shouts of "Allez, Mah-ree" wafted from the stands. When a Seles supporter responded with, "Come on, Monica," he was roundly booed.

For much of the first set, Pierce and Seles were like two pool sharks, directing balls into the corner and side pockets. At one point, Seles punished a short ball and followed it up with a screaming swinging volley, a sure winner. The ball headed straight toward Pierce. In a fluid motion that recalled the court's eponym—the nimble Lenglen—Pierce took three loping steps to her right, leaped, and fired a forehand between her legs. The ball bounded past a stunned Seles, alighting just inside the line. The crowd was apoplectic. Seles recovered and won the set, but the fates seemed to have decreed the outcome. (The next day Pierce would describe the shot to anyone in the locker room who would listen. "It even made the Play of the Day on CNN," she chirped.)

The astonishingly high level of tennis continued in the second set, which Pierce took 6–3. As Seles departed for a momentum-stopping bathroom break, which has become practically automatic for the player who drops the second set, the crowd started doing the wave. As it moved past her, Pierce, seated in her chair courtside, raised her arms. The crowd laughed and adored her again. "It's a lovefest," joked Pierce's brother, David.

With the crowd still buzzing, Pierce broke Seles early in the third set, but surrendered the break and suddenly trailed 3–2. The crowd grew palpably restless during the changeover, bracing for another

Pierce flame-out in Paris. But they had nothing to fear, as Pierce elevated her game, winning the next three games. Serving at 5–3 she played conservatively, waiting patiently for Seles to commit the error. When Seles obliged, dumping a routine forehand in the net on match point, the fans erupted. Again, Seles had played a top player tough. Again, by the third set, her fuel gauge was on empty and she dropped the match.

After the match underneath the stadium, Seles's coach, Bobby Banck, shook his head and smiled weakly. "Too good," he said softly. "Mary was just too good." Seles knew it too. Unlike her reaction to other recent defeats, Seles was surprisingly upbeat, though her best chance to win a Slam in 2000 had just passed her by. "Those storybook endings," she said with a sigh, "haven't happened for me yet."

Meanwhile, the French fans were going into paroxysms of elation over Pierce. "Tous Avec Mary"—"We're all with Mary"—screamed a headline in the national sports daily *L'Equipe*. Outside Roland Garros in the Bois de Boulogne, Pierce posters were selling briskly while photos of Cedric Pioline, the top French male who lost in the fourth round, had been slashed to half price. Pierce even received handwritten notes of encouragement from Prime Minister Lionel Jospin and President Jacques Chirac, who passed along "a thousand bravos" as well as a promise, "all French people will be on your side." In the past, these awkward patriot games, the vacillating fan support, and the pressure of playing with a nation's weight on her shoulders—broad though they are—would have unnerved her. Now, they only bolstered her resolve.

Two days later, by the time Pierce and Hingis had stifled their giggles, climbed the stairs outside the locker room, and stepped onto the court for their semifinal match, the stands were packed and half the television sets in France were tuned into the match. The crowd jeered Hingis's every move, and she once again succumbed to hubris and tried to match the power of a heavier hitter, instead of breaking up rallies and forcing Pierce to change direction. If anything, Pierce outflanked Hingis, pinning her behind the baseline and then unfurling feathery, sharply angled shots that died when they hit the clay.

After winning the first set 6–4, Pierce held a match point at 5–4 in the second set. When she floated a backhand long, the crowd sighed. The groans were even louder ten minutes later, when she dropped the set, 7–5. Earlier in her career, Pierce would have wilted under the weight of the moment. At her brother's urging, though, she breathed deeply during the changeover and collected her thoughts. After getting an early break in the third set, and fighting off cramps and dehydration that would later necessitate an IV drip, Pierce prevailed, 6–2. She was now a match away from becoming the first, French—well, sort of French—female since Francoise Durr in 1967 to win her country's signature event, needing only to beat Conchita Martinez in the final.

Though still occupying the top spot in the rankings, Hingis had lost her fifth straight Slam. Another opportunity to win the French had eluded her, yet she was surprisingly casual about the loss, a far cry from her Roland Garros meltdown the previous year. "I need oxygen to live," said Hingis, who, as consolation, would team with Pierce to win the doubles title three days later. "I don't *need* the French Open."

As a girl growing up in the small Spanish city of Monzon, Conchita Martinez would run home from school, grab her tennis racket, and then run to the factory where her father, Cecilio, worked into the night as an accountant. Hitting against a wall, she would emulate her favorite players and their styles, the attack game of Martina Navratilova, the corkscrew serve of John McEnroe. It didn't take long for her to learn a simple lesson. "The wall never lost," she says. For the next two decades, she would incorporate that insight into her game. With loopy, baroque strokes that yielded parabolic, topspin-heavy shots, Martinez penetrated the sport's upper reaches by playing classic defensive tennis. Her leisurely paced game is an acquired taste, but it made her a fixture in the top ten for the better part of a decade. The biggest moment of her career came at Wimbledon in 1994, when she beat Martina Navratilova to win her only Grand Slam title—albeit without hitting a single volley winner in the final. Her career had stagnated since, as tennis's new breed exploited her deficit of power. In 1999, distracted by her father's faltering health, she fell out of the top twenty for the first time since the 1980s. Instead of retiring, as many thought she might, she regrouped, worked harder, and was suddenly back in the top five by 2000. In addition to working intensely with her psychologist, Guillermo Perez, she retained her doubles partner and close friend Pat Tarabini as her coach. "People think she's just a typical European baseliner," says Tarabini, an affable Argentine. "But there's more to her game than meets the eye."

The same can be said for Martinez's personality. Shy with the media, she has never captivated the public or been on the front lines of any WTA Tour marketing drive. But she is one of the circuit's livelier personalities, a Harley-Davidson fiend who owns an oceanside home in San Diego and tours vineyards in Bordeaux during the off-season. Fluent in English and German as well as Spanish, she is among the more popular players and holds the unofficial title of the best karaoke impresario on the circuit.

Veterans like Martinez are supposed to be immune from the pressure of big matches, but in women's tennis, the opposite is often true. It's the younger, callow players who have little to lose and can swing freely. The old hands are fully aware of the significance of the occasion— and the finite number of chances they'll have to return to such a big stage in the future. On yet another brisk autumnal day, Pierce and Martinez waited outside the locker room for their court call. As Pierce smiled gently and thanked well-wishers who passed, Martinez tapped her foot nervously and stared ahead blankly. Once on the court, she looked scared. And she played scared. After nearly breaking Martinez's serve in the first game, Pierce won thirteen of the next fourteen points and took the first set 6–2. With Pierce attacking her backhand mercilessly and a stadium full of fans rooting against her, Martinez could barely hit a ball in the court.

Martinez steadied her nerves in the second set when she began driving her one-handed backhanded rather than slicing it. Tied at 5–5 and the chorus of "Allez Marie" raining from the stands, Pierce broke Martinez to serve for the title. On her first match point, she lined up a forehand that landed in the net. En masse, 15,000 fans moaned. Four points later, she had another match point. This time she spanked a crosscourt backhand wide. The restless natives groaned. "Breathe, Mary, breathe," David Pierce muttered to himself.

Two points later, Pierce had her third shot at the title. "You know what went through my head?" Pierce said later. "I remembered the religious significance of the number three and said to myself, 'This is the one.' " With no dilatory histrionics—neither "babe-ing" nor "re-babe-ing"—Pierce took a ball and casually inspected it as if shopping for fruit at a Parisian market. She bounced it once, twice, then belted a serve down the middle of the court. When Martinez's return fluttered innocuously into the net, Pierce raised her arms in triumph. When she collapsed into her chair, she was overcome by emotion. She fiddled with her rosaries, buried her face in a towel, and said a prayer while the fans offered a rousing Hail Mary.

There was barely time for her to savor her victory. She was called to the PA mike to address the crowd and deliver a thank-you speech, in flawless French. She said a few words in English, adding; "Dad, I'm sure you're watching. Thanks for everything." While David took long drags on a cigarette, Mary posed with the trophy, ricocheted from one interview to the next, and felt her cheeks go numb from smiling. It wasn't until two hours after the match that she finally left the complex to go join her mother, brother, two aunts, an uncle, and three cousins for a celebratory dinner.

As Pierce signed one last autograph and was about to hop into her courtesy car, she stopped, turned, and took one last look at Roland Garros. Buffeted by memories and conflicting emotions, she smiled. The 2000 French Open winner knew she had subdued another ghost from her past.

PLENTY OF ANNA-TUDE

For all the superlatives heaped on Wimbledon—oldest, most prestigious, rainiest—you can add one more: most schizophrenic. This tournament is half Merchant Ivory, half Jerry Springer. On the one hand, it oozes tradition and civility from every pore. The endearingly antediluvian grass surface is the most obvious manifestation of that. The Championships, as Wimbledon proudly calls itself (as if there were no others), are devoid of modern blights like luxury boxes, blimps, and sprawling food courts. With the exception of a tasteful Rolex logo on the scoreboard and a Slazenger decal on the umpire's chair, there is no commercial presence on Centre Court. Linesmen wear jackets and lineswomen skirts, ball kids roll the balls to players rather than do anything so gauche as throw overhand. Four o'clock tea is still very much an institution. Pete Sampras is right when he likens Wimbledon to a cathedral—most everything about the place demands a sort of respectful silence. Immediately, one feels the power of the place.

With that rigid conservatism and resistance to change comes a thick slab of old-fashioned sexism. Gone are the days when married female competitors were known by their husbands' names (remember Martina Navratilova's archrival, Mrs. J. M. Lloyd?) but today married and single players alike are referred to as Miss, whether they like it or not. When the umpires call the score, it's "advantage Sampras" but "advantage Miss Williams." The female players come to Wimbledon knowing that they will get inferior court assignments and practice times. What's more, the Wimbledon purse for women is nearly 20 percent less than the men's; that's the biggest disparity of any Slam. When asked about the prospect of equal prize money, Wimbledon officials cite a dubious study few have actually seen, which allegedly indicates that fans vastly prefer men's matches to women's. Besides, a Wimbledon executive added that if the tournament augmented the women's purse, "we wouldn't have so much to spend on petunias." He was kidding. Maybe.

Despite all this formality, clubbishness, chauvinism, and "snob-bery," as Mary Pierce called it, there's the other face of Wimbledon. Befitting the country that inspired Austin Powers and gave us Bridget Jones's diary, a thick fog of gossip and titillation hangs over Wimble-don. Scan any of the half dozen daily tabloids during Wimbledon and you'd never know there were actually tennis matches afoot. The head-lines cackle about "Bonking Boris" Becker, the former champ whose sluggish play one year was attributed to excessive intercourse and "Monic-Ugh Seles," who grunts "as loud as a Learjet." (This deter-mined by a "Grunt-o-Meter" no doubt as scientifically precise as the fans-prefer-men-over-women poll.)

Twice in the past few years, Wimbledon matches have been inter-rupted by streakers. (The club's response after a naked female ran across the court during the 1996 men's final: "Whilst we do not wish to condone the practise, it did at least provide some light amusement for our loyal and patient supporters.") Wimbledon is where Anne White, an American player of little distinction, made tennis history when she came out for a first round match in a formfitting, full-length bodysuit and was met with earsplitting whistles and catcalls from the crowd. It's where flashbulbs click like cicadas whenever female players remove a spare tennis ball from under their skirts and inadvertently show "a lit-tle bum." Oh, behave! "It's all about sex, isn't it?" says Martina Hingis.

"They always ask me the silliest questions here and, I'm like, 'Don't you have anything better to do?'"

Apparently not. There is a story that Centre Court was moved to its current location on Church Road and expanded in 1922 just so more fans could get a glimpse of the raised hemlines of Suzanne Lenglen, tennis's poster girl of the Roaring Twenties. Even the Wimbledon Museum currently displays an underwear ad from the 1940s for "The Best Lines on Centre Court," next to a picture of a busty player clad in a "fully-fashioned, seamless, pre-shrunk girdle." Against these lurid underpinnings, what better time and place to a take a break from tennis and discuss Anna Kournikova?

Because of a dispiriting second round loss at the French Open in May, Anna Kournikova wasn't even among the top sixteen seeds when she arrived at the Championships. She still hadn't won a professional tournament in her career and had lost to eighteenth-ranked Chanda Rubin at the Wimbledon grass court tune-up event at Eastbourne. No matter. The contagion known as Annamania was raging as the players arrived at their third Grand Slam of the year. The face that launched thousands of Web sites and had recently graced the covers of *Sports Illustrated* and *Forbes* was everywhere in England. The tabloids devoted page after page to her. Flashing a coquettish, Mona Lisa smile, her visage was plastered on 1,500 billboards, 25 feet high, all around London promoting Berlei sports bras. The cheeky slogan, "Only the balls should bounce," became the catchphrase for the tournament. Rumors of her hitting sessions had hundreds of fans scrambling from their seats to get as close to the Aorangi Park practice courts as possible.

When Kournikova took the court—Centre Court of course—for her first round match against Sandrine Testud, there were thirty-six photographers with lenses pointed in her direction. (Never mind that Testud, then tenth in the world, was the seeded player.) "Being with Anna," complained her coach at the time, Eric Van Harpen, "is like being on the scene of a movie." It took only a few games for a fan to yell, "Anna, Will You Have My Baby?"

Many attractive women have played professional tennis. Well before the sultry Gabriela Sabatini, blond beauty Carling Bassett, and elegant Chris Evert, there was Gussie Moran and her lace knickers and, before her, Lenglen and her gossamer dresses. But no player has ever had Kournikova's impact, and the X-factor to supplement her abundant natural beauty. Exceptionally photo- and telegenic, Kournikova is drawn to the spotlight as if it is her oxygen. Her slight accent, her icy demeanor, the persistent whispers of alleged ties to the Russian Mafia, the bizarre love triangles, and the conga line of revolving suitors imbue her with a sense of mystery and a lightning bolt of eroticism. Whereas the diffident Sabatini was described as having "tennis elbow of the personality," Kournikova knows how to play the crowd and enflame the boys.

It doesn't much matter that she rarely makes the finals, or plays on worldwide television. Fans need only own a computer and a browser and, anywhere in the world, they can download Anna. She is the first tennis pinup girl for the Internet age. Ulf Dalhstrom, formerly an Adidas executive, who now works for Kournikova's management agency, Octagon, gushed to *Sports Illustrated* that "Anna is everything."

The more she ignores the panting men—or better yet, disses them, saying, "You can't afford me," as she did to one ill-suited suitor years ago—the more desirable she becomes. No matter that her relationship with the media has all the warmth of a Siberian winter. No matter that she once denied a Madison Square Garden elevator operator an autograph because his craft moved too slowly, showed such impertinence that a U.S. Open employee filed a formal complaint against her, and was sufficiently petulant on an American Airlines flight to warrant an FBI investigation. Her popularity inexplicably burgeons.

And rest assured that Kournikova's imperious demeanor and black hole of self-absorption is no facade. "I love it when people say, 'Oh, it's Anna's image,'" says Marat Safin, a top men's player who grew up with her in Moscow. "I like Anna, but it's no image. She's been like that all her life. Since she was a little girl she is thinking she is the best and the prettiest."

Kournikova is one of the most popular tennis players ever with the fans, but she is among the least popular with her colleagues. Nearly every one of them has felt the back of Anna's hand. As someone recently observed, women's tennis today is like the Tom Lehrer song "National Brotherhood Week": "Oh, the Catholics hate the Protestants, and the Protestants hate the Catholics, the Moslems hate the Hindus, and everybody hates the Jews." In tennis the lyrics are: "Serena hates Martina, and Martina hates Venus, and Venus hates Lindsay, and everybody hates Kournikova." Asked, for instance, by Rennae Stubbs to become more active in Tour politics, Kournikova responded without pause, "Why should I? I'm doing great." When Kournikova plays her matches, a raft of other players sit in the stands and root silently for her opponent. At the 2000 Australian Open, Kournikova and Barbara Schett played doubles against Sonya Jeyaseelan and Patty Schnyder. Before the match, Schnyder, who makes no secret of her Anna-mosity, asked Schett to give her a short ball so that she could drill Kournikova. "Anna is pretty much a sideshow," says Lisa Raymond, one of the brighter and more highly regarded players on Tour. "Let's just say there's not a lot of mutual respect going on."

Kournikova doesn't care. Her beguiling combination of beauty and attitude—Anna-tude, it's called in the locker room—has made her obscenely wealthy. With endorsement contracts from companies ranging from Adidas to Berlei to Yonex to Omega watches and a Mexican telephone company, Kournikova is a one-woman multinational conglomerate. Though rival agents claim that Kournikova's endorsement figures are exaggerated by incentive clauses, she has scant chance of reaching, even the most conservative estimates have her earning, more than $10 million annualy in off-court income, including exhibitions. Before Venus Williams signed a $40 million deal with Reebok later in the year, Kournikova reaped far more in endorsements than any other female athlete. The $10 million is also fifteen times the $640,459 she made in 2000 for playing singles. Kournikova can command more money for a weekend "hit and giggle" exhibition than most of her colleagues will make from playing a year's worth of tournaments.

She even generates her own synergy. When, for instance, she posed for *Forbes,* her Octagon handlers made sure that her Yonex racket and Adidas shoes and apparel were prominently displayed in the photos. In effect, her sponsors received a free color ad in one of the world's largest financial magazines. "We try to maximize value for all of Anna's business partners," says Octagon president Phil de Picciotto. And consider this scene from late November 2000: Kournikova flew to New York to announce her partnership with Omega watches. The festivities included the unveiling of a sixty-by-sixty-foot billboard in Times Square. After changing out of a low-cut dress and into a low-cut, diaphanous silk blouse, Kournikova walked across the street to MTV for an appearance on Carson Daly's show *Total Request Live.* When Daly interviewed Kournikova, naturally, the cameras panned the Omega billboard. Everybody won. Omega received the equivalent of a free commercial on MTV; MTV secured an interview with the hottest female athlete in the world; Kournikova (and Octagon) showed Omega why she's worth the megabucks. And since Daly did his part and plugged the product, Kournikova presented him with an Omega watch in the green room after the show. Cha-ching.

Kournikova stars with Mary Joe Fernandez in a popular television commercial for Charles Schwab. Fernandez deadpans to the camera that "some of the other players are kinda jealous of [Anna's]" . . . cut to a swaggering Kournikova, in a flattering red dress, her blond hair billowing around her shoulders . . . "portfolio." It's a clever, playful gag, but it's actually dead-on. Players really are envious, less of Kournikova's comeliness than of her earning power. The other irony of the ad is that Fernandez's husband, Tony Godsick, is Kournikova's former agent and helped build the portfolio in question.

For many players, Kournikova's wealth and popularity represents a disquieting trend. As Nathalie Tauziat wrote in her controversial book, *Les Dessous du Tennis Feminin (The Underside of Women's Tennis),* which appeared in Europe in the spring, "Aesthetics and charisma are winning out over sporting performance." Tauziat is quick to mention that she has nothing against Kournikova personally, but she resents that a player who has never won a tournament is promoted more heavily than better players. Tauziat writes, "For the WTA Tour, Anna is a real cash till, a blond windfall." Tauziat describes watching a match between Kournikova and Davenport played in Key Biscayne several years ago and being amazed by the "lynching" Davenport received by the fans. "I went to the WTA Tour office to see how they felt. One of them said, 'You know, Anna is so pretty.' " Tauziat responded, "What do you think this tennis is, a casting ground for the next James Bond movie?"

In her book, Tauziat takes particular umbrage with the Commitment List, a cloak-and-dagger ranking of players based on their marketability. If the twenty players on the list play the requisite number of Tier I and Tier II events (in most cases thirteen, not including the Grand Slams) they receive a bonus based on their Commitment List rankings—de facto appearance fee money. The top sixteen singles players automatically make the list, as well as four other players, but a committee of international Tour tournament directors determine their rankings. So while Kournikova collected $100,000 in 2000, players with superior match results but lower Commitment List rankings received less. Mary Pierce, for instance, finished 1999 ranked seven places higher than Kournikova but was eligible for only $50,000. Rewarding sizzle over steak, Tauziat argues, not only runs counter to a meritocracy, it unfairly punishes older, less attractive players.

Tauziat, not surprisingly, is a prime victim of this zeitgeist. She was born in Africa, where her French father sold bathroom fixtures in the Congo. After playing for a decade in obscurity, she reached the Wimbledon finals at age thirty, the biggest achievement of her career. Just her luck, it occurred on the same weekend in July of 1998 that her cousin, Didier Deschamps, was leading France to the World Cup in soccer. At age thirty-two, Tauziat would beat Serena Williams and reach No. 3 in the world in 2000. But because she isn't mistaken for a runway model—and, in fairness, partially because she is notorious for being uncooperative with sponsors—the Tour does little to promote her. Despite beating Kournikova in the rankings, Tauziat was nine spots lower on the Commitment List, eligible to earn a mere $15,000 bonus.

Though more than $2 million was allocated for the Commitment List—Lindsay Davenport, Martina Hingis, and Venus Williams were each eligible for $400,000 in 2000—the Tour downplays the list merely as a way to entice the biggest draws to play as often as possible. "Certain players sell tickets and others don't," says Bob Arrix, who runs the Amelia Island tournament and is a former WTA Tour board member. "It only makes sense to reward the players you need to have in your draw." But others fear that the imprecise science of assessing players based on their perceived Q-rating and not their empirical rankings is a slippery slope. "If we're just here to sell tickets and make money, not win matches," says Tauziat, "why have rankings in the first place?"

The Tour isn't shy about giving Kournikova and other charismatic players attention and money disproportionate to their results on the court. And the unremorseful emphasis on good backsides as well as good backhands has done wonders for women's tennis, cementing its status as the world's most popular and financially successful women's sport. Including her Commitment List bonus, Martina Hingis earned $3,857,049 in 2000, more than double the $1,865,053 earned by Karrie Webb, the top-ranked LPGA's top golfer, who quietly won two majors in 2000. And while forty-eight WTA Tour players earned at least $200,000, the average salary in the WNBA in 2000 was just $55,000— so low that some of the league's top stars have to supplement their income playing for overseas teams in the off-season.

Flesh peddling is now a part of the business and it extends far beyond Kournikova. At larger tournaments, the Tour offers "photo calls" at which players pose for photographers away from the court. At the French Open, there was a "call" for Magdalena Grzybowska, a strikingly attractive player but one so unaccomplished she had to qualify for the main draw. Olga Barabanshikova, a marginal player but a marginal player with a pierced navel who reportedly turned down a six-figure offer to bare all for *Playboy,* was asked to recline in a bikini poolside at Indian Wells. How this related to tennis is unclear. Tour officials openly root for Germany's Jana Kandarr, a twenty-four-year-old who has yet to crack the top fifty, but looks wunderbar. "Today, fans expect athletes to be more than athletes. We're never going to stop selling sex," says Jim Fuhse, the Tour's director of player promotions.

"If anything, I'd like to see us be *more* risqué and take more chances. Look, if a player doesn't sell tickets because of her tennis, she has to do something else to contribute."

The Tour defends its "if you got it, flaunt it" stance not as a sellout but as a triumph of feminism. Far from undoing the gains of Billie Jean King and Martina Navratilova, it claims that this vamping is the ultimate expression of women's lib—strong women using their unique assets to move product. "I don't think there's anything wrong with wanting to be ladylike or wanting to be considered attractive," says Hingis. "Fans want you to be more than just a tennis player. If you can give them that, why not do it? It's like, Girl Power, you know?" Even Bart McGuire, the Tour's straight-laced CEO, makes no apologies for the marketing strategy. The women he governs are attractive, have arresting personalities, and bundles of attitude. What's wrong with cashing in on that? "We're not in the sexploitation business, but we are in the entertainment business," he says. "I don't apologize for having attractive players any more than Hollywood studios apologize for Julia Roberts."

That analogy doesn't quite work. Looks are a prerequisite for many film roles, but they are incidental to success on the tennis court. And unlike in film, there are objective measures for gauging a player's ability. (Did she—or did she not—get her clock cleaned in straight sets?) McGuire's larger point is well taken. Sports and entertainment are comingling, and if showing some leg helps sell the game, what's the harm? It's not as though women are the only ones playing this game. Didn't at least *some* of the appeal of Joe Montana, Oscar De La Hoya, Joe Namath, and even that famed Hanes skivvies pitchman, Michael Jordan, stem from their looks? And where was the hue and cry and indignation when men's tennis, tacitly admitting the women were on to something, launched the testosterone-driven "New Balls Please" campaign?

Some of this piety about exploitation may just be a cover for the fact that a lot of players just plain hate Kournikova. And she gives them plenty of reasons to do so, often putting her own interests before the

good of the Tour and the good of the sport. After committing to the
Oklahoma City event in February, Kournikova pulled out, citing a
desire to play fewer tournaments. She played in a lucrative exhibition
in Mexico that week instead. According to multiple sources, when
Kournikova took the court for her doubles match in Mexico, she said
to her partner, Natasha Zvereva, and their opponents, Barbara Schett
and Anke Huber, "I have to lose because I want to get out of here."
Huber and Schett retorted, "We want to get out of here too, Anna." In
spite of their best efforts to lose, Kournikova and Zvereva nearly were
leading in the third set. But with a few games to go, Kournikova
abruptly retired with an "injury" to her wrist, leaving Schett and
Huber seething. (Thankfully, Kournikova was healthy enough to play
in Scottsdale a few days later.)

In the fall, Kournikova was one of several players who blithely
ignored a Tour rule forbidding a player from competing in a non-Tour
event within 60 days prior to and within 125 miles of a Tour event.
When she played an exhibition in Vienna a few weeks before the Linz
tournament, the Tour warned her that she was committing a finable
offense. No problem. The fine was so negligible compared to her
endorsement fee, she played anyway. In 2000, she also left exhibition
promoters in Memphis and Baltimore scrambling when she reneged
on commitments to play exhibitions in those cities. "She just does
whatever she wants," grouses one WTA tournament promoter. "But
you take it with a smile because you want her to play for your event in
the future."

Fortunately, women's tennis has thus far been able to balance the
slick packaging of Kournikova with the quality products of the
Williams sisters, Davenport, Seles, and Hingis. But many still bristle
when Kournikova is lavished with endorsements, is the top drawing
card at most events, and even gets her picture on the cover of the WTA
Tour's media guide at the expense of more accomplished but less rav-
ishing, colleagues.

Still, players and agents know that Kournikova sells. Over and
over, they describe prepubescent juniors as "the next Anna." (Rest
assured, it's not because they use the same forehand grip or emulate

Kournikova's service motion.) One of these "Kourni-klonas" is thirteen-year-old Maria Sharapova, who has already signed with IMG and trains at the IMG-owned Bollettieri Academy. Another "next," Monique Viele, is a Florida junior whose brain trust published a brochure extolling her as "more like a supermodel than a tennis player," with "long, lean, tanned muscular legs." She was thirteen at the time. Team Viele threatened to sue the Tour on the grounds that the Age Eligibility Rules were "not only unconstitutional, but un-American." The Tour granted her a minor, face-saving concession and before she played her first professional match—an unqualified fiasco—she parted with IMG and hired Donald Trump's T Management to represent her, with an agreement to leverage her singing and modeling ambitions as well as her tennis. "Have you seen her?" Trump asked a reporter after he had already signed Viele. "I hear she's better than Kournikova!"

In *Les Dessous du Tennis Feminin,* Tauziat writes that she fears the system will crush Kournikova and "she will feel very alone the day the press starts to treat her with the indifference they do Conchita Martinez." What will happen to Kournikova, she wonders, when her shelf life expires, the klieg lights dim, and the next It Girl comes along? The answer: she will be very rich.

The conventional wisdom is that if Kournikova ever breaks through on the court her popularity will increase exponentially. "If she won just one major," Charlie Pasarell told *Sports Illustrated,* "she'd become the most famous athlete of all time." Some think such talk is just a feeble attempt to justify the tidal wave of testosterone. "The attention she gets is totally inappropriate," says Sue Levin CEO of Lucy.com, one of the Tour's major sponsors. "Saying that all she has to do is win a tournament is like saying all Brooke Shields has to do is win a tournament. Right now Brooke has about the same chance. If Anna were my client right now I'd be ripping my hair out."

Kournikova, usually defensive and disingenuous with the media, put her mouth where her money was during Wimbledon. At a press conference sponsored by Berlei bras, she took questions from the throng of reporters. Asked whether she was wearing an engagement ring, she snapped. "My private life is private." Without any irony, she then said, "I'm here to talk about my bras."

The paradox for Kournikova is that she truly does have game. Despite what her detractors say, she plays tennis better than all but ten or twelve women in the world. "She may not be the MVP of the league yet," says de Picciotto, "but she's definitely an All-Star." She has beaten most of the top guns at least once, she has reached the semifinals of Wimbledon; she finished 1999 with the Tour's top ranking in doubles and wrapped up 2000 ranked eighth in singles. She competes in more events than all but a few players, and in spite of the perception that she divides all her nonplaying time between juggling men and cultivating her caramel tan, she's actually among the hardest workers on Tour. Her practice sessions are sweat-fests—tough, intense workouts that put to rest any doubts about her commitment.

Her problem is that as a player she is neither fish nor fowl. She lacks the consistent, percussive strokes to rally with the Williams sisters, Davenport, and even Hingis; and neither her serve nor confidence are strong enough for her to become an attacking player. And despite her abundant ego off the court, she often collapses under pressure. (She once double-faulted an unheard of sixty-eight times in three matches—yet when it was suggested that she consult a psychologist, she responded testily, "Why should I?") Nonetheless, she has the talent to beat solid players like Testud, which she did, to the tabloids' delight, in her first round match at Wimbledon.

When one considers the intense pressure Kournikova is under to win—from her ubiquitous, pigtailed mother, Alla, to the corporate sponsors paying her millions—she almost becomes a sympathetic figure. Almost. One's instincts for compassion are aroused when a half dozen players claim that they saw Kournikova furtively smoking cigarettes in the locker rooms of various events. Lindsay Davenport might even have a point when she says, "I know Anna brings it on herself sometimes, but no one wrote about Chris Evert's exploits. Anna does one thing and it's all over the world. She didn't ask to be this pretty."

Kournikova is smart enough to know there's little honor in being tennis's George Hamilton, famous merely for being famous and having a killer tan. She says she wants desperately to win and hastens to add that tennis is her top priority. Besides, she points out, the media created her. She would have been happy as a nondescript player, but now she is the victim, helpless to stanch the hemorrhaging hype. "I can't do anything about it," she says plaintively. "I want to be like all the others." And of course if she's disliked by her peers, it has nothing to do with her caustic personality. It's because "tennis is an individual sport so naturally all the players won't get along."

But if Kournikova is so scornful of superfluous publicity, why does she flash her Buick-sized engagement (?) ring at every press conference? If she really wants to shuck her Lolita image and be the Mary Magdalene of tennis, surely there are better products to endorse than a sports bra, replete with a wink-wink, nudge-nudge catchphrase. (And did she really have to tell a newspaper, "My breasts are really good because they don't sag. They are firm and perfect"?) If she is genuinely trying to tone down her image, what was she doing on the cover of *Sports Illustrated,* sporting a come-hither look, clad in a negligee, clutching a pillow? Contrast this with Davenport, who declined to pose for *Sports Illustrated for Women* wearing a T-shirt that read "Bitch," wary of what kind of image it would project.

Like the dependable femme fatale on a long-running soap opera, Kournikova plays out her scenes with numbing predictability. The script goes like this: Anna plays on the prime court and is showered with whistles, hoots, and cheers. After a few games, some Humbert Humbert asks for her phone number, or for her hand in marriage, or if she'll bear his child. (Crowd erupts in laughter.) The chair umpire repeatedly asks fans to cease using flash photography. (Crowd erupts again.) Anna plays well, but as the match tightens, so does she, unable to change tactics, unwilling to attack the net. She looks to her mother for support but gets an urgent, icy stare in response. She loses. (Crowd groans. Players in the locker room rejoice.) She heads to the interview room, where she is asked barbed questions about her sustained futility in winning a tournament and salacious questions about her off-court activities. She gives a few surly answers, most of which blame the media for her shortcomings.

Kournikova followed the script to perfection in her second round match at Wimbledon. Against Anne-Gaelle Sidot, a talented but temperamental lefty from France, Kournikova played unimaginative tennis and froze like a lawn ornament on key points. As the crowd moaned, Kournikova went down in straight sets. A gleeful Sidot reacted as though she had won the tournament.

An hour after the match, Kournikova was asked whether she had any message for her legion of fans who were disappointed once again? "No." Naturally the loss was big news. "Kournikover!" a tabloid headline screamed the next day. "Anna said she was more than a bimbo, but oops she's out again." Just like that, tennis's little-ingenue-that-couldn't was back to her role as a well-compensated pinup girl.

A DISH BEST SERVED COLD

THE "CHAMPIONS PARADE," WHICH WAS held on the middle Saturday of the 2000 Championships, honored living Wimbledon winners and provided a rich historical tapestry of the game's evolution and current incarnation. The procession included three pioneers who ushered in the current era of power and money in the women's game: Billie Jean King, Chris Evert, and Martina Navratilova strolled onto the court arm-in-arm-in-arm. Bjorn Borg, whose life has taken some hairpin turns—including a suicide attempt—since he claimed his five titles, returned to Centre Court for the first time since 1983 and dropped to his knees in a spontaneous gesture, kissing the grass. Bunny Austin, the last British man to reach the finals and the first man to wear shorts on Centre Court, flashed a grin as he was wheeled onto the court. He died two months later on his ninety-fourth birthday.

Venus Williams forlornly watched the parade on the TV in the locker room, biting her lip. It was, to borrow a phrase from her father, a party to which she wasn't invited. The parade was yet another reminder that Venus' career had, until now, been marked by underachievement and unfulfilled promise. "I thought to myself, 'If I had just been more serious, if I had won this tournament, I could have been there too,' " she said wistfully. "But it was too late. I thought, 'Now you'll just have to be the first champion of the new millennium.' "

In the past, Venus had had a particularly rough time at Wimbledon. In her maiden match in 1997, at age seventeen, she faced a little-known Pole, Magdalena Grzybowska, who was ranked No. 91. Leading 6–4, 2–0, Venus surrendered control of the match and dropped seven straight games. As Serena sat in the stands, barely looking up from the pages of *A Tale of Two Cities,* Venus went down in three sets. "This was my first Wimbledon," Venus said breezily afterward. "There'll be many more."

She was full of bluster and optimism then; but with each subsequent loss in a big-ticket event, her confidence eroded. In 1998, she reached the Wimbledon quarterfinals, but again folded under pressure. In a tight match with eventual champion Jana Novotna, a close call went against Venus. "Why is this happening to me?" she wailed. The outburst came in the heat of battle, but it was a telling admission: clearly she didn't feel in full control of her destiny. She lost 7–5, 7–6; and the schadenfreude in the locker room was palpable. "I have watched Venus and Serena play, and they're not that good," Anna Kournikova said richly. "They don't know how to play points or how to win." Martina Hingis, who would lose to Novotna in the next round, said, "I don't know with Venus—she is always trying to do a show, not playing real tennis." Hingis had a point. Venus had generated plenty of buzz, so much so that many players declined to discuss either Venus or Serena in interviews. But for all the talk of her beads, her skimpy outfits, her unprecedented power, and her boundless potential, she had yet to demonstrate the consistency needed to win a major title. She was as likely to smack a no-way-in-the-world winner as she was to bang one off a courtside placard. Her tenacity was lacking as well. In 1999, Venus again made the quarterfinals but lost to Steffi Graf in one of the better matches of the year, 6–2, 3–6, 6–4. "It's the biggest tournament and for some reason I can't bring out my tennis," she said. "Very frustrating."

During the first few matches of Wimbledon 2000, it looked as if Venus' frustrations would continue. Her game was still tinged with rust and her swagger was missing after four months off with the wrist injury. In the third round, she committed a welter of forehand errors and was pushed to a second-set tiebreaker by Nathalie Dechy. In her next match, she held a 6–4, 5–0 lead over Sabine Appelmans, and then took a four-game mental holiday, as the Brits would say, before closing out the match 6–4, 6–4.

Inevitably, Venus was compared with her younger sister, who looked sharp and had swapped her signature beads for a purple feather bow. Showing no ill effects of the knee injury that had sidelined her for the French Open, Serena was playing tennis that she described as "scary good," dropping only thirteen games in her first five matches and losing her serve only once.

The ascent of Serena—and the eclipse of Venus—was a hot topic in the players' lounge. Martina Navratilova opined that Serena's serve was more difficult to return than Venus' and "she comes at you a little bit more." Andre Agassi thought that Serena was "fundamentally a better player than Venus." Lindsay Davenport said that Venus wasn't nearly as feared as her sister, as it had been years since she'd beaten a higher-ranked player in a Grand Slam. The snipers in the salon pointed out that Serena's forehand was more reliable, her service motion more fluid, her killer instinct better honed. By the middle of the tournament, even the London bookies were picking eighth-seeded Serena to finish stronger than her fifth-seeded sister.

While Venus was pensive, solemn, and businesslike, Serena was charming with the fans and the media. She treated her postmatch interviews like open-mike night at Ye Olde Comedy Shoppe. After dismantling her second round opponent, she was asked about the spate of inter-tour romances: Steffi Graf and Andre Agassi, Jennifer Capriati and Xavier Malisse, Martina Hingis and Magnus Norman, and Lleyton Hewitt and Kim Clijsters. "I guess there's a lot of action going around," Serena said smiling. "I've been away. Every day I see things, my eyes light up. 'Whoa, I didn't know.' " When the laughs subsided, Serena was asked if she would date another player. "Right now, I'm focusing on my career," she said. "It's really hard to get involved in a relationship. Next thing you know your game goes down, all kinds of things happen." (Forsaking her goal of being more diplomatic, later that afternoon Hingis retorted: "I don't know if Serena's had any experience, so how can she talk about that?")

The banter continued. A reporter asked Serena to respond to the criticism that, despite their "great bodies," she and her sister weren't as "strategically aware" as other players. It's an observation rooted in the most pernicious of racial stereotypes. Venus and Serena may not have Hingis's intuition—who does?—but they play every bit as creatively as most players. Rarely has Anna Kournikova, Jennifer Capriati, or even Monica Seles been asked to defend their "strategic awareness." In a sense, the sisters' go-for-broke mentality *is* a conscious strategy. Were they simply playing on instinct, they would likely push the ball back to the middle of the court and avoid making errors. And somehow it went unnoted that, in addition to singles, both Venus and Serena played six rounds of doubles *and* practiced every day. You'd be hard put to find two players who spent more time working on their games during the tournament. Serena riposted tartly: "They're right. We definitely have great bodies. Yeah, nice, slim, sexy shapes." Next question.

Race is generally a nonissue on the Tour. But it simmers closer to the surface at Wimbledon than anywhere else on the Tour perhaps because everything here—the fans, the lines, the dress code—is conspicuously "lily-white," to invoke Richard Williams's depiction. Further, the signs for the "members" dressing room, the immense, foreboding black gates, even the Kipling quote near the Centre Court portal, bespeaks an ambiance of exclusivity. So somehow it seemed only fitting that the lone racial flare-up of the year came at the Championships.

Following her first round match against the Hungarian Rita Kuti Kis, Alexandra Stevenson prattled on about her admiration for Julia Roberts and her own aspirations of winning an Academy Award someday. After Stevenson lost her next match to the Austrian player Patricia Wartusch, the reporters gathered for another round of inane, innocuous musings from the attention-starved nineteen-year-old. But this time, Stevenson came out with guns ablaze. First she fulminated about Damir Dokic's drunken outburst earlier that day. She recalled that when she and Jelena played doubles at Hilton Head, "her dad showed up drunk. My mom said, 'You're not playing with her again.' He needs help."

Then she dropped her bombshell. She accused French player Amelie Cocheteux of calling her "a piece of shit black girl" during a recent match in Strasbourg. Stevenson also charged that Cocheteux's friend Anne-Gaelle Sidot, also motivated by race, hit Samantha at the same event over a mix-up about practice courts during the same event. (Cocheteux vigorously denied the allegation. "I've never said those words, I've never insulted her," she told the French sports newspaper *L'Equipe.* "It's purely invented.")

What Stevenson failed to mention was that she and her mother had already filed a complaint and that the WTA Tour officials had investigated and "found no conclusive evidence that Ms. Cocheteux made this remark." Further, the Tour determined that Sidot never struck Samantha but rather flicked the brim of Samantha's cap. "No discipline was warranted," the report said. Mariaan de Swardt tried to tell Stevenson that all this "was just part of the trash talk" and she should pay it little mind. Another coach explained that it was girls being girls. "But I'm a girl," Alexandra said, "and I don't do that."

When Alexandra's press conference ended, her mother jumped into the fray, flailing her arms and gums. On the day that the Tour formally announced that nonplayers were banned from the locker room, Samantha—a constant, irritating presence in the changing rooms—gave a dramatic demonstration of why that policy was enacted. The former journalist held an impromptu press briefing for a small pack of reporters. Practically hyperventilating, she explained that Sidot and her boyfriend had seen Alexandra on a practice court and said—inexplicably, in English—"Let's get her." Added Samantha: "My only fear was that it was going to be a Tonya Harding incident." (She neglected to mention that Sidot's goon boyfriend was the French pro Arnaud Clement, who is five-eight, at least four inches shorter than Alexandra.) As Stevenson fulminated, Belgian player Kim Clijsters and her boyfriend, Lleyton Hewitt, walked by and rolled their eyes.

The rants by the Stevensons were their final publicity-grabbing salvo before they disappeared into the oblivion of wild card groping and qualifying draws. Now that all of those points gained during her improbable 1999 Wimbledon semifinal run had dropped off of her ranking, Alexandra had gone from a hot commodity to a marginal player barely ranked in the top hundred. The flaws in her game were obvious—"The first thing she needs to do is to get into shape," said Nick Bollettieri, part of Stevenson's sizable brain trust of coaches. "Alexandra's a nice kid," says one former coach. "The problem is the mother. She thinks she knows everything and she's completely unrealistic in her expectations."

Neither Venus nor Serena—Alexandra's good friends, to hear Samantha tell it—offered a word of public support on these charges of racism. Nor did other African-Americans, like Chanda Rubin or Mashona Washington. While Zina Garrison recalls not being allowed into tournament sites because security guards didn't believe she was a player, and of losing out on millions because she wasn't "right" for an endorsement contract, she has never alleged that there is institutional racism or instances of overt bigotry on the WTA Tour. Of course, it would be disingenuous to assume that the Tour is devoid of prejudice, but as women's tennis has become increasingly international, tolerance has increased. As Lori McNeil, who at the age of thirty-five was still playing doubles, said: "Out here, everybody pretty much respects differences."

Wimbledon officials, unaccustomed to such an outburst, tried to gag Samantha Stevenson. "You don't want to talk, *do you*?" press officer Geoffrey Newton told Stevenson. Naturally, she did. As she was all but shoved into a courtesy car, she scribbled her cell phone number on a piece of paper and encouraged the journalists to request that Alexandra come back into the press room after her mixed doubles match the following day. "Alexandra will be back to win Wimbledon!" she yelled desperately to reporters before the car door slammed and the driver stepped on it.

Samantha Stevenson wasn't the only tennis parent making life easy for the tabloids that day. It was barely past noon at the All England

Club when Jelena Dokic dispatched Gala Leon Garcia in the second round of the Championships, but Damir was already clearly plastered. After the match, he walked through the grounds wrapped in the St. George flag, unleashing a rambling tirade: "The queen is on the side of democracy. The rest of the country is fascists!" He also proclaimed that "fascists and criminals" were running the WTA Tour.

On a balcony outside the press lounge, British journalist Mark Saggers asked Dokic if he'd like to share his ruminations on camera with SkyTV. Dokic asked to borrow Saggers' cell phone, then smashed it into three pieces and raised his arm as if to fight. In a quintessential postmillennial moment, Damir then calmed down and beckoned to his wife Liliana, who was standing nearby, looking distressed, to hand him his gold card. Plastic in hand, Damir offered to pay Saggers L500 for the broken phone. Saggers declined and Damir was carried away by three policemen and detained in a makeshift holding cell under Centre Court. Jelena had to cancel her post-match interviews and negotiate with Wimbledon authorities for the release of her father. She promised that he would leave the grounds and would cause no more disturbances. Ninety minutes later the family returned to their hotel.

Jelena stood steadfast behind her father: "I owe everything to my dad," she said. "He knows my game more than anybody else and he's someone that I can work with." And just about the only person she's allowed to work with. Before Wimbledon, Damir dismissed the venerable Tony Roche, a former French Open champion, as Jelena's coach and installed himself in that role. "Even though Jelena is Australian and seems like a perfectly nice girl, we never really have a chance to talk to her," says Nicole Pratt. For the second year in a row, the Dokic family lodged not in the village of Wimbledon or at the tournament hotel but in a hundred-dollar-a-nighter in Putney. (A few weeks later, the Dokic family announced that Jelena would not play on the Australian Olympic team unless she were excused from staying with the other athletes in the Olympic Village.)

Displaying a Steffi Graf–like ability to block out the distraction of a hard-drinking, hard-driving father, Jelena finds refuge on the court.

She seemed to be imperturbable at Wimbledon. Relying on her effective, if uncomfortable-looking, technique, and clever shotmaking that belies her years, she won five matches and reached her first Grand Slam semifinal. It was a stellar achievement for a seventeen-year-old, the highlight of her promising career. Yet when Jelena lost to Lindsay Davenport in the semis, she was still lingering around the players' lounge hours after the match had ended. Was she was afraid to go out and face her father? As Martina Navratilova observed later in the summer, "I see fear in her eyes when she looks up at her father. She's afraid of failing and you can't play tennis in that environment."

Another father in the press's crosshairs was Richard Williams. As Venus and Serena advanced through the draw, Richard had trouble adjusting to a different culture and country. Unaccustomed to narrow English roads and to driving on the left side of the road, Richard almost totaled his car maneuvering between the Wimbledon courts and the family's rented house three kilometers away. "I was lost and then I had to swerve out of the way of the other car but then I was in a driveway and I nearly got myself killed," he cackled. "Look, I still have goose bumps." Richard decided to walk from his house to the courts for the rest of the tournament, even though he feared that the additional exercise might mean "there would be less of me for my wife to love."

In the quarterfinals, Venus took on Hingis on Centre Court, while Serena played Lisa Raymond on the adjacent Court One. Before the match, Raymond had taken exception to the Williamses' imperious attitude in the locker room. "I don't know why they have to be so unpleasant," Raymond said. "Lindsay Davenport has won three Grand Slams and she still manages to be cordial to the other players. They should be able at least to say 'hi' in the locker room." Serena proved just as icy on the court. In forty-two minutes, she played perhaps the most dominating match of her career and smoked Raymond 6–2, 6–0. Afterward, Raymond was despondent until she looked at the stats—she had converted 63 percent of her first serves and come to the net thirty times. Her problem was that Serena simply refused to misfire. All manner of serves, volleys, ground strokes, returns, and passing shots found the lines as if guided by lasers. Late in the match, Richard Williams stopped by the court. With Serena up 6–2, 4–0, Richard turned to Raymond's coach, Oliver Messerli, and to Raymond's friends Kim Po and Gigi Fernandez. "Sorry to ruin y'all's Fourth of July, but my daughter is too good," Richard crowed. On the next point, Raymond hit one of her few volley winners of the match, and Richard taunted, "How come you guys aren't excited? You got to get into the match. If you were my fans I'd be disappointed." At 5–0, with Serena's victory well in hand, Richard left to watch Venus' match. When he was out of sight, Serena's supporters—Lori McNeil, a shoe company representative, and Zina Garrison—apologized profusely to the Raymond contingent for Richard's behavior.

It is often said about boxers that contrasting styles make good fights, and that observation epitomizes the rivalry between Venus Williams and Martina Hingis. Though the two were born just three months apart, one would be hard-pressed to find two more different players. One is willowy and angular; the other is short and solid. One is the fourth of five sisters, raised in a blighted L.A. neighborhood; the other is a quintessential only child, reared first in Czechoslovakia and then in Switzerland. One is coached largely by her scatterbrained father, the other is tutored by an intense, exacting and publicity-shy mother. They are perfect foils—and their differences play out beautifully and dramatically on the court.

   Their matchup is characterized with typical—and lazy—connotations of "power versus guile" or "strength versus savvy." NBC announcer Dick Enberg described it as "the power of Williams versus the cerebral nature of Hingis." (Enberg was later out-clichéd by his colleague Chris Evert, who remarked that Venus was "playing like a caged animal.") In truth, their matches are far more nuanced. They play at different paces, they prefer different angles and utilize different parts of the court. Hingis's anticipation and unpredictability counters

Williams's pace. Williams's long arms and legs neutralize Hingis's angles and test her stamina. Nor does it hurt that there is plenty of personal animus between them—despite their attempts to downplay it publicly. Hingis was once asked if she felt any bond with Venus, given their many epic duels. "No," she said, puzzled by the query. "It doesn't mean you like someone more just because you have good matches."

Nearly ten months after losing to Hingis at the 1999 U.S. Open, Venus admitted she still had nightmares about it. During that match, Venus watched Hingis's face go flush from exhaustion, saw that she was breathing heavily and chomping on energy bars during changeovers. Venus knows she had Hingis on the ropes but couldn't put her away. She'll never forget what she said to herself during the match: "'Venus, could you do anything more wrong?'" Once upon a time, Venus had her sights set on beating Davenport—The Big L., as she derisively called her—and asked her hitting partners to simulate Davenport's booming strokes and limited footwork. But ever since the 1999 U.S. Open, she had told her partners to slice, dice, and retrieve like Hingis. As Venus walked onto the grass of Centre Court to play Hingis, she knew that she had waited—and worked—nearly a year for this rematch.

The encounter was rich with significance for Hingis, as well. She had developed a bad habit of surrendering to hubris and trying to swap blows when she encountered a more powerful player in a high-stakes match. Urged by her mother to stick to her strengths, she was determined not to enter an arms race with Williams. This time, she erred toward the other extreme. Pushing back balls that barely cleared the service line and spinning in cream puff *first* serves that could have been clocked with a sundial, Hingis dropped the first set 6–3. Watching in the locker room, Davenport couldn't believe how tentatively Hingis was playing. In the stands, Melanie Molitor sat stone-faced, her fingers making a steeple under her chin. Down a break in the second set, Hingis tried desperately to dictate points, and had some success, stealing a break and then closing out the set, 6–4. In the final set,

Williams and Hingis swapped four breaks of serve, but Williams held at 2–2 and cruised from there, her baseline missiles as accurate as they were powerful. (When someone later suggested Hingis might have added more depth to her shots, she responded tartly: "You want to go out there and try it yourself?")

Serving for the match at 5–3, Venus betrayed no sign of nerves, spanking a 118-mph ace. When the ball bounded past Hingis, Venus let out a euphoric yell and jumped up and down like a kid on a pogo stick. She had crossed the Rubicon. She had won a seminal match in her career. She was now the player the rest of the Tour had been dreading for years. Watching a replay of the match on tape, sitting on a couch in the NBC lounge, Evert shook her head. "What do you say to Martina? 'Go back to the gym, try to put on thirty pounds and try to grow five or six inches.' That's the way it's looking." Venus' combination of power and athleticism had long been unimpeachable, but she was often undone by her inconsistency. Now, she had found her radar, reduced her unforced errors, and kept her nerve. In one match, it seemed, the balance of power in the women's game had shifted.

As Venus shook Hingis's hand—or, more accurately, perfunctorily brushed against her palm—she smiled at Serena in the box. Richard was doing an impromptu jig. "That Hingis, little miss smarty pants, thinks she knows all the answers," Richard said later. "But she don't know the answer to Venus or Serena." An hour after the match, Hingis was leaving the dressing room toting her racket bag. Removing a drink from the refrigerator, Venus inadvertently blocked her path. Hingis swung her bag to hit Venus and snapped, "Do you ever get out of the way?"

This was the triumphant moment Richard Williams had dreamed of—and loudly predicted—for two decades. His daughters, raised in "gang-infested Compton," were now going to play against each other for a spot in the Wimbledon final. His sanity had been called into question, his methods assailed, his immodest predictions dismissed as ugly braggadocio. But there he was, the father and coach of two Wimbledon semifinalists. Surely this was among the happiest days of his life. But Richard, being Richard, promptly announced he would not watch his daughters play; instead he would be going to the funeral of the friend of an RAF member he had just met. "When Venus plays Serena, it's going to be like a funeral, anyway," he reasoned. "So I might as well go to a real one." When the cameras stopped rolling, Richard softened. "I've seen enough already," he said quietly. "It's Venus and Serena. I've already won."

The clash of the Williams sisters was *the* story at the Championships. The press corps suddenly swelled with writers and photographers; columnists flew in at the last minute to cover their historic match. Camera crews lined the practice courts three-deep whenever Venus and Serena were rumored—falsely it turned out—to be hitting together. Hundreds of fans clasping Sharpies and assorted Williams paraphernalia converged on "Autograph Island," a patch of asphalt near the players' underground entrance, praying that the sisters would walk by them.

Among them were Ariel Gooding, thirteen, and his brother, Jamiel, nine, who had begged their mother to bring them to Wimbledon from Bristol, England. The two brothers had been desperate to see their two favorite tennis players, Venus and Serena Williams. A few years ago, only a thirteen-year-old with a fondness for wedgies would have admitted that his athletic hero was a heroine. Betraying not even a whisper of self-consciousness, Ariel bragged that it was Venus—not MJ, Zizou, or Shaq—whose posters covered his bedroom walls. It was nothing sexual. It wasn't even racial. She was simply his favorite athlete. "She plays the best," he said with a shrug.

As the brothers stood in line, hoping that their idols would emerge, their mother tried to explain the appeal of Venus and Serena. "They're strong black women who love each other and have a soft side, but I reckon they're tigers on the court. Kids needs someone they can relate to. Tim Henman seems to be a gentleman, but he grew up in this," she said, motioning to the plush surroundings, the manicured lawns, the ambient whiteness. "What the Williams family has done is inspiring for everyone, but especially ethnics."

Much like Tiger Woods in golf, the Williams sisters are changing the face of tennis's image and demographic. Their cachet, their "street

cred," is such that when Venus and Serena made an appearance on
Hollywood Squares, Whoopie Goldberg met them in the green room
and performed the *Wayne's World,* we're-not-worthy genuflect. When
NBA players learn that a reporter also covers tennis, they will say: "I
love the Williams sisters. What are they like?" Or, as NBA All-Star
guard Gary Payton once said to a reporter, "Serena's just a mother-
fuckin' animal, ain't she?"

Rodney Harmon, a former pro who now oversees multicultural
development for the USTA, estimates that 42 percent of the 260,000
new tennis players in 1999 were minorities. There have never been
more top-ranked African-American juniors, including thirteen-year-
old Jamea Jackson, daughter of NFL cornerback Ernie Jackson, who
made it to the fourth round of the girls draw at the 2000 U.S. Open.
According to both an ESPN–Chilton poll and a Nielsen Media
Research study, 11 percent of African-Americans consider themselves
avid professional tennis fans, compared to 4.7 percent of whites and 5.7
percent of the U.S. population as a whole.

"In black neighborhoods, tennis isn't considered a sissy sport any
longer," says Willis Thomas Jr., who runs the Fila/Arthur Ashe Tennis
Academy in Washington, D.C. "My kids see the Williams sisters, and
say, 'Hell, I want to be like them.' I even had guys wearing their hair in
braids because of them. I don't know if I should say this, but Venus
and Serena have done more than [previous African-American players
like Ashe, Washington, and Jackson] because kids relate to them better," says Thomas. "They look like them, they speak like them, and
they seem to go out of their way to 'be black.' They've got the right
personalities." Thomas, who coached both Zina Garrison and Lori
McNeil on the Tour, believes that the earlier wave of African-
Americans in women's tennis like Zina, Lori, and Chanda Rubin
"spoke well and acted a certain way, so as not to upset anyone or rock
the boat." When their success spawned a second wave of minorities,
there was less novelty, less emphasis placed on politesse, and the black
athletes could show more fire and more charisma. "With Venus and
Serena," says Thomas, "they say the hell with fitting into the sport;
they just want to hit the stuffing out of the ball."

"We know black people are our top supporters," says Venus. "And it feels really good when black kids—boys and girls—say I want to be like you one day." At the same time, one rarely gets a sense that they see themselves as anything more than two American teenagers with a multitude of interests who happen to be black. The notion that the Williams sisters are "hostile racial separatists," a term one journalist used to describe them, is ludicrous. They are proud of their heritage, and haven't compromised their racial identity in order to become "crossover" stars. Serena complied with the NAACP boycott and withdrew from April's Family Circle Cup event in South Carolina because of the Confederate flag controversy. (Venus claims that were she not injured, she would have boycotted for political reasons as well.) Contrast this with Tiger Woods, who appeared in a Nike ad saying, "There are still courses in the U.S. I am not allowed to play because of the color of my skin." Yet asked whether he would boycott playing in South Carolina, he told *Sports Illustrated,* "I'm a golfer. That's their deal, you know?"

But unlike their father, the Williams sisters rarely initiate discussions of race or prejudice. They don't bemoan the homogeneity of tennis crowds, and have never publicly mentioned the pile of bigoted hate mail—most of it anonymous—that their mother turns over to Florida law enforcement every few months. "Yes, they're black, that's pretty obvious. But they realize the person inside matters more than the color of their skin," says Oracene. "I think they want to be role models, or whatever you want to call it, for all kids, not just black kids."

In the dark of night twelve hours before their historic semifinal, Venus and Serena were lying on adjacent beds in their rented house in Wimbledon Village. They had come a million miles since they had shared a bunk bed in their modest house in Compton, but the dynamics between the two remained remarkably unchanged. As kids, they had listened nightly to an urban symphony of car horns, screams, sirens, and the occasional rat-a-tat of gunfire.

"Venus," Serena would whisper.

"What is it, Serena?"

"Don't go to sleep before me."
"I'm tired, Serena."
"Well, I'm scared."

Venus would sigh, but she would force herself to stay awake until Serena had drifted off. "Same thing every night," Venus recalls, shaking her head. "That was Serena, getting her way." ("My responsibility in life is to be the annoying little sister and I've always taken that responsibility seriously," responds Serena with a laugh.)

Constantly seeking the imprimatur of four older sisters—six parents, it sometimes seemed—Serena could be competitive, feisty, and "just plain nasty," her father says. "No fighting" was one of the cardinal rules of the Williams household. For the most part it went unbroken, but Serena was the one who pushed it. The eldest Williams sister, Yetunde, now a nurse in San Francisco, recalls Serena joining the family games of Monopoly and cheating flagrantly. She'd flip the Community Chest cards until she found one she wanted. She would steal from the bank. She would sneak hotels onto her properties without paying for them. When a dispute erupted, Serena would turn to Venus, knowing that she would defend her. "I think Serena just didn't understand the rules," Venus would say. "Let her take her turn over again."

Their bond is just as strong on the tennis court. Serena made an unremarkable professional debut at age fourteen at a small tournament in Quebec. Endowed with precocious power but little court sense, she lost to American Annie Miller, 6–1, 6–1. "I played like an amateur," Serena said at the time. More than a year later, Venus faced Miller in an early-round match at Indian Wells and thrashed her in straight sets. As they shook hands at the net, Venus stared coldly at Miller. "That's for beating my sister," she growled.

As Richard Williams's master plan for world domination neared fruition, there was an obvious problem. If Venus and Serena were going to vie for tennis's top ranking, they would have to play each other and that might threaten their close friendship. "It's pretty weird when the person on the other side of the net is family," says Patrick

McEnroe, who played his brother, John, in the finals of a Chicago tournament in 1991. "You want to win but you don't want to win. John and I were at different stages of our careers—he's almost eight years older than I am—so it must be that much harder for those two."

The Williams sisters had faced each other four times before the Wimbledon semifinal. Venus held a 3–1 lead, but Serena had won the last encounter. When the sisters played in the final of the 1999 Key Biscayne tournament, Venus won in three atrociously played sets. After that match, Venus sat in the backseat of a station wagon on her way to the trophy ceremony on a Miami beach. No sooner had the car pulled out of the parking lot than her cell phone beeped. "Hi, Serena. I know. Can you believe she said that? Me too." When she hung up with her sister, Venus erupted in laughter. "They love each other so much they're almost like a husband and a wife," says their mother, Oracene.

At Wimbledon, before the Williams sisters' semifinal match, 14,000 fans crowded into the Centre Court stadium. Millions were watching when Venus and Serena, who had practiced together for half an hour that morning, took the court. The crowd was seemingly uneasy, unsure of who they should support. The inevitable cheer of "Let's Go, Williams" was greeted by peals of laughter. The crowd wanted either sister, it didn't matter which, to elevate her play and take control of the match. Beset by anxiety, neither player deployed much strategy or played with passion. When Venus took the first set, 6–3, the applause was awkward.

If the crowd was unclear about how to act, so too were the sisters. There was virtually no interaction between them. They stared into their strings as they passed each other at the net post on changeovers, neither casting even a furtive glance at the other. There was no clapping of the hand on the racket in applause when the other hit a winner, no appealing to the other's sense of fairness on a close call. "We're both competitors and we tried our best," Venus said later. "You guys tried to make a big deal out of it. We wanted to treat it like any other match."

Down match point, Serena kicked in her sixth double fault of the afternoon, an appropriate coda to an ungainly and unpolished match.

Momentarily frozen, she wobbled to the net like a punch-drunk boxer, unable to choke back tears. In one of the biggest matches of her life, her poise had deserted her along with her game. The player the odds-makers had picked to win dropped as many games against her big sister as she had in her previous five Wimbledon matches combined.

Instead of doing an exuberant dance, as she had after beating Hingis, Venus showed no joy either. Never mind that she won a chance to play in her first Grand Slam final since 1997; her feelings for Serena prevailed. Her facial expression froze rictuslike as she looked over at her kid sister and they hurriedly packed up their bags. The armies of photographers poised for a Kodak moment were disap-pointed. There would be no hamming for the crowd, no curtsies, and only a tentative, demi-wave to the vacant Royal Box. Slinging her racket bag over her shoulder, the big sister turned to the little sister, clearly in pain. Determined not to let the press harass her, Venus lightly touched Serena's shoulder and said: "Let's get out of here."

According to a source close to the family, the morning before they had played each other in the Key Biscayne final in 1999, Richard gave his daughters explicit instructions that Venus was to win in three sets. Another source, self-described as "a former confidante of the family" claims that Richard didn't care who won but he told both daughters: "This is on national television and a lot of endorsement money is rid-ing on this. Whichever one of you wins the first set, you should let your sister win the second set." Though both sisters were playing superbly entering the final, they combined to commit 107 unforced errors, as Venus won, 6–1, 4–6, 6–4. (Richard steadfastly denies any role in the outcome of that match.)

Now at Wimbledon, many wondered again whether the paterfa-milias was pulling the strings. Was it now Venus' "turn" since Serena had the won the U.S. Open? Lindsay Davenport echoed the thoughts of many when she said: "I thought Serena was playing better tennis going into the match, but I personally thought Venus was going to win for outside reasons." Indeed in March of 2001, the *National Enquirer*, admittedly not the most august of sources, published a front-page story with the alarmist headline: "Wimbledon Fixed?" Quoting a live-in nephew and an alleged former lover of Richard's, the article asserted that Richard instructed Serena to lose the match.

Asked by *Sports Illustrated*'s S. L. Price to address the speculation, Richard went bonkers. "That's a goddam shame that people come up with that bullshit," he said. "When McEnroe and his brother played, when Chris Evert and her sister played, no one asked about that. But everyone comes to us with a goddamn bunch of bullshit when it comes to that. You got the two best girls in tennis right here, and if it wasn't for Venus and Serena, this bullshit tennis would be dead, because Hingis and the other girls aren't worth selling. And people come up with a bunch of bullshit like that? That is disgraceful."

While one puts nothing past a man who claims to be buying Rockefeller Center for billions, Williams had a point. For starters, too much was at stake for one sister to throw the match. Had Serena won, she would have beaten out Monica Seles for the final spot on the U.S. Olympic team. And even though Serena aspires to a career in acting, it's hard to imagine that she could manufacture the emotions she exhibited after the match. Besides, there are more plausible reasons why the match fizzled. First, the sisters match up poorly, as they play a similar style that doesn't allow for much contrast. They also know each other's game inside and out. After practicing together for years, it wasn't as if one sister could unveil a secret weapon the other had never seen before. Most important, of course, how does one get motivated to thrash an opponent with whom you long shared a bedroom? History tells us that it's virtually impossible. The Williamess' predecessors—Manuela, Katerina, and Magdalena Maleeva, whose careers overlapped in the eighties and early nineties—were notorious head cases when they had to play each other. Though each of the Bulgarian sisters was a top ten player, they weren't nearly as high in profile and stature as the Williams sisters, so their intrafamily matches went largely unremarked upon. Which is probably a good thing because they were so ugly and freighted with awkwardness that their mother and coach, Yulia, couldn't bear to watch. In more than twenty professional matches among the sisters, the older sibling won every time but once.

The lone exception came when Manuela retired against Katerina after sustaining an injury mid-match. "It was no fun for anyone," recalls Magdelena, who returned to the Tour in 2000 after a shoulder injury and cracked the top twenty. "You were wishing there was some rule saying you didn't have to play against your sister."

Despite Venus and Serena's claims, it strains credulity that the sisters should achieve some cognitive dissonance and regard each another simply as foes and not siblings. Overwhelmed by the situation, overwhelmed by the futile exercise of trying to muster competitive feelings for the person who refused to let her go to bed scared, Serena was beaten before she took her first step on the grass.

After cloistering herself in a toilet stall in the locker room and, other players say, sobbing for half an hour, Serena arrived at the press conference with red, puffy eyes, a baseball cap tugged low on her head. No longer the poised comedienne who had lit up the room during the past week, she answered questions with either acidic or monotonous responses. Both sisters, but Serena especially, pride themselves on being impervious to emotion, immune to pressure. Yet here, with the world watching, Serena had been so overcome by the occasion that she, in essence, choked.

More than an hour after she walked off the court, Venus, too, was unwilling or simply unable to summon much elation. Maybe if the match had been the final, it would have been different. But at the moment, Venus's sisterly solicitude and empathy eclipsed any triumphant feelings. "She's a real competitor, probably even more than I am," Venus said of her sister. "So this really hurts her deep." In the afterglow of perhaps the biggest win of her career, Venus was a big sister first and a tennis player second.

Venus tried to pooh-pooh the difficulty of beating her sister with the world watching, but it had been a miserable experience, "real bitter," she said later. Yet there was at least some benefit from their clash. Venus derived so little satisfaction from the win and was so subdued afterward that it entombed her in an unshakable calm going into the final. There was no celebration and thus there would be no letdown against Lindsay Davenport, who, as usual, had been flying below radar.

The match against Serena had also infused Venus with an unwavering sense of purpose. Richard Williams had made the tactless pronouncement that "this final is Venus's party and Lindsay isn't invited." And though Venus had the good form not to ratify her father's statements publicly, that's essentially how she felt too. "After going through all that with Serena," she said a month later, "there was no way I was going to lose the next match against Lindsay."

While a bruise-colored sky spit rain on the morning of the women's final, Venus sat in the locker room reading and rereading note cards she had written for herself. *Stay relaxed. Stay focused. Bend your knees.* Davenport, who hadn't dropped a set in three previous Grand Slam finals, sat idly and asked attendants for the latest weather report. When the rain ceased and the players took the court twenty minutes later than scheduled, it was clear from the start that the match would be aesthetically unremarkable. Venus was broken by Davenport in the first game. But taking advantage of Davenport's stolid movement, Venus broke back at love. Venus held in the third game, and began to find the range on her percussive strokes, playing judiciously and belting winners whenever Davenport served up a short ball. She also frustrated Davenport with her superior court coverage. On point after demoralizing point, Davenport hit what, against other players, would be a baseline winner only to have the ball come back across the net. After thirty-two minutes, Venus had a 6–3 lead and stood a set away from winning her first Grand Slam.

During changeovers, Venus calmly continued to read her note cards. Her father amused the crowd by holding up bizarre messages on a greaseboard. *We Love the Duke and Duchess. The British Fans are the Best in the World. Hello Mrs. Williams I Love You and Miss You.* Where was Oracene Williams? Watching nervously on television back home in Florida? Hardly. She was driving back from Mississippi with her mother, where they had visited her grandmother's grave. She didn't even know the outcome of the match between Venus and Serena until she got a call on her cell phone outside of Tallahassee. "Oh, really, Venus won," she said nonchalantly. "Well, good luck in the

finals, V." Was she sorry not have been at Wimbledon? "Are you kidding me? They dragged me to Australia and that was enough. I have
my own life to lead."

In the seesaw second set, Davenport regrouped and surged to a 3–1
lead. But Venus served herself out of trouble to go up 5–4, only to have
Davenport break her and then take a 6–5 lead. Now serving to stay
in the set, Venus played a game that demonstrated her evolution as
a player. When Venus went down 0–30, former champion Jana
Novotna, sitting a few rows behind the far baseline—a player only too
familiar with Wimbledon meltdowns—buried her head in her lap.
But Venus wouldn't choke. On the next point, she resisted the tempta-
tion to play tentatively and tagged the baseline with a backhand. She
then belted an ace down the middle. At 30–30, Davenport hit a shot
that would have given her a set point, only to have the ball called out
by the chair umpire. On game point, Venus waited patiently in a baseline rally and induced a forehand error from Davenport. "I amaze
myself sometimes," Venus said later. "I don't know how I got out of
that game."

In the tiebreaker, Venus reeled off five straight points and served
for history at 6–3. "I said to myself, 'Venus, you came and you didn't
play great, but you've been waiting for this opportunity and there's no
way in the world you're losing this.' " Following a baseline exchange,
Davenport attacked, but her volley bounded awkwardly into the net.
With that, a reservoir of Venus' steely resolve morphed into jumping,
spinning joy. Then she gripped Davenport's hand at the net, and
shrieked. Ignoring her father, who was dancing maniacally atop the
NBC broadcast booth, Venus made a beeline to the friends' box.
There, she pushed past the omnipresent business adviser, Leland
Hardy, and reached to embrace her semifinal opponent. As the two sis-
ters hugged, both fought back tears. "You did it, Venus," Serena whispered. "Great job."

Just three weeks after her twentieth birthday, Venus had redemption.
The burdens she had been shouldering three years had vaporized.

There were no longer doubts that she was capable of winning a Grand Slam. There were no longer doubts that she was capable of equaling her little sister's prowess. There were no longer doubts her wrists would prevent her from playing her best tennis. As she jumped into her sister's arms, Venus had never felt lighter.

When the Duchess of Kent handed her the trophy, you would have thought Venus Williams had been raised as a member of the gentry. Witty and gregarious, she charmed a crowd that looked nothing like her, showing aplomb that suggested she had been preparing for this moment for years. She clasped her trophy—aptly named the Venus Rosewater dish—and gazed approvingly at her reflection and said, "I have to say, it is better than the men's cup in my opinion."

The following night Venus wore a long lavender gown she had optimistically picked out before the tournament for the Champions' Dinner at London's Savoy Hotel. She and Serena sat at different tables but exchanged knowing looks the entire evening. They shook their heads in disapproval when Pete Sampras, fresh from his record-breaking victory over Pat Rafter in the men's final, ambled in around midnight wearing a jacket, a tennis shirt, and gray sweatpants. At 12:30, the Williams clan left the party; Venus and Serena still had to play the doubles final the next day—which they would win. It was well past one in the morning when they returned to their house. Serena, resplendent in a pink bodice and a long silk skirt, stopped and admired herself in a mirror. Venus looked at her sister, who as a little girl insisted on going to sleep first. "Serena, we have a big match tomorrow," Venus said wearily. "You need to go to bed."

As Venus became only the second African-American champion to win the Wimbledon women's singles title, the first African-American champion was watching in her modest home in East Orange, New Jersey. It had been forty-three years since Althea Gibson won the first of her two consecutive Wimbledon titles. She's in her seventies now, retired and long out of the public eye, living alone on a meager income. Owing to a degenerative disease, she bears scant resemblance to the powerful, five-eleven woman who defeated Darlene Hard in 1957. Fiercely proud, she rarely leaves her home. Countless journalists have tried to interview Ms. Gibson, only to be rebuffed. Year after year, officials from the United States Tennis Association invite her to the U.S. Open, but she politely declines. When American Express contracted Gibson to be in a recent ad campaign, she agreed but instructed them to use an old photograph. "I think that she wants people to remember her as she was, not as the old, thin woman she is today," says Frances Clayton Gray, Gibson's assistant and the CEO of the Althea Gibson Foundation in Newark. "She's not really able to travel anymore but she's very alert mentally."

At a time when blacks in parts of the United States were still being forced to ride in the backs of buses, Gibson's Wimbledon title was momentous. She was the toast of the Champions' Dinner at the All England Club. Gibson, in keeping with tradition, shared the first dance with the men's champion that year, Lew Hoad, and then danced with various members of the British Royal Family. As she said at the time: "Dancing with the Duke of Kent was a long way from not being allowed to bowl in Jefferson City, Missouri, because white customers complained."

When Gibson won her title, the players were still amateurs. She earned not a dime. Venus Williams earned roughly $650,000 for her feat—and, by extension, millions more in endorsements. Shortly after taking her title, Gibson returned to her seventy-five-dollar-a-week job at a sporting goods store. When her tennis career ended, she played on the women's professional golf tour, did some singing, gave tennis demonstrations before Harlem Globetrotters games, had a bit part in a John Wayne movie, and later gave tennis lessons at parks and clubs on the East Coast. "She has her good days and her bad days," says Clayton Gray. "But she's not a bitter woman at all. She takes very seriously her role as a pioneer." Today, Gibson is an avid golf and tennis fan. Her weekend usually includes grabbing a glass of Ensure dietary supplement and sidling up to her forty-eight-inch television to watch sports. She likes Tiger Woods and Pete Sampras but, not surprisingly, feels a special kinship with the Williams sisters. Venus met Gibson a decade ago, though she doesn't recall precisely where. Awed by the occasion, Venus retreated into a shell and recalls Gibson asking playfully: "How come you're so quiet?"

The day before the 2000 finals, Gibson telephoned Zina Garrison in London and asked her to deliver a short message to Venus: "Move your feet, girl, and bend those knees." Wary of distracting Venus and cluttering her mind, Garrison didn't convey the message until after the match, but it hardly mattered. Venus moved her feet just fine. When the match ended, Gibson sat up straight in her black leather chair in New Jersey, whipped out her remote control, and punched up the volume so she could hear Venus's speech. "She called me up and said, 'I told you: it's their time now,' " says Clayton Gray. "That right there very well could be the happiest day of her year."

When the Wimbledon trophy ceremony was over, the frail African-American woman who shared the same title on the same court nearly a half century ago raised a glass of ginger ale in a silent toast. After more than forty lonesome years, she at last had company.

OPEN SEASON

IF EVER A TENNIS TOURNAMENT CAN BE SAID to take on the qualities of its host city, it's the U.S. Open. Like New York City, the Open is at once energizing and exasperating. Everything about it is massive and monumental. It boasts the biggest purse, the biggest stadium, and the biggest crowds of any event. The pace is frenetic, the fans are loud, the personnel are usually brusque—and occasionally venal—tempers run short, and attitude runs high. Appropriately it was at the 2000 U.S. Open that one photographer *bit* another while jostling for space in the photographers' pit.

Like most of Manhattan, the tournament is barely affordable for those outside the monied class. In 1997, the National Tennis Center, host of the U.S. Open, underwent a sterilizing, soul-sapping face-lift—worthy of newly Disneyfied Times Square—the crown jewel of which, Arthur Ashe Stadium, is a monument to avarice. Access was replaced by excess, as the stadium—too cavernous for tennis—has all the charm of army barracks, and the plethora of corporate boxes pushes the common folk far from the court into vertiginous seats. The bottom line: it's hard to argue with the bottom line—the two-week event grosses well over $100 million and makes more money than all but one American sports franchise, the New York Yankees.

WIPED OUT

Hampered by injuries to both mind and body the first half of 2000, Venus Williams was rumored to be a candidate for early retirement.

WONDERS DOWN UNDER

Davenport (right) was elated to kick off 2000 with a win in Australia, but was miffed about having to doll up and pose with her trophy (middle) on the Yarra. Tanned, toned, and well-armed, Capriati (bottom) began her transformation from cautionary tale to fairy tale with a strong showing at the 2000 Australian Open.

Bill Frakes / *Sports Illustrated*

Bill Frakes / *Sports Illustrated*

NOT A SELES MARKET

Monica Seles started strong with a win at the IGA Superthrift Classic in Oklahoma City (above), but the rest of her year was as dry as the Dust Bowl.

#1 WITH A CAVEAT

Despite failing to win a Major, Martina Hingis held on to the top ranking while her improved relationship with her mother, Melanie Molitor (left), helped her achieve peace off the court.

COMMITMENT-PHOBIC

The WTA's controversial Commitment List (left) rewards players according to their marketability, not match wins.

V. Sanex WTA Tour 2000 BONUS POOL.

A. Gold Exempt Commitment Contracts & Deductions for Withdrawals

There will be a total of $2,020,000 in Commitment Contracts awarded to the 20 Gold Exempt Players. Each Gold Exempt Player will receive a Commitment Contract for committing to the required 13 Tour events exclusive of the Grand Slams and the Chase Championships. A player will receive a deduction from her commitment contract if she misses a commitment tournament.

2000 Gold Exempt List	Commitment Contract $2,020,000	Deduction from Commitment Contract
1. Hingis	$400,000	$60,000
2. Davenport	$400,000	$60,000
3. Williams, V.	$400,000	$60,000
4. Williams, S.	$225,000	$25,000
5. Seles	$100,000	$20,000
6. Kournikova	$100,000	$20,000
7. Pierce	$ 50,000	$10,000
8. Sanchez-Vicario	$ 50,000	$10,000
9. Mauresmo	$ 50,000	$10,000
10. Coetzer	$ 50,000	$10,000
11. Schett	$ 30,000	$ 5,000
12. Halard-DeCugis	$ 30,000	$ 5,000
13. Martinez	$ 30,000	$ 5,000
14. Testud	$ 15,000	$ 5,000*
15. Tauziat	$ 15,000	$ 5,000*
16. Van Roost	$ 15,000	$ 5,000*
17. Capriati	$ 15,000	$ 5,000*
18. Dokic	$ 15,000	$ 5,000*
19. Lucic	$ 15,000	$ 5,000*
20. Stevenson	$ 15,000	$ 5,000*

Bob Martin / *Sports Illustrated*

THE LITTLE INGENUE THAT COULD

There's more to tennis than winning tournaments, as Anna Kournikova's robust endorsement portfolio and fan following proved.

Bob Martin / *Sports Illustrated*

THE EGO HAS LANDED

Never shy about promotion and self-promotion, Richard Williams (above) had the images of his meal tickets painted onto the back of his bus. At Wimbledon, Williams (left) made sure the Centre Court crowds were watching him as much as they were watching his daughters.

SISTERS SLEDGEHAMMER

Giggly and affable off the court, Serena (above) and Venus (below) played with fearsome ferocity between the lines.

TRIED AND TRUE
Oracene Williams said that her daughters, Venus and Serena, were "so close they're like husband and wife." Which is why their historical match in the Wimbledon semifinals (below) fizzled.

Caryn Levy

TOP OF THE WORLD

With two Grand Slams titles, two Olympic gold medals, and a $40 million endorsement deal, Venus Williams stood tallest in 2000.

Stroll through the players' lounge and ask the competitors to describe the event and answers range from "hell," to "chaos," to "prison," to "boot camp." Then there are those who don't like it. For players, if they can make it there, they can make it anywhere. Gone are the days when planes landing at nearby Laguardia Airport flew so low they were in danger of being hit by a lob, the locker rooms were roughly the size of an airplane lavatory, and the scent of rancid grease from ten-dollar hamburgers wafted over the courts. But the list of gripes from the players is still long. Chief among them are the traffic that can make the eight-mile drive from a midtown Manhattan hotel last an hour, the capitulation to television scheduling that causes matches to be shuffled like a version of three-card monte, and the abundance of night matches—in the city that never sleeps, matches can last well into the infomercial hours.

Still, like its host city, the Open succeeds in spite of itself. Splendidly in fact. With the Unisphere, that massive, metallic globe serving as a symbolic backdrop, players from all over the world come to Queens for the final Slam of the year. Played on the most democratic surface, DecoTurf II, the U.S. Open crowns the year's true tennis champions. It may lack the prestige of Wimbledon, the charm of the French, and the bonhomie of the Australian. But there's a distinct sense among the players that, finally, it's the Major that matters most. There are dozens more events and buckets of ranking points and prize money still on the table for the rest of the year after the Open. But, for all intents, you can cue the credits on the tennis season in Queens the weekend after Labor Day. The U.S. Open is the year-end blowout, the season finale of a year's worth of episodes. It's where conflicts are resolved, the subplots culminate, and the characters reveal their true colors. By the time the tournament ends, and summer has imperceptibly transitioned into fall, everything in tennis has crystallized.

Venus Williams came to New York playing the best tennis of her life, the proprietor of a nineteen-match winning streak that included three hard-court titles since her triumph at Wimbledon. Her manifold gifts coalescing, she had finally blossomed into the dominating player her father envisioned so many years ago. She was covering the court better than any player in history and retrieving balls that would scarcely draw a wave from others players. Though her matches were still pocked by too many double faults for her liking, her simplified service motion was paying off handsomely. Her first serve was regularly exceeding 120 miles an hour and her *second* balls were flying over the net at 100 miles an hour, an unheard-of velocity in women's tennis. Scouting reports on Venus uniformly list her forehand—particularly the crosscourt variety—as the stroke most likely to fall into disrepair under pressure; but it was now every bit as reliable as her backhand. At the Open, she was the third seed in name only. Everyone knew she was the odds-on favorite; the real drama was whether she would take on Serena in an all-Williams final.

Like most players, Venus' demeanor swings in lockstep with her match results. Late in the summer she was fairly giddy with self-assurance. "I must say I've been playing pretty unbelievable," she said with a wide smile before the Open began. "There's nobody out there hitting the ball like I am." Not even Serena? "Nah, I don't think so. I'm sorry, but I don't."

A player who had been written off for dead just a few months earlier was now the most feared woman in tennis. And she knew it. "I definitely think that when players walk onto the court with me they feel a little intimidated," Venus said. "I don't think they feel they can run through me, or even win the match. I think they're going to come out and give a good effort, but I don't really think they feel in their hearts they can win."

As well as she had been playing, she knew her redemption would be incomplete unless she emerged as the queen of Queens. A year before, she suffered through perhaps the lowest moment of her life, losing to Hingis in the semis. Now she was back at the scene of the crime. While Serena, the defending champ, was omnipresent—appearing on the network morning shows, showing off a stunning lilac tie-dye outfit, ringing the ceremonial opening bell on Wall Street—Venus kept the lowest of profiles. With a detached look on her face and ramrod straight posture, she walked purposefully and regally around the grounds, stopping for no one. During a changeover in one of her matches, she was so focused, staring into her racket strings, concentrating on the task at hand, that she missed her chair and plopped down on the macadam.

The confidence that had eluded her earlier in the year was back in full force. But Venus quickly learned that, in tennis, uneasy lies the head that wears the crown. Throughout the two-week event, she was a marked woman, the target of potshots from players and the press. Early on, Pete Sampras took an uncharacteristic swipe at her, claiming that she had little idea where her powerful serve was headed. Though Venus downplayed the comment—"I think I know where it's going," she said—she was hurt that one of the players she respected most (and the object of a brief crush) would diss her. During the second week, Venus and her sister were the enemies in a catty axis between Martina Hingis and Lindsay Davenport, who vowed to make the final a no-Williams affair. An even nastier, and more protracted, attack came from John McEnroe.

Not long after the Williams family had moved from California to Florida, Serena and Venus saw McEnroe play on television. "Look at that ugly forehand," they screamed, then perhaps nine- and eleven-years-old. "We can beat him! We can beat him!" The next day they told their coach, Rick Macci. "Get us a match against McEnroe!," they demanded. "He's not that good." The match never came about, but a decade later the roles were reversed. At the U.S. Open it was McEnroe who acted like the snotty brat, clamoring for a match against the sisters.

In a profile in *The New Yorker,* McEnroe declared that "any good male college player could beat the Williams sisters, and so could any man on the senior tour"—i.e. John McEnroe. The statement served little purpose other than to demean the Williams sisters specifically and women's sports generally. But perhaps fearful that he would slip from the public consciousness after his forthcoming resignation as Davis Cup captain, McEnroe wasn't finished. He then challenged either sister to a winner-take-all charity match. "I think they are great players, but let's call a spade a spade," he said, using an incendiary bit of slang. Donald Trump, a man unencumbered by taste, beat the drums and his chest, offering to put up $1 million. McEnroe offered to move to Tanzania if he lost, the one prospect that made the match slightly tantalizing.

The House of Williams deftly brushed McEnroe off like he were lint on their flared lapels. "You want a piece of me?" Serena said facetiously. Venus added, "I don't know if I can fit him in my schedule right now. Besides, I don't think it's fair to put a twenty-year-old against a fortysomething person. So I'll let that pass." Bjorn Borg jumped into the fray as well, boasting that, at age forty-four, he too could beat the top women. More amused than offended by all this bravado, Hingis laughed it off as "male vanity." Rarely one to pass up an opportunity to talk trash, even Hingis had to roll her eyes this time. "It's kindergarten stuff," she said. Richard Williams was less entertained. He marched into the USA network's office under Arthur Ashe Stadium and warned McEnroe, who was covering the matches, not to mention his challenge on the air. "My daughters are trying to win a damn tennis tournament and they don't need no distractions," barked Richard. McEnroe's response: "I knew Richard was a smart guy and this only reinforced that. Richard knows it's best to keep his daughters away from Johnny Mac."

The sisters' indifference only annoyed McEnroe further. After the tournament, he told the *London Sunday Telegraph* that Venus and Serena both "lack respect and humility." He added: "They are as cold as ice. Would it kill them to say hello to people in the locker room? Is it that hard?" The irony of one of the most ill-behaved players in tennis history dispensing tips on decorum made the spat particularly surreal. It was also absurd that the same man who repeatedly bemoans the absence of compelling figures on the ATP would take aim at perhaps the two most dynamic figures in women's sports.

On his original point, though, McEnroe is right: the Williams sisters probably couldn't beat a lot of male college players. Just as the best female basketball player wouldn't last a minute in the NBA, Marion Jones would get dusted by Maurice Greene, and Karrie Webb wouldn't make a cut on the PGA Tour. The Williams sisters, in fact, had already competed against a male player. At the 1998 Australian

Open they took turns playing sets against Karsten Braasch, a quirky, thirtysomething German ranked outside the top two hundred, who is best known for inspiring an ATP Tour edict that prohibits players from smoking during changeovers. The closest either sister came was 6–2.

But . . . so what? The gap may be narrowing, but physical, psychological, and even hormonal differences between genders will always make it impossible for women to compete with men at the elite levels of sport. And why should they? The beauty—the hypocrisy, critics might say—of women's sports is that it's one of the few areas where females aren't seeking integration. A woman's sport exists for itself; the objective is not to play with the boys. Just as many fans prefer college basketball to the NBA, the superior players don't necessarily yield the superior product and the superior entertainment. The wealth of arresting personalities and the textured rivalries in women's tennis generate infinitely more intrigue than the men's game that features the technically better, but infinitely blander, stars. Venus finally put the issue to rest by saying it most eloquently: "I'm a lady. I don't *want* to play with the men's tour. The ladies' tour is where it's good to be right now. I want to be right here."

Besides, Venus had more pressing concerns than a no-win proposition from an increasingly less relevant man. In her third round match, she faced the young American Meghann Shaughnessy in Arthur Ashe Stadium. A reed-thin baseliner who had never won a pro title, Shaughnessy, twenty-one, figured to offer little resistance against the hottest player on Tour. But as a sticky shroud of evening humidity descended on Flushing Meadows, Shaughnessy jumped to a 3–0 lead, fearlessly attacking Williams's serve from inside the baseline, taking the ball on the rise and "hitting out" whenever possible.

Venus steadied her game and closed to 4–3 but Shaughnessy smacked a forehand winner on break point to go up 5–3. That only served as Williams's cue to dig in. She broke back and pushed the set to 6–6, by gradually directing Shaughnessy off the court and then wailing away on a short ball. In the first set tiebreaker Venus suffered her fifth and sixth double faults and was down 1–2. Most players would have played cautiously, but on her next service, Venus cranked a colossal 118-mile-an-hour stinger to the corner. After Venus won the tiebreaker, she settled into something resembling a rhythm, and took advantage of a few loose games from Shaughnessy. She cruised home, 7–6, 6–1, extending her winning streak to twenty-two matches. When Venus left the court, she offered a perfunctory wave, tinged in disappointment at her performance.

The lackluster match was a source of encouragement in the women's locker room. If a borderline top fifty player could serve for the set and take seven games from Venus, perhaps she was not invincible. Even Shaughnessy said: "I definitely think she's beatable." But on closer examination, Venus' victory should have been dispiriting for the rest of the field. This throwaway match said as much about her evolution as her subsequent throw-downs with Davenport and Hingis. On an off night, she extricated herself from peril by battling through her errors and summoning the "Plan B" she is too often accused of lacking. The days of her breaking down, packing it in, or mysteriously contracting an injury when she was on the verge of defeat were clearly in the past tense. "I just feel like whatever it takes, I'm going to get it done," Venus said after the match. "Losing is just not in my vocabulary right now. That's a good feeling to have."

Only three months earlier, Alison Bradshaw had been a member of the Arizona State tennis team. Now, on the first Friday of the U.S. Open, she was playing former champion Arantxa Sanchez Vicario for a spot in the fourth round. A nineteen-year-old from San Diego with flame-red hair and swimming-pool-blue eyes, Bradshaw took a wild card to get into the main draw of the Open, her first Tour event. She made good use of it. In her first match, she blasted away Sarah Pitkowski, a top fifty player, and then exacted revenge on Marissa Irvin, her rival in the juniors and in college. Hitting flat, penetrating strokes and a big serve, Bradshaw played like a seasoned pro, opening up the court and showing the "controlled aggression" that junior coaches are forever preaching.

Afterward, her facade of poise collapsed in the players' cafeteria. At the stage in her career when pro tennis still has an Omigod luster, she looked as though she was there on a backstage pass, not a competitors' badge. She nearly got whiplash craning her neck to peer at Lindsay Davenport and then Pete Sampras as they walked by. When college friends called on her cell phone—a "turning pro present" from her parents—she picked up without first checking caller ID, a dead give-away that she was a novice pro. "I know, it's soooo cool," she whispered into the phone, absentmindedly fingering her constellation of earrings. "I'm doing an interview right now, but I'll call you right back when I'm done."

For all of her pop-eyed awe, Bradshaw, had some sense of the Tour's culture before she turned pro. Her mother, Valerie Ziegenfuss, was one of the original nine insurgents who founded the women's tour nearly thirty years ago. To her slight embarrassment, Bradshaw admitted that she is fuzzy on the details of her mother's struggles. But even that shows how far women's tennis has come. Bradshaw got $35,000 for reaching the third round. To her, the days of women playing a tournament with a total purse of $7,500 and fighting for opportunities to play may as well have been the Paleolithic Era. In fact, as Bradshaw played, four promoters were meeting with Bart McGuire, vying to pay the Tour millions for the rights to hold a new Tier II event during the less-than-ideal third week in September. "You could say things have changed a lot," said Bradshaw with a shrug. "I know that much."

In her next match, against Arantxa Sanchez Vicario, Bradshaw learned the difference between a fourteen-year pro and a fourteen-week pro. In front of her mom and grandparents, Bradshaw overcame a spasm of nerves and played a strong first set against Sanchez Vicario and pushed her to a tiebreaker. Though her scouting notebooks are still thin, Bradshaw knew enough to pressure Sanchez Vicario's uneven forehand and attack her second serve. In the second set, how-ever, Bradshaw started feeling the physical effects of playing three matches in four days and wilted, losing 7–6, 6–0. Still, neither she nor her mom, now a USTA junior coach, could suppress a smile when the match ended. Suddenly ranked in the top two hundred, Bradshaw had instant validation for her decision to quit school and become a second-generation WTA Tour pro.

As Bradshaw's career got off to an auspicious start, another American reached the inevitable end of hers. Debbie Graham could have turned pro in 1988, when she was the top-ranked eighteen-year-old in the United States. Her goal, though, was to become the first college graduate to be ranked in the top twenty, so she went to Stanford. After earning her degree in economics and political science in just three years, she joined the Tour full-time in 1992 and was named Newcomer of the Year. At six feet, Graham had a booming serve and a deft pair of hands that made her a top doubles player. By age twenty-three, she was a top fifty player, a Fed Cup team member, and for a brief spell in 1993 was America's top-ranked female pro.

Her career took a scary turn after she lost in the first round of Wimbledon in 1995. On the flight home, Graham's leg began throbbing and she iced it for hours. When the plane touched down in San Francisco, Graham disembarked, but just inside the terminal, she fainted and went into seizures. In the ambulance from the airport to the hospital, Graham's heart stopped beating and was restarted only after she was given an injection of adrenaline. She woke up in the intensive care unit of a local Catholic hospital, surrounded by friends and family. Wary of scaring her, they told her that she had fainted. Lindsay Davenport, a good friend, called Graham a few hours later from Wimbledon. "Oh my God, are you okay?" Davenport asked.

"Yeah, I just passed out," Graham said.

"Uh, Debbie," Davenport said. "You need to find out what really happened."

What really happened was that Graham had suffered from deep vein thrombosis, a blood clot in her leg that carried to her lungs. After ten days in intensive care, she was released, but she shudders to think what might have happened had she passed out while the plane was in midair or had Patty Fendick-McCain, an American player with her on the flight, not suggested the possibility of clotting to paramedics.

Following eighteen months of recovery, Graham returned to the

Tour in 1997, but her singles ranking had imploded. Now taking blood-thinner medication, Graham promised herself she would take it easy and make a concerted effort to enjoy her privileged life as a tennis player. She concentrated primarily on doubles, got involved in Tour politics, and cultivated friendships with other players. "Before, I was trying to make as much money as I could, missing weddings and losing touch with friends," she says. "As a human being, I felt like I was stagnating."

In January 2000, she and her doubles partner, Nana Miyagi, reached the quarterfinals of the Australian Open, but two months later, at a Challenger event in West Palm Beach, Florida, she contracted another clot spanning from her left calf to her thigh. She had a hellish experience in a local hospital, waiting hours to be seen by a doctor and then being told that she had cancer. With the help of Corina Morariu's father, a doctor at a nearby hospital, her clot was correctly diagnosed. Immediately put on blood thinners, she recovered quickly this time, but it was a clarion call for her to retire. "It's frustrating because I can still play," she said. "But when you're not supposed to sit still very long and shouldn't take long flights, it's hard to be a professional tennis player."

Graham scheduled her swan song for the week of her thirtieth birthday at the U.S. Open, the tournament that first gave her a wild card in 1988. She had hoped to play her last doubles match with Davenport, but when that didn't work out, she paired with Katarina Srebotnik. Playing together for the first time, they won their opening round match, as Graham's parents and boyfriend looked on. Two days later, Graham and Srebotnik pushed the seventh-seeded team, Anke Huber and Barbara Schett, to three sets before falling. As she packed up her racket bag for the last time as a pro, she had conflicting emotions: disappointment, elation, nostalgia, insecurity about leaving tennis, excitement about moving on. Most of all, she was disgusted with how she had played. "I thought it might be romantic playing my last match at the U.S Open, but not when you play like this," she said with a dramatic sigh an hour after the match. "Oh well. Real world, here I come."

Sandwiched between Bradshaw's alpha and Graham's omega, the career of Croatia's Mirjana Lucic was at a crucial middle stage. A Wimbledon semifinalist in 1999, Lucic was among the twenty players on the Tour's Gold Exempt Commitment list for 2000 and was eligible for a $15,000 bonus from the Tour simply for entering the requisite number of tournaments. No less an expert than Steffi Graf proclaimed that Lucic was destined for greatness. Yet after her success at Wimbledon and finishing 1999 ranked in the top fifty, her game went into free fall. Having won just three matches in 2000, Lucic, eighteen, came to the U.S. Open a week earlier than she had expected to, because she had to endure the indignity of winning three qualifying matches just to make the main draw.

Lucic can't pinpoint why, when, or where it happened, but at some point she misplaced her work ethic. She fell prey to the vicious cycle that has afflicted countless other players. The more she lost, the more her confidence and motivation flagged; the more her confidence and motivation flagged, the more her fitness level dropped; the more her fitness level dropped, the more she lost. As the defeats mounted, she parted ways with her coach, Joe Guiliano. Her management firm dropped her as well. "Once you lose your focus and confidence, it's trouble," says Lucic, who speaks perfect English, "It's not like you can get it back the next day."

Lucic's decline is clearly tied to her relationship with her father. Lucic says that the day before her sixteenth birthday in 1998, she lost to a lesser player. Marinko Lucic punished his daughter by forcing her to spend her birthday locked in her room. At night, she says, she was permitted to leave in order to practice her serve. A few months later at Wimbledon, her father beat her, she alleges, after she lost the doubles final. "I went through terrible things people my age just shouldn't have to go through," Mirjana says. After the Wimbledon assault, Mirjana, her mother, and four siblings left Marinko in Croatia and moved to a three-bedroom home in Florida. Mirjana has had no contact with her father since.

In the summer of 2000, Lucic asked Harold Solomon, the career resuscitator, to apply the defib paddles to her floundering game.

Within a few weeks of hooking up with Solomon, she had lost nine of the twenty-five pounds she wanted to shed. With a blond, butt-length ponytail dragging behind her like a rudder, she was back to pounding her ground strokes and using her six-foot frame to bludgeon serves. But she was still a long way from her former self. In her first match at the U.S. Open, she fell to an inferior player, Kristie Boogert, in three sets, done in by her poor conditioning. Afterward, Lucic was realistic. "I'm not happy with how I played," she said. "But things are going in the right direction. Little by little, I'm going to make it back."

Though she was one of the most promising teens on the circuit, Jelena Dokic was better known for her father's boorishness than for her tennis. By the U.S. Open, Damir Dokic was such a constant source of strife that Tour officials had discussed banning him from events, much as they did with Jim Pierce. Part of the problem, though, was Jelena, who wanted her father around and vigorously defended him. Not only did she reject offers of help from administrators, but she blamed Tour officials for the troubles her father faced.

On the first day of the Open, Damir was on his best behavior. After watching Jelena dissect Israel's Anna Smashnova, he even sat down for a rare interview with Filip Bondy of the *New York Daily News*. He proclaimed his great loves to be "women, wine, food, and kids—by women, I mean women. Not wife." He added that he'd had nothing to drink that day. "Today, I skip. I just smoke." His ride on the wagon didn't last long. The next day, Jelena finished her doubles match and joined her father for lunch in the players' cafeteria. Served a ten-dollar portion of salmon that was too small for his liking, Damir exploded. "What is this? This is ten fucking dollars? This is it?" he screamed at the cook, Mattie Jones. A U.S. Open employee since 1988, Jones responded, "Yeah, that's it." Reeking of alcohol, Damir called Jones a "cow" and bellowed, "Fuck the U.S. Open! I'm not paying for this shit!"

The tournament's security chief, Pete Pistone, ushered Damir out of the cafeteria through the upstairs lounge, and then tried to eject him from the facility. Passing Jim Fuhse, Damir threw his credential at him. He also lightly pushed Brenda Perry, one of the Tour's directors. When Damir physically resisted his ejection, Pistone grabbed him by the scruff of the neck. "You want to get smart with me?" Pistone asked. "You're a fascist man!" Damir yelled as he was tossed out. With players nearby transfixed as if watching a schoolyard fight, Damir continued his rant in the parking lot. At one point he grabbed his daughter's credential off her neck and tossed it in the air. He also got nose to nose with Fuhse, and screamed, "This is the biggest fucking crime in the world! WTA Tour steals from little girls!" When Damir noticed that his daughter was crying, he gave her a tight hug, kissed her face repeatedly, and wiped the tears from her eyes. He then tried to reenter the grounds, only to be rebuffed by Pistone. Damir was eventually pushed into the passenger seat of a courtesy SUV and, with Jelena crying in the backseat, driven back to the Intercontinental Hotel in midtown Manhattan.

Were it not for a lapse at the French Open, Damir might well have pulled off the first Grand Slam for obnoxious behavior—he had now created an ugly scene at three of the Majors. Barely an hour later, the USTA issued a statement that Damir Dokic had been ejected for "abusive behavior" and was barred from returning to the tournament. Photos of Dokic were also distributed to the tournament guards in case he tried to sneak in to watch his daughter, though it was hardly necessary as his unmistakable bearded visage would be splayed on the back page of the *New York Post* the following day.

The prevailing sentiment in the players' lounge was massive sympathy for Jelena. "I feel sorry for her," Australian Mark Philippoussis said a few hours after L'Affaire Damir: Part Three. "She's so young, she should be enjoying herself. When I played mixed doubles with her in Hopman Cup [the annual one-week, coed equivalent of Davis Cup] she didn't look like a happy sixteen-year-old girl. She's not. She's not smiling out there."

In the women's locker room, compassion for Jelena was coupled with unbridled disgust for Damir. Players are generally unstinting in their criticisms of the Tour. The purses are weak, the season is too

long, the management groups have too much pull. But when an outsider embarrasses their sport, they close ranks. With unconcealed dismay, players correctly predicted that the day's matches would be writ
small by Damir's latest eruption. Particularly at the biggest tournament of the year—when deals are cut, sponsors are courted, and the
media coverage is unparalleled—the players deeply resented the
sideshow Damir had yet again created. "This has happened a number
of times and it's probably time he be reprimanded," said Lindsay Davenport. "I don't know if he's doing it for attention or if he just likes to
insult people. I'm not really sure, but it's a shame."

As she had at Wimbledon, Jelena exhibited a remarkable ability to
compartmentalize her father's sociopathic behavior. The following
day, six television camera crews trailing her from the locker room to
the court, Dokic overpowered the Netherlands' Miriam Oremans.
Jelena declined to answer specific questions about her father and deftly
parried all innuendo. Two days later, as Damir watched from his hotel,
Jelena beat Italian qualifier Francesca Schiavone to advance to the
fourth round. On Labor Day, Jelena faced Serena Williams in Arthur
Ashe Stadium for a berth in the quarterfinals. Time and again, Jelena
reflexively peered into the players' box, looking for her father, only to
realize he was elsewhere. But forty minutes into the match, she was
playing superb tennis, hitting winners and matching Williams' power.
At one point she even pumped her fist *at* Williams, an act of true
courage—and disregard for her physical well-being. Up set point in a
tiebreaker, Dokic took a ball in the middle of the court and rifled a
backhand that appeared to clip the sideline. The ball was called out,
the chair refused to intervene, and the match effectively ended right
there. Williams went on to win the set and took the second 6–0. Dokic
later all but admitted that she'd packed it in once that close call went
against her. After a chaotic week, she had finally reached her personal
break point.

At an age when the majority of her peers cringe at the notion of
being in the same area code as their parents, Jelena continued to show
a strange lack of embarrassment for her father's Vesuvian eruptions.

"I've said this many times. I have a great relationship with my dad. I like having him around," she said nonchalantly. "It doesn't bother me at all."

In the players' lounge, Mary Pierce, who had been through similar experiences, shook her head. "Nothing's going to change until she wants it to change." The day after the tournament ended, the WTA Tour announced that it was banning Damir Dokic from all Tour events until April 1, 2001.

As for the other reliable circus act in women's tennis, Annamania raged as fiercely as ever at the National Tennis Center. Her practice sessions were mobbed. The "Anna, Will You Marry Me?" banners abounded. An autograph session at the Chase bank corporate booth drew more fans than the men's match going on simultaneously in Arthur Ashe Stadium. "The madhouse continues," Jim Fuhse said, amusedly shaking his head. "Don't these people ever get sick of her?"

Kournikova came into the Open playing what she characterized as the best tennis of her career. Having dumped her coach, Van Harpen—who promptly complained that Kournikova lacked discipline and was every bit the prima donna she's made out to be—Kournikova had scored wins in the California tournaments over Davenport, Testud, and Tauziat. In Queens, she was on schedule for a rematch against Davenport in the fourth round and needed only to beat Justine Henin, a talented but hardly battle-tested Belgian teenager who had been sidelined with a wrist injury for most of the year. Henin has the soft, cherubic features becoming a Vermeer subject, but she is tough. Her mother, Francoise, died in 1994 after a battle with cancer. Her father, Jose, quit his job as a post office manager to tend to his wife, strapping the family financially. Mature beyond her years, Henin is like a miniaturized Davenport, focused on winning matches and impatient with all the ancillary pomp and publicity. Effectively deploying a gorgeous one-handed backhand and a crisp forehand, she too had taken a set off Davenport two weeks before the Open in Montreal and had beaten Kournikova late in 1999. On this day, she single-handedly reversed Kournikova's summer progress.

Before a packed house at Arthur Ashe Stadium—Davenport, a former champion, a higher seed, and an American, was simultaneously
relegated to Louis Armstrong Stadium—Henin won a tight first set
6–4 and then surged to a 3–1 lead in the second. A point from 4–1, she
opened the court masterfully and positioned herself for a gimme volley. Henin, though, tightened. Inexplicably, she pushed the ball back to
Kournikova, who uncorked a lob over Henin's head. Henin froze in
disbelief and her coach, Carlos Rodrigues, buried his head. Dazed, she
chomped on her lower lip and slogged back to the baseline. It was the
type of squandered opportunity that can turn a match. Sure enough,
Henin dropped that game and the next. With Alla gesticulating desperately for her daughter to attack the net, Anna was suddenly serving
for the set at 5–4.

With the match in her grasp, it was Kournikova's chance to choke.
Playing a style that Henin later described as "no variety," Kournikova
simply batted the ball back over the net. She lost her serve and the
second set went to a tiebreak. Clearly the more nervous player,
Kournikova continued playing tactically vacant tennis, taking only a
few seconds between serves, eager, it appeared, to get off the stage.
Down match point, she pushed a short ball to the middle of the court
that Henin was obliged to attack. Henin hit a mediocre approach and
then floated a sitting duck of a volley back to Kournikova. With ample
time and a multitude of options, Kournikova smacked a forehand into
the net, that, even had it cleared, was directed right at Henin. Just like
that, the most watched streak in tennis had extended to seventy-eight
tournaments.

When the match ended, gleeful security guards at the lip of the
players' entrance exchanged high fives. "She lost! She lost!" one guard
shouted to his colleague posted in front the women's locker room. "All
week she and her mom have been acting like they're God's gift," he
said euphorically. "Now they're both outta here." Kournikova
deployed her usual charm with the media afterward.

Anna, how disappointing was your loss?

"Disappointing."

How do you really feel?

"Disappointed."

Do your outside interests distract you?

"I don't have any. I don't have any. I don't have any."

Henin pumped her fist fiercely at the pro-Kournikova crowd after taking match point, but otherwise there was no celebrating. Possessed of a champion's mind-set, she perceived the match not as an upset but as a perfectly logical result. "I showed that when I was aggressive, when I went to the net, when I attacked, I was better than her," Henin said. "She likes her look and everybody likes her look. But I am here to play tennis and I think that's most important. I am not here to do cinema." It all made for compelling theater nevertheless.

When she took the court against Martin Hingis for their quarterfinal match, Monica Seles was trying desperately to forget the 6–0, 6–0 pratfall in Key Biscayne. Since that low moment, she had played steadily, improved her fitness, and managed to avoid injury. One cogent statistic, though, summed up Seles's year: she hadn't dropped a match to any of the forty-six lower-ranked opponents she had faced, but she had yet to beat a higher-ranked one. On a chilly, blustery evening, form held.

Thanks to snarled traffic in Manhattan caused by the United Nations Millennium Summit, the seats and boxes at Arthur Ashe Stadium were perhaps 10 percent filled when Hingis served the first ball of the match. Thirteen minutes later, fans were trickling into the stands, and the first set had already gone to Hingis, 6–0. Betraying the body language of a defeated player, Seles had won just five points and had dispensed errors like so many Halloween treats. Dating back to their match at Indian Wells, Hingis had now won more than twenty consecutive games from her. Seles could easily have packed it in, but to her credit, she didn't. After dropping the first game of the second set, she held her serve to the delight of the crowd. There was something heartrending about a former champion being showered with hosannas for winning a solitary game; but the attention and support galvanized Seles. She broke Hingis at 3–2, firing up a little something for the memory banks with her signature two-fisted return at an impossibly acute angle. The two exchanged baseline sniper fire for the next five games and suddenly the score was 5–5. Hingis had surrendered more games in the previous twenty minutes than she had in any of her four previous matches. "All of sudden I looked at the score," Hingis said. "I was like, 'I've got to take control of the match again.' " As if it were no more difficult than that, she clicked her heels, whipped a few lasers, took advantage of several Seles short balls, and closed out the evening 6–0, 7–5.

As Seles exited the court, there was the obligatory raucous ovation and shouts of "We Love You, Monica!" She waved, smiled, and then disappeared into the locker room. "I hate playing Monica," she said, and grinned. It was an odd sentiment, given that she clearly had Seles's number and had allowed her all of five games in their previous four sets. "Not for the tennis," Hingis later explained. "It's the fans. Wherever we play—the States, Europe, Asia, Australia—they are always for her and against me."

Disheartened with her performance, Seles had a massage and then cleaned out her locker like a baseball player after the season's 162nd game. Her coach, Bobby Banck, sat in sullen silence in the players' lounge, staring emptily at a blank television monitor, wondering how, as he put it, "Monica could take that next step." Seles's mother, Esther, sat quietly near Banck, the family's Yorkshire terrier, Ariel, in her lap. A good ninety minutes after the match ended, Seles emerged from the locker room, her tumescent blue Yonex bag slung over her shoulder. The faith of a small cluster of loyal fans that had waited outside the players' entrance for Seles was finally rewarded. As Seles scrawled "MS" on an oversized tennis ball, the holder said, "I know you'll do better next year, Monica." As if trying to convince herself, Monica said, "Thanks, I think I will too." Her face expressionless, Seles then climbed into the backseat of a Lincoln Navigator. As the door slammed, the car drove off into the cold night, the sun having set long ago.

VENUS ENVY

AT ARTHUR ASHE KIDS DAY, A TENNIS CAR-
nival held on the National Tennis Center grounds the weekend
before the U.S. Open, a young girl no taller than a net post inquired to
Lindsay Davenport how long she had been playing tennis. "Too long,"
Davenport growled.

Following her torrid start in 2000, Davenport's year had slowly disintegrated. Since beating Hingis at Indian Wells in March, she hadn't
won another title. And after failing to win a tournament on the summer California leg that she had dominated for the past few years, she
was forced to withdraw from the Canadian Open with a foot injury.
Add to that a chronically sore groin and a back that still stiffened at
inopportune times and she was a walking Ace bandage. She had a
boyfriend at home, stockpiles of money in her back account, and a
body that seemed to be crumbling. The bellwether for "well-adjusted"
in a culture of divas, she was once amused by tennis's ambient psy-
chodrama and dysfunction; now the scene simply repelled her. In
short, Davenport was at a professional, if not an existential, crossroads.

She still coveted Grand Slam titles. She still hated to lose, particularly to the Williams sisters. And she still had years of obligations left
on her endorsement deals. But what was she chasing? To this point,

her career had been unexpectedly brilliant. When she joined the Tour, no one—not least herself—would have predicted that she'd win three Grand Slam titles and achieve the top ranking. She had surpassed all expectations. But at age twenty-four, she was now too old to pursue immortality and make a push to join the pantheon of legends with names like King, Court, Evert, Navratilova, and Graf. How much longer could she endure the string of injuries, an atrophying game, and the peripatetic lifestyle that put her in one nondescript hotel suite after another? "In the summer, it was probably the first time I was thinking, 'I don't know why I'm still doing this,' " she conceded. "Eight years—it's a long time for anyone to do a job as taxing as this one."

But with most of the attention and the high-intensity lighting directed on the Williams sisters, Davenport stealthily advanced, playing her best tennis in months at the Open. She dropped a set in her second round match to Belgium's Kim Clijsters, a future top ten player, but by the time she faced Serena Williams in the quarterfinals she was moving well and hitting the ball cleanly. "Tennis is a lot more fun when you're healthy and playing well," she observed. "You try not to take your results off the court with you, but that's easier said than done."

During Labor Day weekend, Davenport was whiling away time playing with her three-year-old niece, Kennedy, in the players' lounge during a rain delay. Mid-pattycake, Hingis happened by. Anticipating—correctly—that Davenport would play Serena in the quarterfinals, Hingis playfully said: "Okay, come on, you have to do this, finally. You never win. *Beat her.*" Davenport told Hingis she expected her to take out Venus in return. It wasn't the first time the world's top two players had had such a discussion. When Davenport lost to Serena at the 1999 U.S. Open, she returned to the locker room to find Hingis clucking her tongue and staring like a disappointed parent. A few weeks later at the 1999 Porsche Grand Prix in Filderstadt, when Davenport pulled out with a wrist injury. Hingis and her mother approached her. Hingis said plaintively: "You gotta hurry back. I can't play the Williamses on my own."

When "the pact" was reported in the papers, Davenport and Hingis said that it was in good fun and had been blown out of proportion. But Oracene Williams was outraged by the ad hoc alliance. She thought there was a lacerating racial edge to it. "It's just the whole black experience. The odds are always that someone is going to gang up on you because they are jealous of the press, or whatever it is. That just comes with the territory with us. I take [the pact] very seriously in that way. Because of who Venus and Serena are, even the worst girl in the world would get up to play them more than she'd get up to play their counterparts. I prepared them for this. There's so much jealousy on the part of the other girls, it's not even funny. Why? They can't compete with Venus and Serena. And I don't just mean on the court. In the Causasian community, in order to be a good athlete you had to look like a man. Well, my girls have shown that's not true. When they act like women, look like women, and still play the game so well and make the type of money they're making, other players have a big problem with that. But that's the reality of being black."

Venus and Serena, as it turned out, were seething too. Venus wanted to publicize the back-biting and express her outrage to the media but was instructed by a Tour staff member to take the high road. "Why do *I* always have to be the one to take the high road?" she protested. But when asked about the alliance the next day, she made light of it. "It's getting like the WWF." Venus laughed. "You know, tag team."

Prior to the match against Serena, Davenport and Van't Hof were cloistered in the small travel office in the players' lounge conferring about strategy. Davenport, they agreed, would lace her shots with her customary pace and depth; but instead of aiming for the corners, she would hit to the middle of the court and "hit back" relentlessly to the same spot. She might not record as many outright winners as usual, but she would eliminate angles, making it difficult for Serena, the superior athlete, to open up the court.

The game plan worked masterfully. In a match that had the attendant buzz of a Grand Slam final, Davenport goaded Williams into twenty-seven errors, most on backhands that sailed three, four, and sometimes five feet past the baseline. At one point, Williams was so exasperated by an errant shot that she cracked her racket on the court. Davenport was plenty intense too. After a line call went against her, Davenport angrily offered the chair umpire a thousand dollars to check the mark and maintain that her call was correct.

After converting a break point by inducing yet another Williams miss, Davenport served out the first set 6–4. From there, she tightened her grip, dashing to a 5–1 lead in the second. Serving to stay in the match, Serena staved off five match points in a twenty-point game that featured breathtaking thunderbolt hurling from both players. When Serena won the game on an ace, Davenport hung her head as she walked slowly toward her chair. Her mood brightened, though, when she looked at the scoreboard. She had been so focused on the previous game that she momentarily forgot she still led 5–2. Energized, she bounded up from her chair and deftly served out the match. Her midlife tennis crisis had been averted.

Serena quickly packed her bag, stifling her tears until she reached the locker room, where Venus arrived to comfort her. Outside, Richard leaned on a trash can and mumbled to no one in particular, "She didn't play with no common sense." In the post-match press conference, Serena was even testier than usual after a loss. "Obviously, no one would want to see an all-Williams final because everybody doesn't really like us," snapped Serena, a thinly cloaked reference to the Davenport-Hingis bloc. "It's going to happen in the future, inevitably. Nobody's going to be able to stop it."

Venus was pained to see her little sister so disconsolate. "I felt bad that Serena had to learn a lesson like that," she said. "I feel that it should have been me, that I should have lost like that so that [Serena] could have taken the example from me and not had to have suffered in such a manner." (Never mind that nearly a year ago to the day, precisely that scenario played out at Flushing.) In the hallway outside the locker room, a triumphant Davenport, suddenly rejuvenated by tennis, made her way by the Williams sisters to meet Van't Hof, who was waiting in the players' lounge. Once Davenport's back was to the Williams sisters, Venus unleashed a scorching stare that screamed, *You beat my sister. You will pay.*

The next day, citing a toe injury, Serena pulled out of the doubles draw—to the delight of Cara Black and Elena Likhovtseva, who were supposed to play the Williams sisters in the semifinals and were now guaranteed $85,000 apiece for reaching the finals—and returned to Florida the next morning. Venus spent the following day at the courts practicing. When she returned to her hotel room, she found a note on her bed: "Big Sis, I went home. See you Sunday holding a big check over your head. Love, Serena."

Anna Kournikova and Elena Dementieva, two blond teenagers, were both born in 1981, ranked in the top twenty-five, reared in Moscow, and learned the game at the same club. The similarities between the two, though, don't go much deeper. Kournikova emigrated to the Land of Bolletieri—IMG lucre in hand—before she turned ten and is now a Miami Beach denizen. Dementieva still lives in Moscow, where her father is an electrical engineer and she takes classes three time a week to improve her English. While Kournikova makes a small country's GNP in endorsement income, Dementieva had to run over to Niketown in midtown Manhattan to buy more tennis clothes during the U.S. Open. While Kournikova received red carpet treatment, Dementieva constantly had to fish for her players' badge before being allowed into the locker room. Above all, while Kournikova's tennis career has stagnated in the morass of her celebrity, Dementieva ascended in anonymity.

Entering the U.S. Open with a negligible Q-rating, Dementieva had her star-making turn in Queens. Displaying the kind of tactical, cerebral tennis befitting a player whose favorite pastime is playing chess with her brother, Dementieva blitzed through to the semifinals, thereby equaling Kournikova's best ever showing in a Grand Slam. The best player she had beaten was an over-the-hill Anke Huber, but Dementieva showed valor to match her searing ground strokes, winning two three-set matches and capitalizing on what coaches call "big points." "In the end," she told the Russian press, "I do what I need to win."

She didn't do quite enough to beat Davenport in the semis, but she sure came close. A player not known for difficulty closing out a match, Davenport held a 6–2, 5–2, 40–0 lead over Dementieva, a point away from a shower and lunch. But Dementieva suddenly saved the match points and took the next three games, matching Davenport's power off the ground. A subdued crowd that figured Davenport would need fifty minutes to crush the blonde was suddenly behind the Russian underdog. Mumbling to herself for the duration of the changeover, Davenport held her serve to force a tiebreaker. Dementieva was up 5–4 when she netted two routine backhand returns to trail 5–6. Holding another match point, Davenport hit a stab (read: lucky) backhand lob that floated over Dementieva's head and alighted squarely on the baseline.

The lob ended a remarkable run for Dementieva, who would go on to win the silver medal in singles at the Sydney Games—losing to Venus Williams in the finals—two weeks later. In addition to winning $220,000 in prize money at the U.S. Open and securing endorsement deals with two companies, she cracked the top twenty and served notice that she would become another prime player in the Tour's colorful cast. "She's definitely the real thing," said Davenport, who would lose to Dementieva two months later at the Chase Championships. Still, the Russian had little interest in moral victories. Five minutes after the match, she knelt in the locker room, buried her face in her hands, and bawled. When she regained her composure, she showed off her improving English, as well as a self-deprecatory humor—further distinguishing herself from Kournikova. "I did stupid mistakes," she said, shaking her head. "I need to improve my second serve. I think my grandmother can do it better."

To the profound disappointment of CBS, the tournament sponsors, the scalpers on the No. 7 train and on the boardwalk, as well as most fans, there would be no Williams-Williams final. But the prospect of another clash between Venus Williams and Martina Hingis, the best rivalry in women's tennis since Chris Evert and Martina Navratilova, was ample consolation. Both players came into their semifinal throwdown riding high. Venus had yet to summon her best tennis in Queens, but still wielded a twenty-four-match winning streak. Hingis had yet to drop more than five games—or double-fault once—in her five matches.

Before the match, Williams and Hingis stood five feet apart outside the locker room, awaiting their court call. Like two gladiators, they didn't look at each other, didn't make eye contact. Melanie Molitor whispered a few last-minute words into her daughter's ear before giving her a kiss and departing to the players' box. Williams stared straight ahead, jumping up and down like a pumping piston, trying to get loose and shake off any gnawing anxiety.

With the late-afternoon sun hurling shadows across Arthur Ashe Stadium, the two foes added to their collection of classic matches. A tasting menu for the virtues of the women's game, the match featured every tennis attribute imaginable: speed, guile, strength, power, pace, slice, spin, shotmaking, quickness, searing volleys, seeing-eye passing shots, blurring serves, and pinpoint returns. All the while, the match's momentum oscillated like a sine curve. After 113 spellbinding minutes, it was Venus Williams who would splay her legs and raise her arms in triumph, forming a perfect X with her body, and a perfect, incredulous O with her mouth. After match point she repeatedly mouthed the world "Unbelievable," echoing the sentiment of the 20,000 fans. Unbelievable it was.

Hingis played painstakingly precise tennis in the first set. Taking her cue from Comrade Davenport, Hingis frequently worked points to the middle of the court, eliminating angles and neutralizing Williams's unparalleled court coverage. Inducing twenty-one unforced errors from Williams (compared to just five for herself) Hingis drew first blood, 6–4. In the second set, Venus found the range on her ground strokes and revealed a deadly new weapon: the full-swinging volley from behind the service line. With both of her parents cheering her on with more animation and intensity than usual, Venus leveled the match, 6–3. In the third set, both players did what they do best:

Hingis confounded Williams with her tidal consistency and some brilliant shotmaking—including an around-the-post winner. Williams slugged a bushel of winners to the remote corners of the court and used her athleticism to prolong rallies, forcing Hingis to hit upward of fifteen shots in a single point. At the changeovers, Williams, swigging Evian, hardly appeared winded, but Hingis looked shopworn. She took off her shoes to rest her weary feet and gobbled down energy bars.

As Molitor clutched the guardrail in front of her as if it were the last chopper out of Saigon, her daughter broke Williams for a 5–3 lead. At 15–0, Williams suffered a rare instance of acute brainlock and attempted an ill-fated drop shot. Richard Williams bounded from his seat, shaking his head, and left. Followed out of the stadium by a number of journalists, he shouted obscenities and jumped into a Lincoln Navigator. Why had he left at such a crucial juncture? "He had a pressing meeting about an Internet initiative," the Williams family flack, Leland Hardy, said later.

Richard missed one of the transcendent moments of his daughter's career. At 30–15, Williams and Hingis swapped twenty-nine blows in one rally, mercilessly working the corners with every weapon in their arsenals. Spying an opening, Hingis attacked the net and Venus threw up a standard-issue lob. Hingis took aim at an overhead. Had she put the shot away, as she would ninety-nine times out of one hundred in practice, she would have held two match points. So fatigued that she saw the ball only as a blur, she swung tentatively and her shot fluttered in the air like a Frisbee. Venus pounced on it, unloading a backhanded passing shot up the line. Hingis shrieked in horror as the ball strafed by her and landed inside the line. As the crowd erupted, Hingis hung her head. There was an ironic smile on her face, but her resolve was punctured. Her shoulders practically slumped to the asphalt.

If mortal combat is an acquired taste, at some point in the year 2000, Venus had grown to like it. Earlier in the season, Venus was asked whether she derived more satisfaction from winning a tight match or a 6–2, 6–2 romp. "A hard-fought match makes you dig," she said, shriveling her nose in disgust. "Six-two, six-two means you're taking care of business." Here she was, locked in the hardest of hard-fought matches, two points from the precipice of defeat, digging like mad. And she relished it. Her eyes at once hot with intensity and coolly calculating, Venus won fifteen of the next eighteen points, prevailing in the show-case match of the year in women's tennis, 4–6, 6–3, 7–5. Her victory had far less to do with muscle mass, height, and power than an inex-tinguishable competitive fire.

Following their customary dead fish handshake at the net, Hingis departed to the locker room. As usual, Molitor was there to greet her and give her a hug. Without saying a word, mother and daughter sat together on a varnished bench. Hingis closed her eyes, and, ignoring the tears that welled, sucked in deep breaths. It had been a devastating loss that would bother her for months, but Hingis was characteristi-cally candid and introspective about it fifteen minutes later. Maybe she was afraid of winning, she bravely acknowledged.

This was the seventh straight time Hingis had entered a Grand Slam as a top seed and failed to win. The gravitas of her top ranking was evaporating without the titles to support it. The book on how to beat her was becoming increasingly thick and her physical disadvan-tages had some wondering whether she would win another Grand Slam, so long as bigger species like the Williams sisters, Davenport, and Pierce roamed the planet. And she knew it as well as anyone. But this time there would be no temper tantrums, no jaunts to Cyprus, no hoof-in-mouth disease. She quietly left for her home in Switzerland and days later was back on the court, trying to keep up with the heavy hitters. Never did she think it might be in vain.

Despite the equal purses at the U.S. Open, there are vexing reminders that women's tennis still gets treated as a sideshow for the men's game. At the other three Slams, the women have their own day in the sun to play the final. The U.S. Open has "Super Saturday," a made-for TV tennis Lollapalooza, with the women's final played after the two men's semifinals. It beats the previous format, which sandwiched the women between the men's matches. But it's still less than ideal. Lindsay Dav-enport and Venus Williams both arrived at the National Tennis Cen-ter in the early afternoon, unsure when their court call would come and, thus, uncertain when to eat, when to stretch, how long to warm up. Two quick men's matches and the women would be on the court by midafternoon. Two five-setters and the women wouldn't start playing until the evening.

In the middle of the afternoon, Venus had a light practice with Brad Thyroff, her hitting partner who moonlights as a real estate developer in upstate New York. Davenport had a quick warm-up with Van't Hof. Both players then lingered in the lounge while Pete Sampras methodically disposed of Lleyton Hewitt in straight sets. The difference between the two camps couldn't have been more stark. Venus was flanked by her four sisters, Richard, Oracene, an army of advisers, and, for good measure, a man covered in pink and white feathers who claimed to be Venus' guardian angel. Shortly after talking with Patti LaBelle, on hand to perform a memorable rendition of the national anthem, Venus was interrupted by a security guard. "Did you find Johnny Cochran?" the guard said. "He came by looking for you."

Ten yards away, Davenport huddled with her entourage. That is, she sat and ate a sandwich, periodically peering up from a magazine, while Van't Hof watched the Nebraska–Notre Dame football game on a television overhead. A few seats down, Ann Davenport was lost in her paperback. At one point, Lindsay retreated to the locker room but wasn't allowed to exit because Bill Clinton, on hand for the men's matches, was on his way out of the building. Then and there, Davenport might have inferred that it wasn't going to be her day.

In a match that would mirror their Wimbledon final nine Saturdays earlier—right down to the brief rain delay—Williams would overcome an initial hiccup, take advantage of Davenport's inability to conjure her best tennis, and prevail in straight sets. It was prime time in New York when Venus took the court wearing a slinky yellow dress, a mass of jewelry, a diamond tiara, and the focused look of a linebacker anticipating a quarterback's snap court. "I just said to myself, 'Here we go, another opportunity. You've done this before. Now do it again. It's not hard.' "

Initially, though, she showed signs of nervousness. After getting broken three straight times, Venus was down 4–1 and two breaks of serve. Then Davenport collapsed, playing a string of loose games while Venus simplified her strategy. *I'm just going to stop missing.* Twenty minutes later, Williams held a 5–4 lead. Serving to stay in the set, Davenport double-faulted at both 15–30 and 15–40 and walked to her chair a defeated woman. A set from victory, Venus played purposeful tennis and refused to relinquish control of the match. And having recovered miraculously from her three-set shoot-out against Hingis the previous day, she showed no visible signs of physical fatigue.

With Davenport serving at 5–6 to stay in the match, Williams played a masterful game that she should proffer as a rebuttal next time her aptitude for strategy is questioned. Put in the rare position of playing defensive tennis, Williams patiently returned Davenport's missiles deep in the court and waited for an error or an opening. When a missed Davenport forehand gave Venus match point, Serena shot up from her seat, clapping. "One more point and it's yours, Venus," Serena thought to herself. "One more and the family will have another Grand Slam."

Less than a minute later, Davenport drove a routine backhand long, and the House of Williams had defended its U.S. Open title. It was a year ago to the day that a hooded Venus had sat numbly, barely able to bring herself to clap, when Serena was awarded the trophy. Now the sisters swapped roles and Venus was the queen of the hill. As Venus reached to hug her mother and sisters, Richard was working his way down a short flight of stairs and onto the court. "Give it up," he said to her. "You're awesome, baby. You are great, V." Gazing at her husband again threatening to steal the spotlight, Oracene Williams's smile suddenly vanished. As Richard did a bizarre celebratory dance, doubtless inspired in part to taunt Davenport, he offered his hand to Venus, inviting her to join him. She took a step back and shot him a look that said: *I'm twenty now, I'm a two-time Grand Slam champion. If and when I dance, it will be on my terms.* Davenport, packing up her gear, averted her eyes. "It's better not to see how they act," she said later.

When Venus was awarded the $800,000 winner's check and a

gleaming trophy, her brief speech pointedly offered no pro forma praise to Davenport. Venus told the crowd that the best part about winning this year was that her name would be engraved both on the Cup and in history, right next to her sister's. Before Venus could exit stage left and reach the tunnel, fans of all ages, shapes, shades, and sizes mobbed her. Suburban housewives elbowed Puerto Rican teenagers in backward Yankees caps for a photo, a sweat-drenched wristband, an autograph, anything, from the winner, the champion, the star. "Hey, Venus, you said you'd give me something if you won," a teenage boy yelled. She looked up, acknowledging her promise, and handed him her tiara. The crowd gasped at her largesse. "It's zirconium," she explained with a smile.

There's a long-standing tournament tradition at the Open in which the locker room attendants douse the new champion with beer. Walking in the tunnel, Venus told Brooke Lawer, one of the Tour's communications officials, that, she didn't feel comfortable getting a Budweiser shampoo. Lawer passed on the word and when Venus arrived, she was showered with confetti instead. Grateful that the attendants had complied with her wishes, Venus spent fifteen minutes before her press conferences posing for pictures and signing autographs for the staff.

While Venus was in the locker room, Richard was busy filling obliging reporters' notebooks, delivering an inexplicably angry, offensive soliloquy. Asked whether Venus' victory was particularly sweet because of the Martina-Lindsay alliance, Richard said: "I think what Martina and Lindsay need to do is come to me to get some advice. It's obvious they don't have the advice because they're losing. Now I know tennis players are dumb. They don't go to school. Lindsay graduated from high school and said, 'Looky here, I'm the one that graduated.' Hell, McDonald's don't hire you no more with a high school diploma." Richard also had some advice for Hingis: "You know, Hingis is an inch shorter than when I first met her. She should come to me and say, 'Master Williams, I want you to help me. I want to be better.' And I could help her. I've got a friend in Compton, and when he's not high, he's a surgeon. He could saw her legs off and attach new legs that are a couple of inches taller."

As usual, Oracene stayed in the background, laughing with her daughters and watching the Brady Bunch movie in the players' lounge. And as usual, she offered more insight into her daughter's triumph in one sentence than her husband would in a thirty-minute diatribe. "I knew Venus wanted to get the second one before Serena," Oracene said. "She was the first on the scene and said, 'I'm the oldest so maybe I should be the one.'"

Shuttling from one post-match interview to another, Venus stopped to accept a congratulatory phone call from Bill Clinton. The five-minute exchange was Venus unplugged. She was playful, irreverent, and sharp and she was unmistakably in control. In the lounge, Oracene Williams switched from watching the Brady family to watching a member of her own famous brood on television. By the time Venus ended the conversation, Oracene was laughing hysterically. "Did you hear her with the President?" Oracene asked. "I love it, I love it, I love it." It was all too perfect. Ten years ago, her two youngest daughters were crammed into a bedroom in their drab, mint green house in Compton, hitting tennis balls on a cracked, weed-infested court. Now, one having supplanted the other as the U.S. Open champ, they were imbued with such confidence and suffused with such bravado that they felt comfortable jousting with the President of the United States, the most powerful man in the world.

It was after 10 P.M. when Venus finally punched the clock and left the National Tennis Center. She, her family, and a merry band of well-wishers and hangers-on headed off to celebrate at the trendy 212 Restaurant and Bar in midtown Manhattan. In the coming weeks, Venus would win an Olympic gold medal in singles, take the gold with her sister in doubles, return to her studies at fashion school, and run her win streak to thirty-five matches. She would also sign a $40 million endorsement with Reebok, the largest deal ever given to a female athlete. Never mind the WTA Tour rankings, which would have her finishing at No. 3. Venus ended the year 2000 as *the* player in women's tennis—and, in private anyway, her rivals grudgingly conceded as much. As she left Arthur Ashe Stadium and walked into a hazy night, euphoria, relief, and a profound sense of achievement simultaneously tugged at her. In one of the rare moments when there were no flash-bulbs or cameras in sight, the biggest star of them all savored the silence, and struck an enduring pose. Beaming with a look of contentment, she raised her arms triumphantly, as if trying to touch the night sky.

Damned if she didn't miss by much.

EPILOGUE

• Following her successful 2000 Australian Open, which placed her on the cusp of the top ten, **Jennifer Capriati** went into a mini-tailspin. Distracted by a burgeoning romance with the young Belgian pro Xavier Malisse and derailed by an Achilles' heel injury, her confidence and physique both sagged. Following a string of poor tournaments in the spring, Capriati split with her coach, Harold Solomon, the man whom earlier in the year she had credited for her comeback. In a move questioned by even her most loyal supporters, she retained her father, Stefano, as her coach. She finished 2000 ranked No. 14, a vast improvement from a few years ago but disappointing given her auspicious start to the season.

Capriati, however, had more than tennis on her mind—the player who had been so moved by cancer patients she met in Australia had a scare close to home. During a routine checkup in the spring, her mother, Denise, was told by doctors that she had a cancerous growth on her thyroid. As Jennifer took the court to play her first round match at Wimbledon, Denise was in surgery in Chicago, having her thyroid removed. Everything went fine, and Denise spent much of the rest of the summer convalescing, but Jennifer was shaken. "Tennis is great," she said, "but it's not life."

But at the end of the year, when other players were on vacation or giving their DVD players a workout, she spent hours in the gym regaining her muscle tone. The hard work paid off handsomely. At the 2001 Australian Open, she fulfilled the expectations heaped upon her a decade ago and, at age twenty-four, won her first Grand Slam title.

• **Lindsay Davenport**'s schizophrenic year continued to be uneven after the U.S. Open. The defending Olympic gold medalist in singles, Davenport won one match at the Sydney Games before pulling out with a foot injury. She contemplated taking the rest of the year off, but came back after a month to snap Venus Williams's thirty-five-match winning streak and then defend her title in Philadelphia. No sooner had she appeared to be back in form than she squandered a match point and lost in the first round of the Chase Championships to Elena Dementieva. She ended the year on a high note, helping the U.S. win the Fed Cup and then taking a break from tennis, going on a Hawaiian vacation with her boyfriend.

• After her endearing fairy tale run at the French Open, **Rossana de los Rios** was finally beset by the demands of being a working mother on the WTA Tour. With her daughter Anna Paula in tow, de los Rios won just one match at a tour event for the rest of the season. Nevertheless she ended the year ranked No. 77, and more important won $82,797 in prize money for 2000, enough to continue playing in 2001.

• With her father, Damir, serving his ban, **Jelena Dokic** reached the semifinal round of the 2000 Olympics in her hometown of Sydney and finished the year uneventfully. At the 2001 Australian Open, however, her family was back in the news. After Jelena drew defending champion Lindsay Davenport in the first round, Damir renewed his charge that the draws were fixed against his daughter. Once she lost the match in three sets, Jelena announced that she was leaving her adopted country and would be playing under the Yugoslav flag. With her father in the background, prompting her in Serbian, Jelena said: "I have been

assaulted by the media and Tennis Australia enough, me and my family, and that's why we have come up with this decision."

• Despite failing to win at least one Grand Slam title for the first year
since 1996, **Martina Hingis** finished 2001 atop the rankings and won a
career-best nine titles including the Chase Championships. Still,
thumbing her nose at those who say that she's simply too undersized to
win Major titles, she defeated both Serena and Venus Williams at the
2001 Australian Open before losing to Jennifer Capriati in the final.

• **Anna Kournikova** finished 2000 with a career-high ranking of
No. 8 in the world. Despite entering a number of smaller, less prestigious events, she found her first tournament title remained elusive.
She ended up marrying neither Pavel Bure nor Sergei Fedorov, but
she still maintained her tabloid-friendly lifestyle. In the fall, she purchased a $7 million mansion in Miami Beach. Her latest rumored
suitor was baseball's $250 million man, Alex Rodriguez.
    Also, her long-simmering rivalry with Martina Hingis finally
boiled over. A few weeks after the two defended their doubles title at
the Chase Championships, they played a singles exhibition in Chile.
After a call went against Hingis, she appealed to Kournikova, who
agreed with the line judge. Hingis lit into Kournikova during the next
changeover. "Do you think you are the queen? Because I am the real
queen," she reportedly said, causing Kournikova to cry midway
through the match. Kournikova prevailed 6–4, 6–4, and according to
various accounts, the two hurled bouquets, glass stemware, and insults
at each other in the locker room afterward. "It was so bad I thought
they were going to beat each other up," said Jaime Fillol, the event
organizer. The next week, Hingis called Monica Seles and asked if
she'd like to be her doubles partner. At the 2001 Australian Open,
Kournikova reunited with Barbara Schett.

• While she didn't win any titles, the return of **Martina Navratilova**
was an unqualified success. Playing with an assortment of partners,

she acquitted herself well and, as she put it, "had a blast the whole time." There was only one match when she showed signs of her age. Paired with Arantxa Sanchez Vicario, Navratilova took on Jennifer Capriati and Anna Kournikova—their combined age equal to Navratilova's—in the second round of the U.S. Open. Navratilova lost two points on her serve and then slapped her forehead and ran to her chair. She had forgotten to put her glasses on after removing them at the changeover. To rousing, sympathetic applause from the fans, she corrected her vision and won the next four points. She and Sanchez Vicario lost in the next round but announced that they would be back as a team to play a limited schedule in 2001. Why not?

• As if **Mary Pierce** had made some sort of Faustian bargain, her promising year fell apart after her triumphant French Open. An injury to her serving shoulder limited her to just two events after Roland Garros and she finished seventh in the 2000 rankings. Opting for rest over surgery, she was healthy again by the Australian Open. No small consolation was that during her hiatus she spent most of her time with Roberto Alomar in Cleveland. A friend claims that by year's end, the relationship between Mary and Jim Pierce was back to being "strained." Also, by year's end David Pierce was pondering attending massage school and both siblings agreed that Mary would take on a new coach for 2001.

After an early loss at the 2001 Australian Open, Pierce played the Gaz de France indoor event in Paris. Looking sluggish and overweight, she lost her first round match to little-known Anne Kremer. She was booed by the Parisian crowd as she walked off the court.

• Though she and her doubles partner, Rennae Stubbs, failed to reach another Grand Slam final after their emotional win in Australia, **Lisa Raymond** quietly enjoyed the most successful year of her career. At the ripe age of twenty-seven, she finished with a top thirty singles ranking, was a member of the winning U.S. Federation Cup Team, and earned more than $500,000 in prize money. Still, her year was tarnished when she was passed over for the "doubles only" position on the U.S. Olympic team in favor of Serena Williams. The decision by team captain Billie Jean King made sense, as Serena would generate plenty of publicity. The problem was that Raymond was the world's top-ranked doubles player. That Serena was being paid handsomely to play for the World TeamTennis franchise owned by King at the time of the controversial decision was another complicating factor. Raymond lodged a legal battle against the USTA and King to claim the spot. In late August an arbitrator harshly rebuked the USTA's selection process but rejected Raymond's claim.

• What was shaping up as a disappointing season ended on several high notes for **Monica Seles**. After winning the bronze medal at the Summer Olympics and anchoring the triumphant U.S. Federation Cup team, she came within two games of beating Martina Hingis in the finals of the Chase Championships. Her inspired play was particularly poignant since the Tour, lured by $1 million in additional prize money, announced it was relocating the year-end event from Madison Square Garden to Munich. After her stabbing, Seles vowed never to play in Germany. "I was hurt," she said of the decision. "It wasn't so much going away [from New York] but that no one called me or said, 'We've done this deal and this is what's happening.' "

As few weeks later, Seles was again reminded of her attack. At the Hopman Cup in Perth, Australia, Seles was packing her bag following a victorious mixed doubles match when an autograph-seeking fan marched unaccosted into the court and tapped Seles from behind. Visibly shaken, Seles was escorted from the court by her partner, Jan-Michael Gambill. After a few minutes, she calmed down and accepted the fan's profuse apologies. Seles, being Seles, gave him an autograph.

• After her allegations of racism at Wimbledon, **Alexandra Stevenson** was a nonentity on Tour for the rest of the year. She won just twelve matches—against twenty-six defeats—in her second year and finished

2000 ranked No. 92 in the world, a drop of more than fifty spots. Owing to her lineage as much as her aptitude, she was still a popular—and well-compensated—draw at exhibitions during the off-season.

• Having ruffled so many feathers—particularly among French players and her country's tennis Federation—with her book *Les Dessous du Tennis Feminin,* **Nathalie Tauziat** was left off of her country's 2000 Olympic team. This, despite ranking as the top eligible French player. Galvanized by this snub, she reconsidered her decision to retire at year's end and announced that at age thirty-three she would play out the 2001 season. Ironically, because of her newfound popularity as a belletrist, she was eligible for $100,000 in bonus money based on the Commitment List she inveighed against in her book.

• **Richard Williams** struck a final grace note for 2000 on the eve of the Chase Championships, the WTA Tour's showcase event. Richard suggested to the *New York Times* that because both Venus and Serena—who weren't in attendance because of purported injuries—had such a favorable impact on television ratings, they should receive money up front from the Tour. A month later, Richard took full credit for Venus' momentous deal with Reebok. "When I said she should retire, Venus got angry and asked why I said that," he told reporters. "Best mental move I could have made. I got Venus to understand her value." He also predicted that Venus would soon eclipse Tiger Woods as the wealthiest professional athlete. The key? A future endorsement deal with her own brand of water "that contains 800 percent more oxygen than regular tap water."

• By the end of 2000, **Oracene Williams** was no longer living with Richard. In 2001, she accompanied her daughters to the Australia Open and, upon returning, devoted much of her time to building the Oracene Williams Literacy (OWL) Foundation. In March of 2001, her concerns about racism in tennis crystallized at the Indian Wells Masters Series event. Minutes before Venus and Serena Williams were to

play each other in a much-anticipated semifinal match, Venus withdrew on account of tendinitis in her knee. She showed no ill-effects of
the injury in her previous match and was elusive and unapologetic
about her default. Many irate fans speculated that Richard had orchestrated the scenario, a theory espoused the previous day by Elena
Dementieva who predicted "Richard will decide" which sister will
win. When Serena returned two days later to play in the final, she was
raucously jeered throughout the match, which she won nonetheless.
When Richard and Venus took their seats in the stands, they were
booed as well. Richard claimed that he was called the "N-word" thirteen times and that one fan threatened to "skin him alive."

Watching at home on television as a stadium filled with predominantly white fans booed her daughter, Oracene Williams was livid.
"They took off their hoods," she said of the crowd. "Richard may go
overboard in talking. But that's no cause for the crowd to treat Serena that
way. If the fans thought [the booing] will hurt Venus and Serena, they're
wrong. It's just going to make them stronger and more determined."

• What was supposed to be a breakthrough year ended up a mild disappointment for **Serena Williams,** who retreated into the background
as her older sister dominated. She won three titles but failed to reach a
Grand Slam final and dropped in the year-end rankings from fourth
in 1999 to sixth in 2000. After her emotional loss to Davenport at the
U.S. Open, Serena played just one tournament the rest of the year. "It
was definitely below my standards," she said about 2000. There were a
few high points, however. In Sydney she teamed with Venus to win the
gold medal in women's doubles. When she returned to the U.S., she
and her sister signed multimillion-dollar endorsement deals with Nor-
tel Networks and Avon.

• **Venus Williams** kept rolling after the U.S. Open. In Sydney, she
added an Olympic gold medal to her two Grand Slam trophies; she
ran her winning streak to thirty-five matches, and signed the largest
ever endorsement contract ever given to a female athlete. Reebok, the
same company that had recently turned its back on stars like Shaquille

O'Neal and Frank Thomas, agreed to pay her roughly $40 million for five years. No less than Billie Jean King hailed the contract as "an unbelievable, uplifting [event] for women's sport." To Venus, it was merely a predictable turn. "You get what you deserve: I had a plan, I worked hard, and I achieved," she said. "If you ask me, I'm worth it."

AFTERWORD

JUST BEFORE THE CLIMACTIC FINAL OF THE 2001 U.S. Open, Venus Williams was standing outside the locker room at the National Tennis Center in New York, making no effort to act casual. Ten yards away, her little sister—who would also be her opponent that night—giggled nervously, absently fingering her blond braids, giving a thumbs-up sign to the ubiquitous television cameras. Venus was having none of it. Much as she disliked playing against Serena, there was a Grand Slam title in the offing. Ignoring her sister and nodding blankly as a security guard whispered instructions in her left ear, Venus burned holes in the wall with her intense stare. When she finally got the cue to head onto the court of Arthur Ashe Stadium, walking briskly but not so fast as to pass the backpedaling CBS cameraman, she said to herself, "Let's do it."

It was a few minutes before 8:00 P.M. on September 8, and for the first time in history, the U.S. Open women's final was being televised in prime time. In tennis's season finale, the two biggest stars in the sport's cast were sharing the spotlight. It was the first time in more than 100 years that two sisters had competed in a Grand Slam final and the first time that two African Americans had ever faced off in the final of a Major. Before the first ball was struck, it had already become a seminal match. "I'm sure Venus and Serena realize this is a big deal," said their mother, Oracene, who was wearing a pink jacket with pin on each breast pocket. One read *Venus,* the other, *Serena*.

Oracene added, "I've been saying they're like Muhammad Ali: you'll only know *how* big a deal it was years and years from now."

The atmosphere was electric, more befitting a Hollywood awards show or a Vegas heavyweight fight than a tennis match in Flushing. As blimps circled overhead and a convoy of satellite trucks ringed the stadium, celebrities arrived in stretch limousines and mingled in the players' lounge before finding their seats. The A-list included rappers Jay-Z and "P. Diddy" Combs, Knicks star Allan Houston, former Jets quarterback Joe Namath, actors Sarah Jessica Parker and Robert Redford, and singer Brandy, a close friend of the sisters, who had brandished a sign earlier in the tournament reading, *It's Venus's Planet. We Just Live Here.* After a prematch fireworks display, Diana Ross sang a spine-tingling rendition of "America the Beautiful."

On this clear autumnal night, the country's collective gaze was fixed on the Williams sisters. The match, pitting the cover subjects of that week's *Time* magazine against each other, would draw 22.7 million viewers, the largest audience of any program that day—sports or otherwise—and more than double the viewership for the Nebraska–Notre Dame football game that aired in the afternoon. The import of the moment wasn't lost on Serena. The night before, she had asked her big sister how to stay calm. "Champions don't get nervous," Venus replied. Now, Serena's nerves were frayed. "No way," she mouthed incredulously as she entered the arena and looked around. "It was really exciting," she said afterwards. "Some of these celebrities are really *superstars*. I didn't think so many people would watch little me play tennis. I guess we're really exciting."

As for Venus, she displayed a much higher threshold for awe. Throughout the warm-up, blind to distractions, she gave herself a pep talk: *You've done this before. You're the defending champion. Just pretend it's 2000 all over again.*

Then again, it wasn't hard to rewind the clock: 2000 had been a mere prologue for most players on the WTA Tour. If women's tennis is indeed sports' most compelling soap opera, the stars cooperated by staying in character throughout the year 2001. Clinging desperately to the No. 1 ranking, Martina Hingis couldn't stave off her slow but steady descent. The list of players who exposed her deficit of power—and, in turn, damaged her confidence—grew to include Kim Clijsters, Jennifer Capriati, and Amelie Mauresmo. After a dismal spring, Hingis split with her coach/mother, Melanie Molitor, declaring her need for change and independence. Six weeks later, they reunited. At Wimbledon, for the second time in two years, Hingis failed to make it out of the first round, losing to little-known Virginia Ruano Pascal. Following a devastating fifty-one-minute loss to Serena in the U.S. Open semifinals in which she failed to win a single point against Serena's first serve, Hingis played just one more event and finished the year ranked fourth, leaving many to wonder whether she was washed-up at age twenty. There was, however, a silver lining to her season. In April, at the trial of a man who had stalked her, Hingis made the acquaintance of one of the prosecutors, Christopher Calkin. When the trial ended with the stalker's conviction, Calkin became Hingis's steady boyfriend.

Lindsay Davenport finished 2001 at No. 1, though, as she was the first to acknowledge, it was more a reflection of the WTA's quirky ranking system than an appraisal of her merit. While Davenport won a handful of tournaments, she was 0-5 against the Williams sisters and failed to reach a Grand Slam final. Aside from battling injuries and staving off malaise, Davenport was particularly hard-hit by the news that her good friend and doubles partner, Corina Morariu, had contracted acute leukemia. As Morariu endured emergency treatment in a Miami hospital, Davenport kept her friend in her thoughts by wearing a sterling Tiffany "C" necklace during her matches.

Once again, Monica Seles's results were respectable, even if she was light-years removed from her era of dominance. Plagued by injuries, Seles missed the French Open and Wimbledon, and even her sponsors openly speculated that her retirement was drawing near. She responded defiantly by reaching three straight finals in August, beating Serena Williams, Jennifer Capriati, and Martina Hingis with her signature two-fisted slapshots. But the Sisyphian Seles backslid at the U.S. Open, losing in the fourth round to an ascending player, Daja Bedanova.

The 2001 season was one of abject disappointment for Anna Kournikova. Owing to a foot injury, she competed in just one of the four Grand Slams, continuing to carry her personal albatross of never having won a tournament. In true Kournikova fashion, her injury, much like her marital status, was surrounded by intrigue, cloak-and-dagger secrecy, and disinformation. On one continent, a German doctor was claiming to have inserted a screw in her foot, while a public relations agent denied Kournikova had undergone surgery. Whatever the truth was, by year's end, she was ranked a lowly No. 74. Still, her earning power remained formidable, and she packed arenas in the off-season for a worldwide exhibition tour. The queen of the Internet, she appeared in a series of sexy commercials, most having no discernible connection to tennis.

The world continued to turn for the WTA Tour's secondary cast of characters: Within a year of winning the 2000 French Open, a profoundly unhappy Mary Pierce had split with her boyfriend, baseball star Roberto Alomar. She dropped below the top 100, with back and shoulder injuries threatening her career. WTA CEO Bart McGuire, unable and unwilling to navigate the Tour's political swamp, announced his resignation. Jelena Dokic, her obstreperous father mercifully absent, cracked the top ten. Pam Shriver recovered from the death of her husband by keeping up her usual busy broadcasting schedule and ended the year by announcing her engagement to a former James Bond, George Lazenby. Lisa Raymond and Rennae Stubbs quietly established themselves as the best doubles team in the world, winning Wimbledon, the U.S. Open, and the year-end championships in Munich. Two Belgians, Kim Clijsters and Justine Henin, each reached a Grand Slam final and led their diminutive country to the Fed Cup title for the first time.

One of the few significant plot twists was the triumphal emergence
of Jennifer Capriati, who garnished her Australian Open title by dramatically winning the French Open and briefly achieving the No. 1
ranking. What's more, Capriati accomplished the feat with an
unapologetic "I'm-in-charge" bravado. *Sports Illustrated Women* called
her "The Ballsiest Woman in Tennis," on its cover. Capriati left no
doubt about how far she'd traveled since her days as an insecure, disconsolate, burned-out teenager. "It's the best story in sports in the past
twenty years," said John McEnroe.

But even Capriati couldn't upstage Venus Williams. In the U.S.
Open semifinals, the two played a match hyped as a battle for
supremacy in women's tennis. Between them, the two power hitters
had won the previous five Grand Slam events. Rifling shots off both
flanks, Venus took barely an hour to dust Capriati and demonstrate
the distance separating her from the rest of the players in the field.
After the match had ended—and Capriati had exited the stadium,
tearfully slamming the door of her courtesy car—Oracene Williams
exulted giddily about her two daughters' upcoming final. "Venus and
Serena in the final means it is a victory," she said. "We're going to celebrate tonight since we've already won."

The Williams clan celebrated over dinner— but there was a
notable absentee. Venus and Serena's father, Richard Williams, was up
to his usual tricks. As his daughters blitzed through the U.S. Open
draw, Richard Williams had spent most of his time courtside in the
photographers' pit shooting hundreds of rolls of film—sometimes
with the lens cap still affixed to his camera. When he wasn't prattling
on about his missionary work in Australia, he was declaring his inten-
tion to write a cartoon book. Before the finals, he decided that his work
was finished and purportedly headed to the airport for a flight back to
Florida.

The rumor among insiders was that Richard and Oracene were
barely on speaking terms. Before the U.S. Open, Oracene had told
both girls that she would soon be filing for divorce from their father.
The couple sat beside one another for several matches, but there was
virtually no interaction. While neither Venus nor Serena would discuss

their parents' break-up, Oracene admitted that the marital strife had affected her daughters. "They've been able to cope with it, but I know it hurts them," she told *Sports Illustrated*. "They won't say anything, but I know. They've been able to deal with it, and they're going on."

Despite the monumental buildup, the Venus-Serena final proved something other than scintillating tennis. Most of their baseline exchanges ended with Serena spanking an unforced error. As usual, the intrafamily rivalry had the awkward, slightly anesthetized feel of an exhibition, not a match fraught with significance—even with an $850,000 check for the winner. Older sister Venus felt a tug of sympathy for little sister Serena, but her compassion went only so deep. "I'd find myself saying, *Come on Serena,*" says Venus. "When I lost a couple of points, I wasn't worrying for her anymore."

When Venus won match point on yet another of her sister's mishits, she hardly flinched. With the faintest outline of a smile registering on her face, she walked to net and greeted Serena with a hug. "I love you, Serena," she said. The last time Serena had lost to her sister in a Grand Slam—in the 2000 Wimbledon semifinals—she had dissolved into tears. This time, she knew she had lost to a superior player. In the end, Venus won 6–2, 6–4, beating her sister for the fifth time in six encounters, preserving the natural family order. Asked if she was a mean big sister, Venus smiled. "No," she said. "I just think I'm one of the best out there."

After the tournament, Venus vowed to upgrade her 2002 schedule with more events, so she could claim her destiny—the No. 1 ranking. Ultimately, it didn't much matter. Still only twenty-one, Venus had won her fourth Grand Slam singles title. Computer rankings aside, she left no doubt that she was the sport's dominant player. For the second straight year it was clear: Tennis *was* Venus's planet. Other players—male or female, related or not—just lived on it.

L. Jon Wertheim
January 10, 2002

ACKNOWLEDGMENTS

MY FIRST AND MOST OBVIOUS THANK-YOU goes to the scores of athletes on the WTA Tour who permitted me entrée into their beguiling—and at times bizarre—subculture. After uplifting victories and crushing defeats, face-to-face and over e-mail, players too numerous to catalog here were perceptive and provocative in discussing their sport. This includes stars like Martina Hingis, Lindsay Davenport, and Venus Williams, as well as qualifiers hoping to get into a main draw. Their generosity of time and candor is greatly appreciated.

So too do I wish to thank other members of tennis' cast, who add so much color and texture to the game. Not only did they unfailingly oblige my numerous interview requests, but they welcomed me into their world with open arms. They include Dr. Julie Anthony, Bob Arrix, Joe Favorito, Mary Joe Fernandez, Gigi Fernandez, Sara Fornaciari, Dr. Alan Fox, Tony Godsick, Debbie Graham, David Higdon, Billie Jean King, John Korff, John Lucas, Bart McGuire, Pat McEnroe, Oliver Messerli, Annie Miller, Melanie Molitor, Phil de Picciotto, David Pierce, Tom Ross, Pam Shriver, Harold Solomon, Willis Thomas, Robert Van't Hof, Oracene Williams and Richard Williams. Likewise, I owe a debt of gratitude to Brooke Lawer and the rest of the

WTA Tour's communications staff: Sally Bradfield, Anne Dries, John Dolan, Raquel Martin, Rob Leslie, Vani Vosburgh, Chris DeMaria, Veronique Beaujardin, and Jim Fuhse.

My bosses at *Sports Illustrated,* managing editor Bill Colson and executive editor Peter Carry, could not have been more flexible and supportive in allowing me to pursue this project. I also benefited greatly from the insight and guidance of other editors at the magazine: Sandy Bailey, Paul Fichtenbaum, Rob Fleder, Myra Gelband, Hank Hersch, Chris Hunt, Stefanie Krasnow, Albert Lin, Craig Neff, Rich O'Brien, and Paul Witteman.

Writing and researching this book was made infinitely easier by the assistance and thoughtful suggestions of friends and colleagues like Scott Price, Richard Deitsch, Kristin Morse, Kelley King, Caryn Prime, Sam Silverstein, Gary Smith, Franz Lidz, Grant Wahl, Jeff Pearlman, Marc Howard, Chris Lewis, and Jeff Spielberger. I am also appreciative of Simon Bruty, Bob Martin, Ron Angle, Mel Levine, Bill Frakes, Miriam Marseu, and Karen Carpenter, for their help in supplying first-rate photography.

Lamentably, the corps of journalists—American journalists, in particular—assigned to cover tennis with any regularity seems to be dwindling. But it is a privilege to be a colleague of pros like Rachel Alexander, Selena Roberts, Doug Smith, Lisa Dillman, Steve Flink, Virginie Saint-Rose, Pete Bodo, Chris Clarey, Joel Drucker, Tom Tebbutt, Sandra Harwitt, David Sparrow, Dan Kaplan, and, of course, the inimitable Bud Collins.

It was a pleasure dealing with my three-headed editor, David Hirshey, Susan Reed, and Bob Roe, as well as David's assistant Jeff Kellogg. Their unwavering encouragement and dead-on editorial suggestions helped immensely. Put simply, this project would never have taken root without the diligence of my agent, Scott Waxman.

Once my parents, Albert and Judy, got over the book's title, they were liberal in dispensing love, support, and frequent-flyer miles—as were my brother, Gerald, and sister-in-law, Raluca. Finally, my deepest gratitude goes to my wife, Ellie. I won't embarrass her here with sap. Except to say that she makes for a great doubles partner.